D0210106

GEORGE ANDERSON

. . . gained the ability to hear voices and see visions from the other side after a paralyzing illness at the age of six. Fearful of skepticism and hostile reactions, he used his gift sparingly—until 1973, when he attended a meeting of a local psychic group and slowly allowed his ability to emerge.

WE DON'T DIE

. . . is the astonishing national bestseller that documents George Anderson's conversations with the other side—a startling account filled with dramatic, and utterly convincing, case histories that prove: There *is* life after death.

WE ARE NOT FORGOTTEN

. . . continues George Anderson's psychic exploration of eternity, a fascinating and wondrous journey guided by voices from the other side. Their message to us all is one of peace and love, harmony and forgiveness, truth and immortality. It is a message that offers warmth and comfort through the journey of life . . . and beyond.

$\triangle$

"A MOST ILLUMINATING BOOK . . . *WE ARE NOT FORGOTTEN* IS THE AMAZINGLY PERFECT RIVAL OF *WE DON'T DIE.*"
—Sri Chinmoy

"I THINK *WE ARE NOT FORGOTTEN* WILL COMFORT MANY PEOPLE. I RECOMMEND IT AS AN ANTIDOTE TO IGNORANCE, FEAR AND SORROW."
—John White, author of
The Meeting of Science and Spirit and
A Practical Guide to Death and Dying

Berkley Books by Joel Martin and Patricia Romanowski

**WE DON'T DIE: GEORGE ANDERSON'S CONVERSATIONS
WITH THE OTHER SIDE**

**WE ARE NOT FORGOTTEN: GEORGE ANDERSON'S MESSAGES OF LOVE
AND HOPE FROM THE OTHER SIDE**

WE ARE NOT FORGOTTEN

◆

GEORGE ANDERSON'S
MESSAGES OF LOVE AND HOPE
FROM THE OTHER SIDE

◆

JOEL MARTIN AND
PATRICIA ROMANOWSKI

BERKLEY BOOKS, NEW YORK

"Rainy Day" by Molly Martinek. Reprinted with the kind
permission of Dennis and Suzie Martinek.
"Gene's" poem reprinted with the kind permission of his sister Kim.

This Berkley book contains the complete text
of the original hardcover edition. It has been
completely reset in a typeface designed
for easy reading and was printed from new film.

WE ARE NOT FORGOTTEN

A Berkley Book / published by arrangement with
Joel Martin and PAR Bookworks, Ltd.

PRINTING HISTORY
G.P. Putnam's Sons edition / May 1991
Published simultaneously in Canada
Berkley edition / March 1992

ISBN: 0-425-13288-9

A BERKLEY BOOK® TM 757,375
Berkley Books are published by The Berkley Publishing Group,
200 Madison Avenue, New York, New York 10016.
The name "BERKLEY" and the "B" logo
are trademarks belonging to Berkley Publishing Corporation.

PRINTED IN THE UNITED STATES OF AMERICA

10 9 8 7 6 5 4 3 2 1

Acknowledgments

Literally thousands of people throughout the United States, Canada, and the world have given generously of their time to make this book possible. We are indebted to them and many others who have contributed to our work in so many ways. It would be impossible to name them all, but we are deeply grateful to each and every one.

We would also especially like to thank those people who shared their readings and experiences with us but whose stories do not appear here. By the time we were ready to write, we realized we had amassed ten times more material than could fit in a single book. Still, you should know that we learned so much from each of you, and we hope that is reflected here.

We owe a special debt of gratitude to those people who gladly agreed to be identified by their real names. With your help psychic phenomena is emerging from the shadows and into the light.

Our thanks, then, to: Bill and Jeannine Ayres, Sri Chinmoy, Dr. Joseph Casarona, M.D., the Compassionate Friends of Wilkes-Barre, Pennsylvania, Josephine Cosenza, John and Nancy Elliot and their family, Dr. Gerald Epstein, Carol Gadell, Fonda Gadell, Daniel Gardner, Kim Gardner, Robert C. Gottlieb, Muriel Horenstein, Patricia Ippolito, Dr. Leonard Jasen, Elaine Kaplan and the spirit of Jason, Roxanne Salch Kaplan, Suzie Kenzakoski, Charles X. Kielhurn, the spirit of David Licata, Carol McIlmurr and family, Eileen Maher, Dennis and Suzie Martin?? seph Matyas, Kristen and Randy Micheletti, C? chinski, Mary O'Shaughnessy, Peter and St? Anna Preston and the spirit of Jessie, Rich? Richard Ruhl, Kristina Rus, John Smit?

family, Pasqual Schievella, Yolanda Schmidt, Elaine and Joe Stillwell, Max Toth, Neil Vineberg, and Robyn Willis.

Special thanks to Stephen Kaplan of the Parapsychology Institute of America for generously sharing his vast knowledge of parapsychology and his friendship.

As always, our most sincere appreciation to our dedicated literary agent, Sarah Lazin. And to everyone at G. P. Putnam's Sons and Berkley for their tireless efforts on our behalf: our editor George Coleman, Faith Sale, David Shanks, Roger Cooper, Marilyn Ducksworth, Patricia Kelly, Suzanne Herz, and Andrew Zeller.

In addition we would like to acknowledge individually the special people who stood by us throughout.

My heartfelt thanks to Joel, the true author of this series, for having a vision that included me, and to George, for giving me several gifts this past year, all more precious than he will ever know. I'd like to thank Robert and Rochelle Bashe whose love renders the suffix "in-law" irrelevant. My sister Mary Romanowski Vitro devoted weeks to processing transcripts and a lifetime to being my best friend. Johnetta: welcome home. As always my husband, Philip Bashe, made everything possible, bearable, and often even fun, during what we will someday look back on as "that year."

—P.R.

I would like to thank my parents, George, Sr., and Eleanor Anderson, and my family: Alfred, Dolores, James, and George Anderson, as well as Janice Goldberg, Donna Koopman, Donald Walker, and family and friends in the United States and in Europe. Thanks to my best friend, Neal Sims, who's always there with a sense of humor, and to Andrew Ribaudo for never failing to represent me so nicely on the telephone, especially since it's so hard for people to get appointments. Finally, thanks to the Unitarian-Universalist Association for allowing me to breathe, spiritually and religiously.

—G.A.

I'd like to express my special appreciation to my family, ... Cohen, the late Charles Cohen, and to Evelyn Moleta.

A special thank-you to my coauthor, Patricia Romanowski, who trusted enough to embark on this journey with George and me with that rarest of gifts, an open mind.

My eternal thanks to Elise LeVaillant for her continuing support and ideas. Her sharing her vast knowledge of both the scientific and the psychic with me has guided a large part of my research for this book. Her love and spirit continue to be my inspiration.

And, of course, to Christina Martin for her years of loyalty and patience, as well as for accomplishing the gigantic task of transcribing literally hundreds of hours of taped interviews. I couldn't have done it without you.

—J.M.

Dedications

"The night approaches . . . bringing dread
of that irrevocable journey to eternal sleep.
Is it so awesome?
Ask the dead."

—LLOYD HARTLEY

"The thought of death leaves me in perfect peace, for
I have a firm conviction that our spirit is a being of
indestructible nature."

—JOHANN WOLFGANG VON GOETHE

"A man's dying is more the survivors' affair than his
own."

—THOMAS MANN

Contents

Contents

A Note About the Readings

Through the years, George and I have kept detailed records and notes on readings, in addition to the hundreds now stored on video and audio tape. Largely because of the success of *We Don't Die* many people contacted us to volunteer their personal readings and experiences. Every full reading that appears in this book is used with the express written permission of the subject. The names of professionals, such as doctors and therapists, are all real unless otherwise indicated. For personal reasons, some subjects requested anonymity, so in a few cases we have changed names and other identifying details. The readings themselves—the words spoken by George and the subjects—are real.

Each reading presented herein was taken verbatim from audio or video recordings, or from handwritten notes I took during the readings, or transcripts kindly provided by subjects from their tape recordings of their readings. These transcripts have been edited where necessary for clarity and brevity. They have also been reviewed by the subject whenever possible for accuracy. However, except for the reading itself, information regarding the subjects, the spirits, and their backgrounds was obtained in interviews conducted *after* the reading. For reasons of clarity only, some stories precede the readings that in real life they followed. The words are presented here in the order they were spoken minus pauses, repetitions, and irrelevant asides, which are noted by ellipses. (George is probably the only psychic medium in the world known to interrupt himself mid-reading to complain about his latest electric bill.)

Are all readings as fascinating as the ones we've included here? Certainly not. Spirits, like subjects, can be surprisingly dull. But lackluster readings are no less accurate than any

others, just less interesting. We wish to stress that we didn't
select readings simply for their level of accuracy in an attempt to make George "look good." In fact, several of
George's most unusual readings are actually less accurate on
some points than most others. Yet because they involve
uncommon circumstances or shed light on the mediumistic
process, we felt they should be included here. We've noticed
for a long time that spirits whose physical lives or deaths
were unusual or in some way dramatic often come forth with
more information in greater detail. Obviously, these readings make for better, more interesting (book) reading.

—JOEL MARTIN

Foreword

Shortly after *We Don't Die: George Anderson's Conversations with the Other Side* was published in March 1988, George, my coauthor Patricia Romanowski, and I began receiving mail from readers throughout the United States and Canada. Subsequent publication in many foreign countries brought us more letters from around the world. Because most of them were sent to our publisher, then forwarded to us weeks later, we were not always able to respond as quickly as we would have liked. Within a few months thousands of letters had found us, and while we made our best efforts to answer as many as possible, we could not answer them all. For this we apologize and thank you all again for taking the time to write to us about our first book. We appreciated your comments and questions, many of which we hope to answer here, and invite you to write again.

As George Anderson, Jr., and I read the letters, we noticed a recurring theme: People needed to know not only that their loved ones continue to exist in some form and dimension, but that they still play a role in their lives here on earth.

By the time of *We Don't Die*'s publication, George had been publicly known as a psychic medium for over eight years, giving readings both privately and live on my New York–area talk-radio program and cable-television show *Psychic Channels.* During that time I worked closely with him and witnessed firsthand not only his remarkable ability to receive communications from people who have passed on to the other side, the as-yet uncharted nonphysical dimension we inhabit after physical death, but its effect on people who had readings with him. Subjects, we call them. The readings performed live on radio and on *Psychic Channels,* for example, were for total strangers. George was never even told their names. Much of the time, in fact, he didn't even *see* his subjects, conducting readings over the telephone. After many years as a media journalist, I am not prone to hyperbole, but simply put, George showed incredible accuracy, not hundreds but thousands of times. Also, during these years he made himself available to scientists and experts from the fields of medicine, psychology, physics, and other disciplines for countless tests and demonstrations. With few exceptions, anyone interested in observing George was welcome.

These eight years were vitally important to George personally as well as publicly. The youngest child of a suburban Long Island family, he showed the first indications of his psychic ability at age six following a nearly fatal bout with chicken pox that brought on an inflammation of the brain and spinal cord known as encephalomyelitis. George, who suffered a raging fever and temporary paralysis, was unable to walk for two months. Several experts have since theorized that perhaps the fever or the virus somehow damaged or changed George's brain in a way that made his communications possible. Other renowned psychics' abilities presented themselves only after a brain-damaging incident; the world-famous psychic Peter Hurkos, for example, was not aware he possessed any psychic ability until he recovered from a four-story fall. Shortly after George's illness, he innocently—and accurately—predicted that a young friend's grandmother would die, and around the same time began seeing visions. His life was changed forever.

George's capacity to receive psychic messages made him different, and he suffered greatly as a child. One nun in the parochial school he attended threatened to "beat him sane," even though his Roman Catholic faith accepted the psychic abilities of saints such as Joan of Arc and Anthony of Padua. When George was in his teens, the school tried convincing his parents to commit him to one of New York State's most notorious psychiatric institutions. Misdiagnosed as a passive schizophrenic, George was prescribed the sedatives Librium and Valium, which he refused to take after a short time.

For years George sought to deny his ability, but as a young man he eventually came to terms with it. In the eight years between his first live readings on my radio program and *We Don't Die,* George grew more confident and convinced there was a clear purpose for his gift. This was crucial, as no one is more skeptical of his abilities than George himself, by nature something of a cynic.

That George's ability is of special interest to the bereaved seems obvious. But in fact, even while George was conducting dozens of readings each week, he and I focused primarily on the readings as a means to an end. We both sought to learn all we could about his unique psychic capabilities. We did this by recording and analyzing the readings. Once we'd identified recurring patterns, we recognized and better understood what appeared to be aberrations. To date, literally thousands of readings have been collected, as well as information about the circumstances of each. Unfortunately, the fact that George loses contact with the other side during severe lightning storms doesn't really tell us exactly how his ability works. But it does seem to suggest that energy and electricity play some role. In appendix one we describe a recent electroencephalogram (EEG) test supporting that possibility. We believe that if the secret of George's ability ever becomes known, it will be through a series of minor discoveries rather than a single dramatic breakthrough.

Following the first book's publication, George embarked on a monthlong national tour, appearing and demonstrating live on such programs as *Donahue, Live—Regis & Kathie Lee, Larry King Live!* and a host of regional television and radio shows. A common setup pitted George against a debunker, or skeptic. These encounters offered few surprises, unless we count the number of times debunkers promised to "re-create" George's demonstration—usually through a technique magicians and phony psychics term "cold reading"—and failed miserably. In several instances, George gave subjects information they acknowledged could have come *only* from their deceased loved ones, only to be attacked after the next commercial break by an "expert" claiming categorically (and with no supportive evidence) that George was a fake.

In many respects, this was old hat for George. For the majority of skeptics, the refusal to believe in a world beyond the unseen borders on fanaticism. Inevitably, these debates degenerated into an attack on George's spiritual beliefs, if for no other reason than he had demonstrated his ability. In those instances where a randomly chosen, anonymous subject confirmed all George's information, and in many cases tearfully thanked him, what was there to debate? When one talk-show host tried to convince his audience that George's readings "upset" his subjects, they shouted him down.

The lack of understanding about psychic phenomena sometimes obscured the real issue. On one national television talk program, George found himself sitting between a psychic who read using cards, a psychic debunker, and a politician intent on passing legislation that would revive the so-called fortune-teller laws which limit or prohibit psychic readings.

The politician had been motivated by a report of a phony psychic who placed a fake "curse" on an unwitting victim and then charged $2,000 to remove it. In a brilliant feat of deductive reasoning, the politician believed that all psychics were fortune-tellers and should be stopped.

George listened politely to the man, then piped up, "I'm not a fortune-teller, but I can remove a curse for $1.98. Why didn't the person just get up and walk out?"

George's answer was greeted by enthusiastic applause.

The host then asked the politician, "Do you think what George does is dishonest?"

"It's entertainment," the lawmaker answered.

"It's an extension of my Christian religious beliefs," George protested. "I feel I'm performing a serious service to help people."

Suffice it to say, the tour was never dull. In fairness, we must also mention and thank the vast majority of program hosts and reporters who judged the evidence fairly. On a West Coast television talk show, George correctly determined psychically that a woman had lost her son. From the other side, the young man's spirit explained to George that he'd pulled his car into a rest area, fell asleep with the automobile engine running, and was asphyxiated. Police labeled his death a suicide, something his mother could not believe.

The spirit told George, "Tell my mother I didn't kill myself. It was an accident. It looks like suicide, but I wouldn't do that to my mom." As George repeated her son's words, the woman's eyes welled with tears of relief. *Moments like this,* George thought to himself, *make it all worthwhile.* Traveling throughout the country, George was struck by the realization that no one could ever satisfy every skeptic and that the only people in a position to judge him were those for whom he'd done readings and open-minded students of parapsychology.

As George became better known, thousands of bereaved from all walks of life sought readings with him. Many had suffered heartbreaking losses: a father whose little girl was wantonly murdered by a neighborhood punk; a mother whose daughter perished when Pam Am flight 103 was blown out of the sky over Lockerbie, Scotland; a woman who suspected her mother had died after having been injected by nurse Richard Angelo, the so-called "Angel of Death"; a distraught couple whose son committed suicide after becoming involved in a satanic cult. The list goes on and on.

Our mail indicated to us that people needed more than theories about discarnate communications and tests. They needed hope and some confirmation that their loved ones who passed over did not die:

Dear George,
I am writing for my mother, who still grieves the death of her mother seven years ago. They had a very special relationship, and I feel the greatest gift I could give my mother would be to arrange a reading with you. . . .

Dear Mr. Anderson,
I'm sure that every letter you receive echoes of personal tragedy . . . this missing is so painful and the longing for an embrace so agonizing . . .

Dear George,
My sister died. I am not much of a believer in heaven or hell or an afterlife. But thinking there is nothing makes this worse. I only want to know if she is all right and if she knows how much I love and miss her.

Dear Mr. Anderson,
I feel you are the only one in the world who can help us.

Our son was killed. If there is anything worse that could happen to a parent, I don't know what it would be. . . . If I could only be you for a minute, Mr. Anderson, I could find peace . . .

The only one of us to have a listed telephone number, Patricia once explained to a caller from California how to contact George for an appointment the following year. He cut her off in mid-sentence. "But you don't understand," he implored. "They just found my wife's body *in the trunk of a car.*"

Over the years, George and I have been deluged with such calls and requests. For many people, having a reading with him and hearing from departed loved ones is the only way they can hope to resolve unfinished business, receive answers to tormenting questions, and find peace through the knowledge that although those we love are no longer with us in this dimension, they are not gone. And, perhaps as important, they have not left us behind. We are not forgotten.

By the tour's end, George had reached a spiritual crossroads. The question boiled down to this: With literally thousands of people waiting to see him, how could his purpose best be fulfilled? By devoting hours each week to reporters and skeptics? Or by helping people get in touch with their loved ones on the other side? The answer was obvious.

Our first book was devoted primarily to introducing George Anderson and his ability, examining the scientifically based data, and placing George in historical context as the most publicly tested psychic medium in America. That done, we now turn our attention to George's work specifically as it pertains to bereavement. And because the focus of this book is not so much on George himself as on what we can learn from his readings, we've included more background material on his subjects, a great many of whom have kindly allowed me to interview them at length after their sessions.

It's vitally important to understand that a reading involves the subject as much as George and the spirits on the other side. Yes, they communicate through him, but their message is for *you.* When people realize that the spirits are coming through to them, and that without their input (responding yes or no to George's statements or questions) the messages would remain intricate puzzles, they see for themselves that death doesn't end "life," relationships, or love.

Referrals to George are made by psychotherapists, bereavement support groups, even clergy, who feel that a reading can help the grieving. For the last decade, Mary O'Shaughnessy has been coleader of a major Long Island hospital's thanatology team, addressing the needs of those who've suffered a loss. She represents a new generation of bereavement experts who believe that the psychic mediumistic process has a value in their work.

"One of the main questions the bereaved express to me," O'Shaughnessy observes, "is, 'Are their loved ones who've passed on okay?' 'Where did he go? What happened to him? How could he have been such a significant part of my life and the world, and then, all of a sudden, he's wiped off the face of the earth, and the world goes on without him?' "

Religion does not always answer these questions or fulfill that need fully, she believes. "For some people it is a comfort, but it's the physical deprivation they have to deal with, in spite of what they believe happens after death as religion has taught them.

"George's readings can be one aspect of their healing, because he can relieve people of anxiety. They feel then that it's okay for them to move on and to readjust themselves. They feel they have not abandoned the person who passed on and that if they move on with life here, they are not betraying that loved one.

"George helps bring back the person who's passed on, to *complete* the bereavement process. The clergy, the thanatologist, the therapist, the psychotherapist, *and* the psychic medium can all work together. You have your psychological, spiritual, physical, and social needs. Somehow if we can integrate them, we can function as a whole."

A man named Jordan is another bereavement expert open to psychic phenomena's use with more traditional counseling. He asked that his last name and hospital affiliation be kept confidential, as not all his colleagues share his enthusiasm for a psychic component in the bereavement process. He has worked as a grief, or bereavement, counselor for nearly ten years and holds a master's degree in psychology.

"I try to give a person who's suffered a loss another perspective," he explains. "I think the only way true grief counseling works is by educating the person about the other side, that people *don't* die, and that the soul is immortal and keeps going on. I really have gotten away from a lot of what I was taught in school. For example, we were taught to talk about the deceased individual's accomplishments and what he meant to his loved ones. When I started doing that in counseling, people got upset and cried, because the final thing comes down to: 'I'm never going to see that person again. Any good things I have of them, our relationship, they've all ended! There's no meaning to it.'

"I've found that most bereaved people believe in the afterlife, but that seems to contradict many psychologists and therapists. In school we were taught to not even discuss it. Why? Because it's not 'scientifically proven.' When I was going to college as recently as the 1980s, it was something you didn't say aloud. It was laughed at. Yet it's the first thing people need when they're grieving.

"There are still those therapists who would try to burn George at the stake for what he's doing," Jordan concedes, adding, "but if they experienced him, they'd see for themselves. Sometimes psychotherapy tries too hard, I think, to give people answers. What George is really saying is that the answers are within each of us. Until you find that peace within and look within, you won't find most of the answers."

George remarked to me one day, "When people suffer the loss of a loved one, there seems to be nothing to hold on to. Many blame their loss on God, and they may turn away. I hope that through my ability I can give them hope and assure them that God has not abandoned or punished them. People need to hear and to know that their loved ones are still alive and well in the next stage of life and that one day they will be reunited with them. There *is* life after death, for you and for everyone you've ever known. This realization can sometimes help the bereaved move on to the next step through their grief."

George was quick to emphasize, however, that he was not a substitute for bereavement counseling and that a psychic reading doesn't instantly cure grief. "It can prove to you that your loved ones do live on, on the other side," he said, "but

there is nothing I or anyone else can do to bring them back."
His advice to the bereaved? "Just know that you are not
forgotten, and that they will be waiting for you on the other
side."

—JOEL MARTIN

Introduction

Few of us can honestly claim not to fear death. While we each expect to "die" but once, in a lifetime we will face the loss of loved ones too many times. In those moments of profound pain and grief we turn to family, friends, and loved ones, clergy, counselors, and support groups as we work through the gamut of emotions a death inspires. The fear, sadness, guilt, loss, and anger will, we tell ourselves and one another, eventually disappear. After all, life goes on.

Our cultural attitudes toward death are rife with contradictions—and delusions. We seem to prefer not thinking about death, yet it is all around us: in the news, religion, movies, books, music, and art. We know so little about death and yet speak of it more than we realize. As too many readers will admit, it's not life that makes religion important to us so much as death. We claim not to know anything about what happens to us after we die, but we expend tremendous energy ensuring that we'll be worthy of going to heaven, or at least evade hell.

Ironically, almost nothing we think or do, as a culture or as an individual, truly *prepares* us for death. While at one time or another the vast majority of us have expressed how we'd "like to go" (as if we have a choice), fewer than one in ten of us prepares a will or makes any preparation for those left behind. With such a seeming reluctance to deal with the most basic facts of life and death, is it any wonder that coping with a loved one's death is so difficult for so many of us?

Despite how little we think about death, we assign to each death its own value, meaning, and degree of tragedy. To die in one's sleep with minimal suffering and in advanced age might be the "best" death. Barring that, to go quickly, to be gone "before I even knew what hit me" is certainly preferable to a painful, protracted death at the end of a debilitating disease or mutilating injury. On the other side of the quick-death/slow-death debate are those who cherish the precious time we can share with loved ones when death is expected. Survivors of those who die unexpectedly are often left to ponder and regret the words left unspoken, the questions that now seem sure to go unanswered forever. Other sudden deaths, those caused by murder, violent trauma, or sudden infant death syndrome, for example, bring to bear on survivors an overwhelming sense that the whole world is unfair, unpredictable, and somehow horribly wrong.

"Death is not the end," George tells people. "It's the beginning. No one you are close to ever dies. People should understand that life is everlasting, and everything that happens in it has a purpose."

But in our time of grief, it is so hard to understand death's purpose. It's one thing if a loved one passes at age ninety and quite another if he or she dies young from disease, an accident, murder, or suicide. Despite our advances as a civilization, far too many people's lives are brutal, violent, and short. How can we make sense, how can we find the purpose of those deaths? And what of children who die a lifetime too early? Or the suicide victim we may feel we somehow failed?

There can probably never be an answer to the universal question survivors invariably ask: Why? Even if there were, it would bring us no closer to learning to live with and beyond our grief. Every death brings a million questions and virtually no answers: Did he suffer? Did she know I was there with her at the end? What is he doing now? Does she know what I'm going through? Will we ever be together again? Will she ever forgive me? Does he know how much I love him? Is she angry at me because I "pulled the plug"? Does she still love me? Does he know of the flowers I left at his grave? If only we could believe that we are not forgotten, that death was not an impenetrable wall between this world and the next, but a bridge to a world beyond where we live forever. Through George Anderson, countless people have learned firsthand that there is indeed life after death.

•   •   •

Few topics are as mired in misinformation as psychic phenomena. We call George a psychic medium in the most literal sense. We use the word *psychic* as an adjective, meaning "lying outside the realm of physical processes and physical science," for it describes the nature, and perhaps the source, of George's abilities. We use *medium* because there is no more precise word and because of all of the other terms that have been or are currently in vogue—channel, seer, psychic, sensitive, clairvoyant—it is the most comprehensive, accurate, and "neutral." For George is a medium, a passive conduit *through which* the spirits communicate to subjects, their loved ones.

In the decade since George went public with his ability, he has undergone countless tests and performed thousands of public and private readings. Invariably, the results are the same: He reveals to his subjects information—about events, experiences, trivia, even nicknames—for which the only possible source is the living, discarnate consciousness, or spirit, of the deceased. In some cases, the spirits reveal information about events that occurred during, even *after,* their own physical deaths. George's many readings for subjects whose loved ones disappear or die under mysterious circumstances are of particular interest because by bringing forth new and later substantiated information, he proves conclusively that telepathy, or mind reading, is not a source. As a matter of fact, George consistently scores very low in tests for telepathic ability.

George is not the only person in the world with psychic abilities; we probably all have some psychic potential. However, in several important ways he is unique among those possessing this gift. First, he is deeply spiritual and views his work as an extension of his personal religious beliefs. Because of this, he insists on being a passive receiver; he will not conjure or "call up" spirits. In other words, a subject may not come to George and put in a request for Uncle Pete, or ask, "I'm having trouble at my job. What does my father think I should do?"

George does not "contact" spirits, he discerns them. An admittedly crude analogy would equate George to a radio or television receiver. From what George's readings tell us, it seems that spirits are all around us, existing as a form of energy, perhaps in another dimension: the other side. For some reason, not all of us can communicate directly with them, just as not everyone can see all the colors in the visible spectrum.

Sometimes spirits mention that they have tried to contact the living through dreams or by giving them a sign. This, combined with the copiously documented sightings of spirits throughout history, leads us to conclude that we probably do receive their messages but are not consciously aware of doing so. This is called direct communication, a subject we explore in chapter eight. Why so many of us can recall one or two such experiences remains a mystery, but based on the overwhelming anecdotal evidence we believe direct communication is real. One possible reason why we remember so few of these experiences is that the conscious mind cannot grasp or retain the messages, just as it cannot recall or make sense of all our dreams. For reasons we may never understand, George's ability to receive messages from the other side is unusually well developed.

George also differs from other psychics in that he remains alert during readings and never goes into a trance (except once, for a scientific test). He works in the light, literally and figuratively, conducting readings in well-lit rooms, public places, and live on radio and television. He is also known to crack the occasional joke about the spirit in question. And George does not have a spirit guide or any other entity "speak through" him, such as J. Z. Knight's Ramtha, Arthur Ford's Fletcher, Arigo's Dr. Fritz, or Jane Roberts's Seth. Spirits close to those for whom George is doing a reading, either by relation or by blood, or close to someone the subject would know, communicate directly to George without a spiritual middle man.

George receives the messages over something like a spiritual party line with an infinite number of connections. It's not uncommon for several spirits to drop in on a reading, sometimes quite abruptly, or for George to hear several voices simultaneously. He has no control over which spirits come through or how long they sustain the communication. Generally, the more dramatic, emotional cases result in longer and clearer readings. We can only guess that those spirits know their loved ones have a more urgent need to hear from them.

Before each reading, George instructs subjects to respond to his statements with the minimum amount of information he needs to determine if he is interpreting the spirits' messages correctly. Usually a mere yes or no suffices. In the readings that George conducts over the telephone and that are broadcast live on radio or on television, the caller may say only "hello" before George begins receiving the spiritual communications. This rules out the possibility of George obtaining information or picking up "clues" about the subject's appearance, gestures, and expressions. George does not know why or from what distance these people are calling. Similarly, he doesn't know anything about those he sees privately but the first names of whoever made the appointment. Many subjects come to him completely anonymously, or assume fake identities.

Confusion over what George does often arises from basic misunderstandings about psychic phenomena. Simply put, the term "psychic phenomena" encompasses any occurrence that cannot be explained by current scientific theory or proven—and disproven—by orthodox, contemporary scientific means. Apparitions, or ghosts; precognitive dreams or visions where one foresees a future event; extrasensory perception; telepathy; out-of-body experience; psychokinesis, or the manipulation of physical objects without physical contact; déjà vu, or the sense that one has been someplace or done something before; dowsing, or locating underground minerals, water, and objects clairvoyantly with the aid of a divining device such as a rod—these are all types of psychic phenomena. We would venture to guess that most people have had at least one such experience, even if it only involved "knowing something was wrong" with a loved one at a time of crisis or death. However, we doubt that more than a few are using their mental powers to bend spoons.

Broach this subject with a group of people, and you will undoubtedly find that psychic experiences are far more common than we imagine. One reason for our distorted idea that they are strange, evil, and rare is the taboo against talking about them. We're afraid others will think we're crazy or losing our minds. Yet 42 percent of respondents to a 1981

Gallup poll claimed to have had some form of contact with the dead. That, coupled with the exhaustively documented near-death experience and hundreds of years' worth of reports of "visitations" from the other side, suggests strongly that some form of human consciousness does survive bodily death.

For our purposes, however, we are concerned only with the five abilities through which George receives the spirits' messages: clairvoyance, clairaudience, clairsentience, sympathetic pain and sensation, and psychometry. Through these means, George receives information that he could not possibly have obtained through any of his so-called "normal" five senses, or, interestingly, through extrasensory perception or telepathy (mind reading). These messages consistently contain information regarding the past, the present, and the future; the subject's and the spirit's relationships to each other and others; the spirit's feelings, thoughts, and attitudes.

Clairvoyance makes it possible for George to "see" in his mind's eye objects, symbols, figures, and scenes. Through *clairaudience* he hears the voices of the spirits as well as other relevant sounds: anything from gunshots, to dogs barking, to explosions, to cars crashing, to a spirit speaking to him. *Clairsentience* is an extrasensory feeling, perhaps best described as a hunch. Unlike clairvoyance or clairaudience, it parallels no direct physical sense. George will simply state, "I have the feeling of being trapped," or "I'm feeling anxious and scared," or "They give me the feeling it was a business deal gone bad."

For reasons George cannot always articulate, he "feels" information, as in this excerpt from a reading:

"A woman close to you passed," he said to a young man, who confirmed, "Yes."

"She's older. I'm getting the feeling of age."

"Yes."

"It's your grandmother."

"Yes."

"It seems as though she passed very recently."

"Yes."

"Because I'm getting the feeling she just got there to the other side."

"Yes, my grandmother died today. This morning," the startled young man said to George, who was equally surprised. While George cannot verbalize what a recent arrival on the other side feels like the same way he can describe the sensation of falling or being hit with a brick, somehow his brain processes it so that he can find the words to express the feelings.

Sympathetic pain and sensation differ from clairsentience, because here George receives very real (and sometimes quite painful) physical sensations. Through this faculty, the spirits send important, specific information about their physical selves on this plane. A sharp stabbing pain in the chest indicates to George that a spirit died from a heart attack, for example. Thermographic imaging tests (discussed in our first book) actually show that the affected area on George's body consistently "heats up" at the instant of sensation. Why, no one yet knows.

Psychometry, perhaps the most baffling ability, involves gathering information about an object through touching or handling it. Through psychometry George might learn whom the object belonged to, where it came from, or in the case of a sealed newspaper story, what it is about without having seen it. In the past, George has done successful psychometric readings in the presence of a subject. Here in chapter four we recount a remarkable psychometric reading done with *no* subject present.

For many years George also scribbled on a pad of paper during readings, sometimes writing out a name or drawing a symbol he had received through clairvoyance, clairaudience, or clairsentience. In *We Don't Die* we termed this "automatic writing," which some readers found confusing, since other psychics claim to receive messages through a similar process. There is, however, a crucial difference between George's doodles and true automatic writing that we may not have made clear. In the purest sense, automatic writing occurs when the medium completely surrenders control of himself to the spirit; he is simply the instrument through which the spirit communicates. We cannot stress often enough that there is *no* time during one of George's readings when he is not in full control of himself and fully conscious of his surroundings. Although in some readings the scribbled notes and figures did provide significant clues—in one case documented in our last book, he received obscure weather symbols only his subject understood—it eventually became clear that the note taking was more a focus of concentration than an independent source of information. Today George still "scribbles," but usually with a capped pen to save a tree.

Though every reading is a "discernment," strictly speaking, George does a type of group reading that we refer to specifically as a discernment. Here he picks up a spirit's communication without knowing to whom in the roomful of strangers it is directed. Following the spirit's direction, George walks up to a subject. From then on, that person acknowledges the information by replying with only yes or no.

After years of reviewing readings, we've seen a distinct difference between public, or discernment, readings and private readings. Why this is true, we can't say for certain. Basically, though, rarely does a spirit communicate anything through George when the subject is among strangers that would not be expressed before the same people were both the subject and spirit on this plane. In one group discernment a deceased man who'd kept his homosexual love affair with a subject a closely guarded secret all his life came through and alluded to that relationship with characteristic reticence and discretion. His lover, expecting more, was disappointed, despite George's remarking that he felt that the spirit was "holding back" about something and everything else communicated was confirmed as correct. While we couldn't guarantee that a private reading with the same subject would be different—more personal, more emotional—based on the research, it's safe to say it probably would. Messages one would expect to hear from loved ones only behind closed doors most often come through in private readings.

Readings, whether conducted publicly or privately, are easiest understood as continuations of the conversations and relationships we had with loved ones while they were here on earth. Most of the time a message from the other side varies little in content or tone from the telephone conversation the subject might have had with that person in this dimension— or the kinds of conversations most of us engage in every day.

Skeptics often criticize George because very often readings contain seemingly similar messages: "Thank you for caring for me prior to my passing" is a good example. That sentiment is expressed in many readings simply because it has been relayed to George from the other side. Even he has sometimes questioned why something so seemingly "trivial" recurs. But then when we review the record it's clear that whenever it does come up, in nearly every case the subject did care for the deceased in some special way.

We must also remember that someone who would refuse to help a loved one in time of need would be far less likely to seek contact with that person after death. That's not to say that some do not; they certainly do. But even in those cases, those who've passed over only rarely come through to criticize and berate those left behind. Whether that's because the other side seems to favor forgiveness, we cannot say.

George could easily avoid the criticism this "redundancy" problem evokes by simply refusing to relay any but the most specific, particular, "spectacular" messages. After all, who would know what he'd left out? However, he feels this would be wrong, since he is a passive receiver and his obligation to his subjects and those on the other side is to impart the messages as clearly and honestly as he can. The fact that many spirits do thank loved ones here for that care does not diminish the validity or importance of that message. By that reasoning we could question the sentiment behind every "I love you" uttered in this dimension because it's being said trillions of times a day. We don't, and the reason why is that here we respond to such expressions not according to what they may mean to someone else, but what they mean to us. Messages from the other side are sent each to a specific subject and should be evaluated by exactly the same criteria here.

For George every reading in progress is a new puzzle without a key. He receives information, which he relays to the subject. Many symbols, for example, have multiple meanings. A car accident can be a symbol for a car accident or *any* accident. In order for him to relay it accurately and decipher the clues he receives, he must have the subject's confirmation or denial of information. Some have criticized George for seeking confirmation, claiming that he is merely fishing for answers. Examine the readings, however, and you'll find that over *95 percent* of George's requests for confirmation elicit yes answers. When George determines something as relatively simple as the number and sex of grandparents passed over, he is rarely wrong, a fact that is all the more remarkable when you consider that there are nine possible "combinations." When it comes to a matter as specific as the spirit's name or cause of death, the possibilities are endless.

As you'll see in the readings that follow, countless times George insists on a given point even in the face of a subject's repeated denials. If George were fishing, he would simply follow the subject's "lead." In those amazing moments when George hits on an unexpected series of events or heretofore unknown facts, it's clear that his contacts are genuine.

Wherever possible, George and I question the subject *after* the reading to determine George's rate of accuracy and, when he receives an unfamiliar symbol or a confusing, contradictory message, its meaning. While many readings are quite straightforward and, one might say, filled with "meaningful trivia," some are highly complex and puzzling. It seems that the spirits are concerned with being properly identified; otherwise why would they stress such seemingly inconsequential facts as their having spoken a foreign language, used a particular expression, or means of death?

Sometimes the message's content is so personal or so cryptically expressed that only the spirit and subject know what is meant—for example, a personal nickname, a song title, an allusion to a shared experience. Conducting post-reading interviews has helped us to understand the symbols' and messages' often numerous and hidden meanings. This is how George learned to unravel such visual images as a broken washing machine, which signifies kidney disease or failure. Or the spoken riddles, as in one AIDS case where a spirit explained that the disease was contracted "through a needle but not with drugs," meaning a blood transfusion.

In effect, every piece of information comes to George "out of context." A good example of this came in a reading for a man who'd been recommended to George by a church-sponsored bereavement support group. Within moments George accurately discerned the spirit of the man's ten-year-old son, killed by an automobile while walking to school. As the reading progressed, George offered the kind of detail that invariably opens the mind of even the most obdurate skeptic.

"I'm seeing an American Indian, psychically," he said to the father, who answered, perplexed, "No, that doesn't mean anything to me."

"Well, I see an American Indian," George insisted.

"I don't know what that means."

"It's a Shawnee Indian. The other side is telling me to say that. Does that mean anything to you?" George asked.

"My God, yes!" the father exclaimed. "That was my son's nickname. His name was Shawn, but I called him Shawnie!"

As wonderful as a reading can be, we want to be very clear about what a reading with George can and cannot do. As you will see, for most subjects, a reading with George is neither the beginning nor the end of anything. We especially want to speak to those people who believe that once they receive a reading with him, all their problems will be solved, and their grief will magically disappear. Nothing could be further from the truth. As George tells subjects every day, "I cannot remove your pain. All I can do is ease it for a while."

In fact, a reading is not for everyone. Young children, for example, may not be able to deal with one, despite the fact that they are often far more open to the subject of death than their elders. Bereavement counselor Mary O'Shaughnessy says, "I think a person has to be stable to go through seeing George. I wouldn't send someone to him who is very vulnerable psychologically. In other words, someone who's not able to perform daily functions, or who may be very depressed. However, for someone who seems to be able to go through the day but is experiencing depression from grief, I believe it can be of value to them, as long as they understand that it's not going to be the total answer to their grief.

"What people should do with the information from George's reading is to allow themselves to look at the life of the person who's passed on and what this person's life has meant to them in their relationships. With the messages that they get through George, they can integrate that deceased person's life into their own identity and move on."

While it is true that many people come away from a reading feeling in some way better than they did before, even the spirits don't always have all the answers. If anything, they are more like reporters than soothsayers. One subject came to George hoping to learn from a recently murdered elderly couple that their son—the subject's childhood friend—did not kill them, as the police maintained. But both victims came through and clearly identified their son as the killer, though they were devoid of anger or revenge. Toward the end of the lengthy session, the mother said in exasperation to George, "What does she want? What more can we tell her? That's all there was to it." Other times what they do have to say is less than comforting, as in the reading where a woman's uncle confessed to having an incestuous relationship with her brother, his nephew. Until that moment, the man had kept it secret. He broke down with the painful truth only after hearing the tape of his sister's reading with George.

This is one aspect of the information George gathers from and about the other side that some believers find uncomfortable, for we find as many conflicts and differences of attitude toward life and death over there as here. In a perfect world a dead daughter's pleas to her father to forgive her killer ends his obsessive homicidal rage, every victim of a gruesome death claims to have passed over quickly and painlessly, and everyone who's passed over is content with his lot. But that's not always how it is.

In a reading for a young woman, George discerned that her husband had suddenly passed on from a heart attack at age thirty-five, leaving her alone with an infant child. "I screamed at him, I was so angry," she admitted. "How could he leave me alone like this? We were married such a short time." Her late husband revealed that when he first arrived on the other side, he too was angry that his time here on earth with her had been cut short. Another spirit, a young boy, came through to advise his mother to pay more attention to his surviving siblings. "Don't be too overprotective of them and don't idolize me. My brother and sister shouldn't have to live in my shadow."

Some who accept life after death find these discrepancies troubling. Throughout history peoples of all cultures and faiths have looked to life beyond as a great equalizer, the one place where all of us (except those remanded to hell) might exist in peaceful bliss. The differences in experience and feeling from the other side only further underscore how human we remain, even in death. Every story, every person, every grief is undeniably unique.

How spirits "should behave," what really goes on in the hereafter, what we can expect when we pass on are all subjects our greatest thinkers and religious leaders have debated for thousands of years. Even in the relatively rigid world of organized religion, concepts of the afterlife have evolved dramatically over the years. Skeptics who claim there is no life after death, no God, and no possibility of communication between this world and the next are uniquely unqualified to judge George or his ability. After all, how can one qualify, verify, or debate something he's already presumed to know doesn't exist?

George does not proselytize. "I'm not looking to convert anyone," he said. "You can accept or reject what I do. That's up to you. I have no acrimony toward anyone who disagrees with me. I would just hope they respect my right to disagree with them."

Shortly after *We Don't Die*'s publication, Andy Rooney, in his nationally syndicated column, wrote about George: "Anyone who claims he can predict the future, tell you what someone else thinks or name a card in a shuffled deck is either lying, fooling you or working with a stacked deck." That George has never claimed to do any of those things obviously didn't temper Rooney's indignation. "Anyone who tells you he has spoken with God or can communicate with someone who has died is crazy, a dreamer, or a con artist."

The veteran resident curmudgeon of TV's *60 Minutes* is well known for his humorous, biting commentaries, and no stranger to controversy. Rooney devoted an entire newspaper column to George and the book about him. "In a recent *New York Times*," he complained, "there was a full-page ad for a book called *We Don't Die*. It infuriated me. It's about a so-called 'psychic' named George Anderson, who, according to the ad, has proved we don't die. . . . What happens to us after we die? There are going to be millions of people, desperate for an answer, who accept it without questioning it or thinking. There are a lot of stupid people," Rooney groused.

We wonder if Rooney meant to include among "stupid people" the billions of every major religious faith for whom the belief in an afterlife is a religious or philosophical cornerstone of their world view. As a 1989 *Newsweek* poll found, 94 percent of Americans believe that God exists, and 77 percent believe in a heaven, or "the other side." The columnist added sarcastically, "If we all go to heaven when we die and can talk to our dead relatives before we do, through George Anderson, why bother with Medicare? If our happiness depends on the stars, on luck and on prayer, there really isn't much sense in our making an effort." Like many skeptics, Rooney seems to suggest that a belief in life after death leads us to neglect personal responsibility here on earth before we pass.

The respected sociologist Father Andrew Greeley reached a vastly different conclusion after years of studying the hereafter. He reported, "Those who believe in life after death lead happier lives and trust people more. The people who believe in heaven are just as committed to this world as those who don't. Belief in personal survival is not the coward's way out."

Those like Rooney, who categorically reject psychic phenomena or label parapsychology a "pseudoscience," ignore a growing body of scientific and medical research on the subject. But open, fair-minded debate, George believes, is healthy, for it ultimately can separate the genuine from bogus claims of contact with the afterlife.

Another common mistake self-proclaimed debunkers (who are largely atheists or agnostics) make is to lump paranormal claims in general, and mediumistic ability in particular, with traditional religious belief. For most skeptics, their argument against psychic phenomena is essentially a footnote to their case against God. However, the two are not necessarily the same. If, in fact, George is a passive receiver for spirit communications, or some kind of energy not yet fully understood, the process can be viewed or studied in nonreligious as well as religious terms.

Those who persist in claiming that George is *not* in com-

munication with the dead or that such a thing is impossible
often sum up their "proof" in the following statement: If
George were really in communication with the dead, his
information would be 100 percent accurate. This statement
presumes three crucial points: 1) that the people George
reads for *always* know *exactly* what the spirit is referring to
and that they can and will readily acknowledge *every* part of
the message (as you'll see, this is not always the case); 2) that
human consciousness after death is in some way superior
(the omniscient dead is a horror-movie cliché), or that we
become smarter or more perceptive after death; and 3) that
all other areas we regard as "sciences," such as medicine and
engineering, are infallible.

First, few people know or can recall the names of every
deceased relative and acquaintance, or the circumstances of
their deaths, or what's going on in a cousin's love life, or how
the deceased might have felt about someone or something.
Some people are so nervous or anxious during a reading that
often George must "remind" them that they have an Aunt
Babs who passed from cancer or a grandfather who drank
before he died.

In public readings and group discernments, which are
witnessed by strangers as well as loved ones and friends,
people are understandably reluctant to acknowledge information concerning such personal matters as extramarital
affairs, homosexuality, abortion, incest, or substance-abuse
problems. When a subject cannot confirm George's information as correct, we count George's statement as a miss. However, it is quite common for people to tape-record the
readings and/or discuss them later with friends and relatives. Often, they contact us several days later to say that,
yes, there *was* an Uncle Fred who died in World War II, or
that the name they couldn't acknowledge was from the
spouse's side of the family. Or, someone may call weeks later
to tell us that an incident George alluded to occurred after
or simultaneously with the reading.

One happy example has come up countless times: George
repeatedly insists the subject is going to have a baby in the
coming year. The subject invariably denies it, only to call
one of us a few weeks later and exclaim cheerfully, "George

was right! I'm pregnant!" She was at the time of the reading, but didn't know it—though a spirit close to her did.

We don't know enough about the nature of discarnate consciousness to determine how, or if, death affects it. We do know, however, that many spirits who come through in readings use the same verbal expressions or communicate in the same emotional "tone" that they used in life. People who were energetic, calm, confused, or upbeat often come through the same way in readings. They use familiar idiosyncratic expressions and words, or "sound" as they did here. Many people are shocked to hear George say that a spirit is cracking jokes or teasing; it doesn't correspond to our deeply ingrained image of white wings and harps. What's important is that personalities seem to retain some consistency from this side to the next.

For example, in one reading, George told a widow, "Your husband says that when he was here, he was an agnostic."

"Yes."

"He says if he were alive, he'd make fun of you for coming to me."

"Yes, he would," she answered, laughing.

In another reading, George remarked to his subject, "Your husband keeps putting his fingers on his upper lip. He's smiling—something about a mustache. Do you understand?"

"Yes," the woman replied. "That's him. Just to annoy me, he'd always tease me about growing a mustache."

Small points, perhaps, yet evidence that individual consciousness and personality do survive physical death.

Finally, there's the matter of science's "accuracy." To hear skeptics tell it, *no* scientific endeavor has been marred by error. How absurd. To extend that ridiculous assertion and claim that nothing George does is valid unless he is 100-percent accurate sets a standard for judging psychic phenomena far more stringent and inflexible than applied to anything else. Certainly this all-or-nothing standard isn't used to measure success in medicine, the space program, or quantum physics.

In our last book we compared George's rate of accuracy to that of the National Weather Service, which despite an army of meteorologists and advanced computer technology still cannot accurately predict the weather with a rate of accuracy anywhere near George's during readings. Living in this era of rapid technological advancement, we often lose sight of our limitations. Despite science's progress in the last twenty years, there's still no cure for the common cold, no explanation for why the swallows return to Capistrano, and no real understanding of how electroshock therapy works, despite its being prescribed for thousands every year. Does this mean that there will never be a cold cure—that we can never understand the swallows, or that their return doesn't "exist"—or that no one should have electroshock therapy? Of course not. What it does mean is that there is more to the world than what meets the eye or can be comprehended by the human brain.

It is possible to know that something exists and yet not know everything about it. This is certainly the case with discarnate consciousness, and, we might add, any number of scientifically studied phenomena, ranging from photosynthesis to black holes, conception to quarks.

For all that we can learn from George's readings, there are very clear limitations that he encourages people to recognize and respect. Communicating with your deceased loved ones is not "the answer" to life's problems. Death is a part of life, and as we believe George's ability demonstrates, so are the so-called dead.

As amazed and surprised as one might be to "hear" from those on the other side, rarely is anyone frightened or shocked by what he or she learns. Most subjects are highly relieved to find that the experience itself is neither "spooky" nor "creepy." And why should it be? If anything, the majority of subjects find it comforting and reassuring, even when the circumstances of death were morbid or the spirit's message surprising. To say that, for some, a reading with George has changed their lives is no overstatement. The spirits seem eager to teach us about the nature of human existence, both here and there.

—JOEL MARTIN

Over on the Other Side

It seems that no matter what is revealed during a reading, people invariably come away with the same basic questions about what the other side is and what happens to us there. To help readers better conceptualize the readings that follow, we're opening with George's responses to some commonly asked questions, along with several readings that illustrate these points.

What actually happens when we pass on?

"Interestingly, when different souls are discerned during a reading, they can almost describe it. The experience is essentially the same, but for most there can be variations. For instance, some souls have described a moment of complete darkness where it's as if somebody turned out the lights. Then they see the light, which can be as tiny as a pinhead, and move toward it. As they do, their relatives meet them and cross them over, or help them in their transition to the other side. A recently deceased person might see a barking dog that has passed on in the family and be attracted, figuring the dog would not take them to an unpleasant place."

George frequently tells subjects who it was who met their loved ones after they made the transition to the other side. Sometimes, as in the case of the following reading, the answer can be surprising.

"A male close to you passed," George said to a couple.

"Yes," both acknowledged.

"A young male."

"Yes."

"It's your son."

"Yes."

"It's a vehicle accident, that's what I'm psychically see-ing."

"Yes."

"He appears to be eighteen or nineteen."

"Yes, nineteen."

"He tells me he's not alone in the car at the time."

"That's correct."

"He's with a friend."

"Yes."

"They were not paying attention."

"Yes, that's true."

"They were a little on the wild side," George observed.

"Yes. They were drinking," the parents admitted.

"Don't blame the friend who was with him. Your son says, 'We were both guilty.' "

"Yes."

"Now he's learning how to behave himself in heaven. He says you'd be proud of him on the other side."

Both parents smiled and nodded slightly.

"His sister has passed," George continued.

"Yes," the couple answered, confirming they had lost a daughter.

"The girl passed was stillborn."

"Yes."

"She crossed him over. Even though she passed years earlier, she was there to meet him when he came over. When your son woke up on the other side, he said, 'What hap-pened?' His sister answered, 'Wouldn't you like to know!' "

But making the transition is not the same for everyone, is it?

"Other souls have described going to what I can under-stand only as a 'receiving station.' There they are met by souls who would be strangers to them here on earth but who may help them out. It seems that it's like walking into a hospital emergency room. After a while there—and who can say how long, since there appears to be no sense of linear time on the other side as we know it here—these spirits help new arrivals adjust to their spiritual body. They 'clear' it and perk them up, more or less. Then they take them to their relatives and family.

"Everyone there who wants to, has a different job. It's

funny, but a lot of people seem to feel that the idea of souls being active on the other side is a concept unique to psychics. In fact, it's quite common in Protestant denominations and has been for hundreds of years. Some people have asked me what I would like to do in the next stage. I would like to welcome people over, especially those who have come to me for readings. I'd love to be able to say to them, 'You see? I told you it was all the way it was supposed to be!'

"It seems that when you get there, the best thing to do is to take your time adapting. Some souls claim they take what we'd understand as a vacation. They take time off, because they want to rest. Again, several faiths accept the idea of souls 'resting' once they cross over. You know, in some ways dying is like moving to a different country. You make the big move, then sit back and say, 'Let me have some time off, to get to know the area, before I go to work and get on with my life.' Some souls need to rest after a long illness, for example, or after a tragedy.

"Other spirits can come to someone's assistance, but if somebody's not ready to see the forest for the trees, figuratively, they may just leave them alone. They may go into a 'sleep,' just as we do here on the earth if we have a problem we don't want to deal with. Eventually the person is ready to accept his death and to realize that we are moving on in our lives—we're not dead—we are living in another stage. Even though you are separated physically from your family, you're not separated spiritually. You can still be a part of it somehow, and once they accept that, things are so much easier.

"Many spirits come through and say, essentially, 'It was my time to go.' Yet there can be a sudden death like a car crash or a heart attack, and the soul feels cheated. Not everybody goes over there and wants to play a harp, which they don't do anyway! They can go over there and say, 'This isn't fair. I had a great family, had a great job, everything going swell, and now I'm dead?' Some people are resentful at first. The other side handles that with love and patience. They don't pressure the person to change; they leave him or her alone.

"But of course everybody's different. Some souls need to be occupied, just as they did here on earth. They can't wait to get into the limelight and start doing things. Some of them cross over, then say, 'Okay, let's get going. What do we do? I know I died. I'm adapting. What's my job?' It all depends on the individual. Some souls like to just sit back and appreciate the fact there's no struggle anymore. No worry about money, taxes, illness—all those wonderful things that make the world go 'round here. They feel very much at peace, and there's a sense of tranquillity.

"Some souls have difficulty throwing off the earth, or the materialism of the earth. Some still feel a craving to smoke, so they can imagine they smoke. Some people miss their car, so they create that image and imagine they're in a vehicle, or living in the great mansion they always wanted here but never got.

"You're allowed to do this because, as the other side says, we are responsible for our own choices, here and hereafter. God gave us each a brain and free will. I think that's made evident in the book of *Exodus* in the Bible, with Cain and Abel. If you read closely you know that God basically told Cain, 'You have your own choice, pal. Take the right road or take the wrong road.' Cain *chose* of his own free will to slay his brother. So it seems to be with almost everything."

People find it easier to settle their differences on the other side. Why is it easier there than it was here?

"Maybe because on the other side you can't run away from yourself. You have to face up to yourself, and you have to deal with yourself. I think souls realize that in order for them to spiritually progress, they have to throw off these things and let go. Some don't do it, though; again, it depends.

"I remember one reading I did where a woman lost her husband, and he came through. Then a few seconds later the woman's mother came in. Apparently the mother-in-law and the son-in-law couldn't stand each other. I actually heard the mother-in-law say, 'Oh! I wouldn't have come near here if I thought *he* was here.' And the son-in-law said something like, 'Ah, I don't want to see you, either.' The daughter said, 'That sounds like them on earth.' I said, 'Well, some things never change.' They've chosen not to throw that off. They're still bickering. And since there is no conception of linear time, that can take awhile."

So there can be hostility and negative feelings on the other side?

"Yes. But it's going to make you feel very out of place over there, because in God's world, it's so orderly and positive, there's no room for the negative. Figuratively speaking, you'll feel as if you're tumbling in space, that you just don't belong. You'll feel like a fish out of water."

You say that you discern spirits, but you can't always see or hear them. What is it like for you?

"When the spirits come through, I feel as if I'm beaming with light inside, and they are celestial beings. The intensity is similar to what you'd feel staring into a light bulb for a long time. I know that's a very poor example, but it's so difficult to describe. The average souls like ourselves give off a less brilliant light. One little boy who passed on claimed to me in a reading that the higher up you go, the more spiritual you become. And the more you progress on the other side, the brighter your light shines. Just as a soldier receives a medal denoting some achievement, on the other side you receive a color that signifies your progression. For example, if you're very loving, charitable, giving, your vibration will have a lot of pink, because pink is love and charity. Somehow I sense that, and it seems to be one way I get an idea of the spirit's personality.

"Every soul, no matter what, has some white, which is the Christ light. It's the presence of that light which tells me I am dealing with something positive. Blue is very spiritual; lavender is like a regal spiritual color. At one discernment years ago, I saw Saint Martin de Porres appear, and although he was very poor when on earth, he was very rich in spirit and had a lot of lavender.

"From what the other side has told me, there are different levels of spiritual progressions. Where you start there is determined by your 'light.' For instance, in a reading I did for a woman whose parents were very abusive to her, I felt that they definitely had a lower vibration. It's not that they were in hell, or any similar place of torture, punishment, or damnation, but their light was dimmed; it was foggy to me. In contrast, if I discern someone the Church has declared a saint, they come through clearer, brighter, stronger."

The following reading did not contain the usual elaborate explanation of gradually progressing through many levels as the overwhelming number of spirits seem to do. Because of the spirit's sacrifice and good deed here on earth, his soul progression was hastened on the other side. This reading brings to mind the biblical quote: "This is my commandment, that you love one another as I have loved you. Greater love has no man than this, that a man lay down his life for his friends." (John 15:13) The subjects were a couple and their fifteen-year-old daughter.

"A male close to both of you passed over?" George asked.

"Yes," the woman answered.

"Did you lose a son?"

"Yes."

"Are you the husband?"

"Yes," the man verified.

"Okay. Because he seems to go here [near the woman], and say, 'Mom.' So I assume the loss of a child must be going to you. He keeps acknowledging everybody, that you're all family."

"Yes."

"I take it you're his sister, because he's saying you're his sister."

"Yes," the teenaged girl replied.

"He passed on tragically."

"Yes," answered the mother.

"He's a very high-spirited guy."

"Yes."

"I feel as if I want to bounce around the room. His passing was accidental?"

"No."

"Wait a minute," George continued, clarifying the brief psychic confusion. "Wait a minute. I don't mean a car accident, but he says it's accidental. All right, I'll let it go for a second and give him the chance to tell me how he means it. Does this happen accidentally? Why does he keep bringing

this up? He's trying to tell me something. I'll let it go again.
It's very sudden. That's what he means by accident. He says,
'sudden *like* an accident.' He keeps pushing that out: 'sudden.' It must mean something else. Did he have injuries?"

"Yes," the woman confirmed.

"Did he have trouble with his legs?"

"Yes."

"He keeps telling me that he's fine. There's no trouble
with his legs now. I felt somebody touch me on the leg, and
I started moving. He says, 'I'm fine now.' "

"Yes."

"Was there an accident?"

"No."

"He says there's an accident. He keeps bringing it up. Did
it have anything to do with his leg problem at all?"

"Yes."

"It's clear," George said. "You told me there's no accident, but he keeps insisting. Did he have trouble with one
leg?"

"Yes."

"Due to an accident." Later we learned their son had
previously been injured in a motorcycle crash. Here the subjects were concentrating so intently on the cause of death,
which they assumed was being discussed, they denied information that proved to be correct. Obviously the spirit offered these clues for identification.

"Yes."

"That's where the accident comes from," George explained. "He's also very sensitive."

"Right."

"There's tremendous depth inside. Maybe he kept a lot to
himself. Or he might have been very sensitive. Anything
affect his chest at all?"

"Allergies," the woman answered.

"It's like I'm having trouble breathing. It could be symbolic. So I'll leave it with you."

"He did at the time."

"Was he also in a coma? Because I feel, I'm kind of
sluggish. You were there when he passed on?"

"Yes."

"He knows you were there. I just felt like you might have wondered, 'Does he even know I'm here?' . . . Anything affect his head at all?"

"Yes," the spirit's mother said, beginning to weep.

"There's pressure up along one side of the head." George described the sympathetic pain he felt. In fact, the young man died when a bullet entered his brain through a nostril.

"Yes!"

"This is not from an accident."

"No, it's not."

"Why does he keep giving me this terrible pressure in the head? I'm going to let it go. His head. He keeps hitting me on the head, as if he's trying to knock sense into me. He says he's hit in the head."

"Yes."

"Was there a shedding of blood?"

"Yes."

"That's why I see the blood burst in front of me. I thought it was like he had a tumor or aneurysm. Something exploded, and I saw blood going crazy. I don't know if this is symbolic. Is he shot?" George asked.

"Yes," the woman answered through tears.

"Okay. Because I'm hearing gunshots. He's murdered."

"Yes."

"He's technically at the wrong place at the wrong time."

"Right."

"He says it's beyond his control."

The woman acknowledged George's statement with a nod.

"Was he trying to break something up?"

"Yes."

"Was it that he was trying to do a good deed?"

"Yes."

"Now, he's not trying to be sarcastic. He says, 'That's what you get for trying to be a Good Samaritan.' He says he was trying to do a good deed and was victimized because of it. He seems to be that type of guy. He'd give you the shirt off his back."

"Right."

"He certainly doesn't wish anybody ill, and he certainly is

not unforgiving, but he just didn't think this person would go this far. There's some sort of altercation. He's trying to be a peacemaker."

"Right."

"Was he witnessing something? Then he tried to interfere because it's a friend or somebody he knows."

"Yes."

"Because he sacrificed his life for a friend," George said.

"Yes," the woman answered.

"That's what he states. It's as if he got in the way. He sacrificed his life on behalf of a friend. He's not the least bit sorry he did it. You know that."

"Right."

"The other fellow is still living."

"Yes."

"You have contact with him?"

"Yes."

"Your son gives me the impression that he calls out to him. 'Tell him you have heard from me,' your son says. . . . I feel as though I'm out socially; a social gathering of some sort. Was somebody bullying his friend?"

"Yes."

"It seems like somebody's starting trouble with his friend, and he tries to break it up."

"Yes."

"They caught the person who did this."

"Yes."

"It's not premeditated, but the guy who shot him did intend to do him harm. I'm not going to say this guy didn't pull out the gun with intentions of killing him, thinking he's going to teach him a lesson. He got him straight in the head. Not that he's holding any resentment. It's not going to make any difference now. . . . Was somebody on drugs or something? Because I feel I'm not in the right frame of mind. Either the guy who did the shooting was on drugs or there's some sort of substance involved. This happened in the South," George continued.

"Yes," the woman confirmed.

"Whoever does this has the manners of a dock-size boat . . . He's a big-shot type of guy. You know what I'm saying.

It seems all your son wanted to do was break it up and leave the premises or get away from it, and this guy who threatened him ganged up on him and shot him in the head."

"Yes."

After the family confirmed ten names George received, he remarked, "It sounds like he called out to Chris."

"Someone close to him," one parent responded. "There are two possibilities," the other added.

"There's someone close—" George said.

"Yes."

"It sounds like he's saying 'Chris.' Is he calling out to somebody named Chris?"

"Yes."

"Chris is a friend."

"Yes."

"I don't know. They seem to be playing a jigsaw puzzle with the name instead of coming right out with it. Because he does call to Chris. He wants that understood, that that's correct. Does your son's name begin with the letter *R?*"

"Yes."

"Is there an *O* in his first name?"

"Yes."

"R - O. Now, is Chris a friend of his?"

"Yes."

"You have contact with him?"

"Yes."

"He does call, he says, 'Tell Chris you've heard from me.' Now this friend's life that he saved. Are you still in contact with him?"

"Yes."

"Because that's what he started talking about. He started talking about the friend's life that he saved. He said, 'Please tell Chris you've heard from me.' . . . Your son's name. It's probably so easy. It's a common name, right?"

"Yes."

"It's simple, and it's staring me in the face . . . *Ronald!"*

"That's it."

"I heard Ronnie or Ronald."

"Yes."

"Does Chris live in the state that you live in?"

"Yes."

"Because when you go home, your son says to call him and tell him you've heard from Ron. Do you think he's open to this?"

"Yes."

"Oh good. He says, 'Tell Chris you've heard from me.' He keeps saying that."

"Okay."

"Your son keeps saying that it says right in the Scriptures that the greatest gift anyone can give is the person who lays down his life for his friend. That's a very spiritual thing to say. Christ says that in the Bible. Your son didn't have any medals or trophies, did he?" George asked.

"No," his mother replied.

"You'll be very proud to learn that he was given a medal, as we understand it, over there because he made the ultimate sacrifice. Your son says that what he did brings him directly into heaven! So as he puts it, 'There's a happy ending to an unhappy story.'"

The three members of the family looked at one another, then at George.

"The person who took his life is in prison?" George asked.

"Yes."

"Your son forgives him. He knows that he's in jail. Your son comes across as very easygoing. He says you miss him, but he's closer to you than you can imagine. He's happy and at peace. Continue to pray for him. Do the rosary. He wants Chris to be at peace and all of you to be at peace, and this will help *him* to be more at peace. Know that he's okay. He's there with all his relatives and the people who have passed on. He says he's going to step aside now so that somebody else can get through. 'This is Ronnie—Ron—signing off with love,' he says. He's a very affectionate individual; a very open person."

"Yes," the woman answered softly.

"Always a busy guy, though," George continued.

"Very."

"You know, even though he says he could take it easy over there because he went directly to heaven, he says he's still quite busy over there on the other side. He still feels he has to have a job, to contribute. That's nice to hear. He's definitely one person you can be guaranteed is in heaven."

• • •

Has anyone on the other side ever suggested to you that he or she has seen God or has felt God, and if so, how does He look?

"They say that they have seen God in the sense of *the light*. It's like being absorbed totally in those ultimate, positive vibrations. That's how you see God. That's how you become pure at heart. 'Blessed are the pure at heart, for they shall see God.' That can happen here on the earth, too, just as it can happen there."

Based on your conversations with the other side, what is your view or definition of God?

"I use the word *God* because that's the word I feel comfortable using. Alcoholics Anonymous, for example, would say 'Higher Power,' and I have no problem with that either. Highest Being. Highest Energy. Love. Whatever. It all means the same thing. God is, in my opinion, the complete essence of all that is beautiful, positive, uplifting, joyful. Every positive vibration is God."

Is there any hierarchy on the other side as we would know it on earth?

"A higher being, a more in-tune, celestial being may suggest what would be a good direction for us, but the decision, ultimately, is left to us."

In other words, no general, no president, no pope?

"No, you are ranked according to what you have achieved, of your own choice and free will, spiritually."

So who's "in charge"?

"God, of course, but not in that authoritarian, punitive way we've been raised to believe. God rules through an essence of complete love and understanding so pure and so right, we cannot help but 'obey' or follow. I believe that God, like Jesus Christ, leads through example. To me, Jesus is the perfect manifestation of God here on earth. He is the Savior, because if we look closely at his example and live according to his teachings, we can't help being brought closer to God. I believe it is in our spiritual nature to seek out what is good and of God. Certain circumstances may cripple that drive, but it is inherent in all of us.

"With time comes wisdom, so the more you learn over there, the more you progress. But that doesn't give you authority or superiority over somebody else. It gives you more experience to be able to help someone to help himself as God helps us. You can't make anyone do anything. Even God cannot. But you can be there to help someone once he decides to progress spiritually."

Let me use the 1981 movie Resurrection *as an example of what I mean by this question: The heroine, played by Ellen Burstyn, passes on, or has a near-death experience or resurrection. I know you've said that movie typifies pretty faithfully what you see on the other side of life. She goes there and meets her loved ones, who appear to be in a mist, but she actually sees the physical forms. Obviously when we leave the physical body, we're not in our physical forms anymore, so when we go to the other side, what is it or who is it we see? How is it that we're able to sense one another?*

"First of all, when souls appear during a reading, which happens frequently, naturally they're going to appear in the way that I can describe them so that you can identify them. They can't all appear in a white, standard-issue heavenly looking gown, because I'd have nothing distinctive to relate to the subject. I think that when we go over, and the other side has explained this in earthly terms, we identify our loved ones through personality and emotion.

"I liken it to an experience I had recently at a friend's wake. A woman approached me and said, 'Maybe you don't remember me, but I met you at so-and-so's house two years ago.' I said, 'No, I remember you. You were there at Christmas Eve, just before you moved to Maryland.' And she said, 'You have a good memory!' I replied, 'The reason I remembered you is because of your personality.' She said, 'I hope that means something good.' 'Yes,' I said, 'you had a very friendly, outgoing, nice personality, which made a nice impression on me, and that impression was remembered.'

"It seems that the physical body definitely dies, but the emotional, the personality, the *essence* of the person survives. And that's what you will always recognize her by. As much as we all have individual fingerprints, we all have unique personalities. For example, your two grandmothers. One was certainly very different from the other, and you certainly would be able to tell them apart just by how they *are*."

Spirits come to you who died here in any number of torturous ways, or who lived with a disability. Yet invariably they come through from the other side and say, "I can see again," if they've been blind. Or the mute can now speak, and the deaf can now hear. Others say, "I am free of my disease. My suffering is over." "I can walk, my limbs are back." We're restored whole, is that true?

"Yes, because it's the physical body that had the illness or the impediment, not the spiritual." This is illustrated in thousands of readings. The following excerpt is distinguished by the overwhelming number of physical problems the spirit suffered on earth. It attests to the fact that physical problems die along with the physical body:

"A male close to you passed," George said.

"Yes," the woman acknowledged.

"It's a blood relation."

"Yes."

"He's like a son that's passed."

"Yes, like one. It's my nephew," she explained.

"He's young when he passes. In his teens."

"Yes."

"He had lots of problems when he was here."

"Yes."

"He was hard on himself here."

"Yes."

"He's happier on the other side," George said. "He calls to his parents."

"Yes."

"He's very independent on the other side, but he had a lot of emotional problems here."

"Yes, he did."

"He had serious health problems."

"Yes."

"He calls to his mother. They were close."

"Yes."

"But the illness he had restricted him."

"Yes."

"Leg trouble hindered his walking here."

"Yes."

"But he says he's back to normal on the other side," George explained. "He says his mother is brokenhearted. He thanks her."

"Yes."

"I'm seeing Saint Joseph, my symbol for a 'happy,' peaceful death. He tells me he went into a coma."

"Yes."

"I psychically see blood tests, needles, and transfusions. He tells me his limbs, bones, and breathing are affected. So is his blood. Everything is affected. He suffered kidney failure."

"Yes."

"He was in a tremendous amount of pain. It was pain and then failure," George repeated.

"Yes," the aunt answered.

"He also had mental problems. He couldn't speak the words, although he could think them."

"Yes, that's because he was brain damaged."

"He says he was unconscious a great deal of the time."

"Yes."

"He's very much alive and at peace on the other side," George said. He paused momentarily, listening as the young man's spirit communicated with him. "He says someone pulled the plug. Now I'm seeing the words 'mercy killing' being spelled out in front of me."

"Yes."

"He wants you to know they did the right thing. You've been worried about whether it was the correct decision, and he wants to assure you and the other family members that it was. He says his physical body held him back. Once the spiritual body separated from the physical, he was okay again. He says that when he was on earth he was physically dead. He also says that he can see again."

"Yes, he was blind."

"Well, the instant he was out of the physical body, he was back to his 'old self' on the other side."

"I'm glad," his aunt answered emotionally.

" 'Please tell my mother she didn't murder me when she gave permission to pull the plug,' he says. 'She sent me to peace. But I know she's on a terrible guilt trip. She did not kill me. She did the right thing. She made the right decision.' "

"I understand."

"He's anxious that you tell his mother that he's okay."

"I will."

"He calls to a brother."

"Yes."

"He looks like a young teenager when he passed, less than sixteen."

"Yes, he was fourteen."

"He says he didn't really know his father because his parents split when he was very young. Do you take the name Mark?"

"Yes, that's his brother, my other nephew."

"Your nephew compares sending messages from the other side to making long-distance phone calls. He shows me the last scene from the film *Steel Magnolias* where the parent remains with the child until the end." For George, an avid movie buff, seeing scenes from motion pictures is not unusual. In some instances, the clues the other side offers can be clarified only by the subject. In this reading, the spirit gave George a visual hint he understood and could interpret for the aunt. "He says, 'My mom held my hand till the very end.' "

"Yes, she did."

"He calls to Katherine, or Katie."

"Yes, that's his mother," the woman acknowledged.

"He sends his love to her and you. He repeats, 'Remember to tell her that she made the right decision when the plug was pulled. Don't feel guilty about it.' He says he's fine and at peace, and he steps aside."

It would seem that the physical body is frail but the spiritual body is invincible. Is that so?

"The only way we can harm our spiritual body is by maliciously and deliberately breaking God's law. I hate to bring organized religion into it, but this is a good example: When a village doctor questioned Saint Bernadette of Lourdes during the apparitions of the Blessed Mother in the 1850s, he asked, 'Do you know what a sinner is?' She replied, 'A sinner is someone who loves evil.' Not *does* evil, but *loves* evil. Thus by loving evil, one does it. And that would be the case, where someone is willingly harming his spiritual body, which is the temple of the Holy Spirit, as we've been told; that he willingly breaks the law; deliberately does harmful things to people, knowing that he's doing bad or wrong things, and enjoying it."

Do we age on the other side? For example, you hear from infants who pass on from sudden infant death syndrome (SIDS), stillborns, youngsters, even miscarriages. You've told parents what sex their unborn baby would have been had it completed its cycle and been born. These children obviously are over there, since they send messages their parents have confirmed. But do they mature?

"On the other side, we 'age' through our wisdom. There is no linear time or a declining physical body over there, so we do not age as we would here. That's why your mother— even though she passed at ninety, may appear to me as a very vivacious twenty-one-year-old woman. Youth is a joy to behold, so it'd be something joyful. When these younger souls come in, remember, the physical body might have been young, but the spiritual body could be growing and maturing very rapidly in the next dimension, and this is why they come across to me as more mature. Again, they have to appear to me as their loved ones would recall them. For example, a boy who died in infancy but who would have been sixteen at the time of his mother's reading may appear to me at the age he died. Or he might appear as a teenager and tell me what age he would have been had he remained here. Otherwise it would be impossible for any of them to be identified. Children have to appear as their parents would recognize them, even though spiritually they may be very 'grown up.' It seems as though the spirit knows how he or she would be most readily recognized by the parent."

•   •   •

The baby that's passed on from SIDS, for example, will come back and communicate. The messages are very adultlike and don't sound like those of an infant.

"Because the baby probably has grown spiritually on the other side and hence comes across older. The physical body is removed, so she's not hindered by its limitations. And talking is a physical act. Simply because someone can't speak because of a young age, mental disability, or a coma, doesn't mean she isn't knowledgeable. Perhaps she just can't communicate it.

"The communication over there seems to be more by pure emotion and feeling. A good example of what I mean is: In my bereavement groups, I warn people, 'Keep in mind that if your grandmother raised you, and you called her Mom, my brain's going to say, "This person's *mother* has passed on." ' They'll say no, and I'll insist, 'But there's a person around you claiming to be Mom.' Eventually somebody will explain to me, 'I was raised by my grandmother and *called her* Mom.' To the other side, being *like* Mom is, emotionally, the same as *being* Mom.

"Or a best friend will come through like a brother, because that emotional, eternal feeling does not die. I'll say, 'You lost your brother,' and a subject will say no, and we'll almost get into a teeth-pulling session, because they don't understand that I'm dealing with something on an emotional level."

People ask constantly: Where, physically, is the other side? Is it way up there in the clouds? Is it around me?

"People ask that because of the way we've been conditioned and programmed by organized religion. I have a habit of kidding around during a reading, of looking up and saying, 'I hear you,' or, 'I know you're up there,' because we're told heaven is up. Actually, it seems that the other side runs parallel to this one. It's here. But it's a *nonphysical* dimension. That's why, I think, they constantly say that they're closer to us than we are to them, because they're not constricted by time, space, and matter. A lot of the souls say that sometimes they're so close to us, they literally walk through us. I think the classic movie *Our Town* depicted that well, where at the end the girl comes back for a day on the earth. She more or less walks through her mother and stands next to her, talking to her.

"A lot of souls, especially children who have passed on and whose parents grieve over them terribly, say that it can be very frustrating on the other side. In a recent reading, one said, 'Recall the scene out of the movie *The Wizard of Oz* where Auntie Em appears in the witch's crystal ball.' Auntie Em can't find Dorothy and calls out for her. And Dorothy taps on the crystal ball and frantically replies, 'I'm here in Oz, Auntie Em. I'm trying to get home to you!' But Auntie Em doesn't hear a thing. They said that's basically what it's like for them: The children see the parents grieving over them, but they can't communicate with them, to comfort them. They're like Dorothy, saying, 'I'm here! Why do you think I'm not here? I'm here!' But they can't get through and know they can't be heard."

To prove his point, George shared with me a letter that showed how the spirits see us and are aware of our activities and emotions here on earth:

Dear Mr. Anderson:
On July 16 I went to you for a reading, which was fairly successful. The next week, after listening to my tape on which our son called eight times to his father, my husband visited you. During the middle of his reading, our son sent a message that Andrew, the son of a couple from The Compassionate Friends, was with him and that both he and Andrew had died of brain tumors under similar circumstances. This meant nothing to my husband, as he did not then know of Andrew or his parents. However, that same evening, while my husband was waiting for his reading, I was at a Compassionate Friends get-together at Malibu Beach, New York, where I talked at length with a couple who had lost their son to a brain tumor. His name was *Andrew!* Needless to say, when I heard the tape of my husband's reading, I knew that my son and Andrew had been with us on the beach that night and that, fortunately for us, he was able through you to let us know.

The spirits have told George that all they require to be in a particular location is to think about the place where they want to be or the person whom they want to be near. Either the son's spirit somehow knew where both his parents were because he is close to them, or the moment he thought about them he could instantaneously will himself, out of love, to be with each of them in separate locations, miles apart. In other words, through God's grace, their son's spirit created his own reality.

You have described the other side as beautiful; you've described it in terms of colors; and in one reading, as "flora and fauna." Is it like the Garden of Eden?

"It almost looks that way, yes. It looks as if there's plant life, flora and fauna, and an essence that is completely contrary to what's here."

And yet if we're in spiritual bodies and don't really see one another, how do we sense that beauty?

"The same way you'd look at a rose here on earth and say, 'Oh, isn't that beautiful? Look at the colors!' But you feel the color. On the other side, since you're not in the physical body, the experience, the pleasure, and the color are sensed more through feeling. You sense it so intensely, it's as if you actually see it, as you would here through your eyes. It seems that what you sense there is the feeling that rose inspires, the emotions you would have if you recalled physically seeing, smelling, and touching it. When I discern, I usually see through feeling. I *feel* what the person's name is, I *feel* what he or she looks like. It's like being hypersensitive."

In a reading for a mother whose little girl had passed on, you described seeing her with another little girl who'd passed on previously. You saw them playing on a beach.

"I remember that. If anybody's ever seen the movie *Journey to the Center of the Earth* with James Mason and Pat Boone, it looked like that beach in the center of the earth, minus the dinosaurs. But it was a much more beautiful setting. The mother later told me that her child had always loved the beach when she was on the earth. I saw her in this beautiful beachlike setting, playing there in total peace and tranquillity."

•   •   •

You also said that you can create your own reality over there, if you want to live in a house, or in a palace, or on the beach.

"That's right. The mind's ability to create is very powerful. Really, you create your own reality here, in a lot of ways."

Is it permissible to do that over there?

"Yes, especially if you've just come from the earth, because this could be the way you get it out of your system. Sometimes people need to throw earthly feelings and desires out of their system. It's like Christmas morning. You've waited so anxiously for a toy, then you finally get it. Once the novelty wears off, you move on to something else. That could be what they're trying to tell us."

Can we sometimes choose the time when we pass on?

"Yes, most of us choose that. The only circumstance I'm still unsure about is murder. Do we die because somebody else chooses to do that for us? Or do we sometimes choose to become involved in a series of circumstances and events that result in our death? Then you have to consider another common situation, like a car crash. Sometimes I wonder, Can we simply be at the wrong place at the wrong time?"

Police officers who are wounded or killed in the line of duty often seem to be at the wrong place at the wrong time. Yet in this reading for a disabled cop named Frank, George learned from the spirits of three policemen killed on the job that it had, indeed, been their time to go. Rather than be in the wrong place at the wrong time, they were actually in the *right* place at the *right* time.

The handsome young policeman had walked on crutches ever since he was partially paralyzed by a bullet from a street criminal's gun. By every definition Frank is a hero cop, one who just barely eluded death. As George began the reading, three police officers appeared psychically to him. They stood together and "pinned" a trio of medals on Frank because, they explained, "He has endured his suffering with immense courage."

The three went on to say that once on the other side, each was given what they described as a "spiritual medal by higher spiritual presences." Then the three were also presented with Saint Michael the Archangel medals. Saint Michael is the patron, or the guardian angel, of police officers. Since the time of the apostles, this saint has been distinguished from other angels and held in the highest esteem as a protector. One of the three archangels referred to in Scripture, he is considered a leader in heaven over the forces of evil.

Even though the circumstances of their passings were tragic, each of the three cops told George that nevertheless it was their time to go. They *chose* to pass, they insisted, and were happy and at peace on the other side. They also said that Frank made the decision to remain on earth. Each spirit gave his name: Phillip, Michael, and Eddie. Each had been shot and killed in uniform.

Why had they come through to someone they'd never known in the physical dimension? "For the comradeship," they claimed, explaining they had greatly admired the wounded officer's bravery and patience, and the fact that he had forgiven his attacker.

Later in the reading, the spirit of an elderly man came through to apologize to the young crippled officer. "On behalf of my grandson who shot you," he said, "and my family, I'm sorry this happened to you. You don't deserve this."

Does the other side ever give advice on how we can best make the transition to the other side?

"In many readings they clearly do."

Mary was a pretty woman with jet black hair and large brown eyes. Animated, energetic, and outspoken, she credited being raised on New York City's Lower East Side for her direct, uninhibited manner. She could be brutally frank, yet warm and gregarious. After her first marriage ended in divorce, she raised her two daughters and in her late thirties remarried. With her second husband, a physician eighteen years her senior, Mary found the happiness that had eluded her much of her life. With the measure of affluence that she now enjoyed, she divided her time between family, bookkeeping and office responsibilities for her husband's medical practice, and painting.

Then, only a year after remarrying, Mary developed breast cancer, the same disease that had claimed her mother years earlier. For the next two years she underwent surgery, radiation, and chemotherapy, an ordeal she endured courageously. Mary's positive attitude never wavered. She viewed the cancer as just another of life's obstacles meant to be overcome.

The cancer went into remission but recurred two years later, spreading to her lymph nodes, lungs, and bones. Again she submitted to chemotherapy, her optimism and resolve undaunted by the doctors' dim prognosis and her increasing weakness.

But Mary was also a realist. She had met George briefly through her husband, who had an intellectual and scientific curiosity about the paranormal in general and George's ability specifically. When she knew her time was drawing near, Mary told her husband and her daughters, "I want to be ready to pass on. I want to know who'll meet me. I want to know what to expect." She felt George could help her.

Through friends, arrangements were made for Mary to talk with George on the telephone. He did not know to whom he was speaking or why, and obviously could not see her. With George's permission, Mary tape-recorded her reading.

"Has there been an extreme tragedy around you?" he asked.

"Yes," she answered.

"Not that long ago."

"Correct."

"It already happened."

"Yes."

"But it's not like twenty years ago."

"Well, yes, there was one twenty years ago, too."

"Oh, all right. But this one seems to be more recent."

"Yes, this is recent."

"So this is the one I want to go with. It's definitely more recent."

"Yes."

"I keep seeing Saint Anthony around you, dressed in black, over your head, which is a sign of loss or tragedy. It did involve a death."

"Not so far," Mary explained.

"Could somebody pass on?" George inquired.

"Possible. Not yet."

"Because there is news of a death. Saint Anthony is right over your head, definitely in black. That's news of a loss or a death."

"Yes."

"There is something along those grounds. Your mother passed on."

"Yes."

"Your father also."

"Yes."

"You're closer to your mother, though."

"Yes."

"Not that you're not close to your dad, but you definitely knew your mom better."

"Yes. Right."

"Do you have any health troubles?" George asked.

"Yes," Mary acknowledged.

"Serious."

"Yes."

"I don't think I'm telling you anything you don't already know, but it doesn't look too good."

"Okay."

"It seems it's getting worse. It has its moments when it's under control. Then it gets worse again. It shows up somewhere else."

"Right, right."

"And your mother says she definitely has been with you through this ordeal, which developed recently."

"Okay."

"Did you lose a brother?"

"Yes. It was a miscarriage."

"You took care of your mother."

"Yes, basically."

"She thanks you for being good to her prior to her passing."

"Oh thank you. Okay. Good."

"Do you have a specific illness?"

"Yes."

"You have something like cancer."

"Yes."

"Is it affecting your lower region?"

"Yes."

"Because I feel like I have it in the stomach or that general vicinity."

"Yes. Right."

"It's also affecting your glands."

"Yes."

"I don't know what they mean by that, so I'm just going to have to say what I've [psychically] heard. Your mother says it affects your lower regions and glands."

"Yes."

"In other words, it's spreading."

"Yes."

"You have been hospitalized."

"Yes. Yes."

"Because I see you in the hospital. You're certainly under chemotherapy and all that kind of treatment."

"Yes. Right."

"Your mother, a very religious woman."

"Yes. Definitely."

"She's Catholic."

"Yes."

"She's very, very religious. Very Catholic."

"Yes."

"She says she's praying for you, but it's almost as though you could go at any time."

"Right."

"You know I don't mean to be morbid by telling you that," George hastened to add.

"No, I've been told that," Mary answered.

"Your mother, she's waiting. She knows that you could pass at any time."

"Okay."

"And she says there is nothing to be afraid of, that she's waiting for you."

"Okay."

"She says you've been praying for her and praying to her."

"Yes."

"I keep hearing bells ringing, which is an alert. It's a symbol of—you know."

"Could you tell her I don't want to come!" Mary blurted out.

"Well, she keeps saying that there is nothing to be afraid of. It's like going from one room to the next."

"Yeah, but . . . okay."

"You know when the time comes, the time comes in any case."

"Yes."

"Was your mom very devout to the Blessed Mother?"

"Yes."

"She was also devoted to the Sacred Heart."

"Yes. Definitely."

"I keep seeing the Sacred Heart of Jesus and Mary burning in front of me," George explained, referring to the psychic symbol he had seen.

"Yes."

"You've been praying to the Sacred Heart."

"Occasionally."

"Your mom says to pray to the Sacred Heart for help and for acceptance of whatever comes to pass, as she did."

"Oh, okay."

"I mean, anything is possible. But if the doctors have already told you anything could happen, the same thing comes from my point of view, that you could pass on."

"Yes."

"But in any case, your mother says if you do pass on, she certainly will be waiting there for you. She'll take you by the hand and lead you into the light. She says there is nothing to fear but fear itself."

"Right."

"Your mom passed on peacefully."

"I would say so."

"Because she shows me Saint Joseph, the symbol of a happy death. It could also be a sign with you as well for a happy death. So it's a peaceful passing." George frequently sees this symbol when the person has passed on during sleep, in a coma, or a persistent vegetative state.

"Is there an Anna passed on?" George asked.

"Yes," Mary acknowledged.

"She knows your mother."

"Yes."

"Because she's there also. She's like an aunt or something."

"Yes, it's my grandmother. My mother's mother."

"Because your mother says, 'Anna is here with me also.' Apparently she's on the alert, too, that you could come over."

"Okay."

"Is there also a Mary?"

"Yes, that was my mother's name."

"Because it's Anna and Mary waiting. I mean, miracles never cease, but at this point it doesn't look like it. There could be one, but it seems you've been battling this for a while."

"Yes."

"I see Saint Peregrine around you. That's also a sign of cancer and terminal illness and things of that nature."

"Right."

"You feel you're being cheated?" George asked.

"Oh yeah. I want to live longer," Mary answered.

"Well, that's the thing. It seems your life is really happy."

"Yeah, I feel cheated."

"Your life has been very happy and constant in the last few years. You finally have purpose and direction. And all of a sudden this happens, and, frankly, it's screwing everything up."

"You got it."

"Your mother says to try to look at it from a spiritual point of view; that whatever you were to do here, has been accomplished, and it's time to move on. You still can work from the next stage of life as well. You're married?"

"Yes."

"You've been married before. This is your second marriage here. Your husband will outlive you."

"Right."

"You have children. Your mother calls out to your children. The one thing your mother impresses you to do is to pray to the Sacred Heart for peace."

"Oh, okay."

"That's the main thing. Pray for peace. She keeps saying that. Did you call her Mama?"

"I used to call my grandmother Anna that. Anna was Mama."

"Oh, okay. That's why somebody said, 'Pray for peace.' I heard somebody say the message was from Mama. I took it to mean it was from your mother, but apparently your grandmother said that. Anna was definitely very religious also."

"Yes, definitely."

"Very devoted to Saint Anthony and different saints."

"Yes."

"Is there a Philomena who's passed on or someone devoted to her?"

"I'm not sure. I have aunts that passed on, but I was very young. I don't remember their names."

"Saint Philomena also represents a happy death," George explained.

"Good," Mary replied.

"Is this affecting your blood, too? Because it seems like it's all over."

"Yeah."

"Your mother is being very fatalistic, in a sense. She says, 'Don't fight it. If it is going to happen, it's going to happen.' Being that your life is so happy, that's why you don't want to accept it."

"You're right."

"Your mother is very family oriented."

"Yes."

"She keeps saying to me, 'What's wrong? You don't want to see me?' "

"Yeah, later!" Mary quipped.

"She's looking forward to seeing you again. Did you lose a pet? A dog?"

"Yes."

"Your mother says, 'The dog's here with us.' "

"You're kidding!"

"The dog will be waiting for you, too. There definitely are a lot of people over there who know and love you. If your time comes, they'll know you, and they'll be there."

"May I ask a question?" Mary inquired.

"Okay," George said. Because George insists on remaining passive, he rarely allows questions, but does so at appropriate times such as this.

"Could you ask her how I could make my passing easier for my husband and children?"

George was quiet for a moment as he listened to the spirit's answer. "Your mother responds: Tell them that you've heard from her, and that you will still have the connections with this dimension. And that someday they'll be with you as well. Tell them to always pray for you and let them know you are near. 'What can I say to make it easier?' She says the loss is going to be taken deeply. You're very well loved. But it's something we all have to go through, sooner or later."

"Right," Mary said.

"Just remember to tell them to pray for you and to know that you are near. Besides, you're open to life after death."

"Yes."

"You'll make the transition. You'll adjust all right because you believe it. Your mother will be there waiting for you. So when you know you're passing on or when you feel you're letting go, that's when your mother says to start thinking of her. She says, 'Start looking for me immediately. Know that I'll be there with Anna and the other relatives, too!' Is there also an Anthony passed on?"

"Yeah. In the family there is someone named Anthony."

"They're all nearby. In any case, she says, 'There is nothing to fear but fear itself.' Pray to the Sacred Heart and know that she'll help you make the transition. It will be a smooth, peaceful transition. She is near. She's going back now."

"Okay. Could I have a time frame? A year? Six months? A week? Go to bed now?"

"You never know the way things can change. You could outlive all of us. But it could be within the year. It does not seem to be that far away, because I don't see anything for your immediate future except what is being talked about now."

"There's experimental treatment for the cancer I have. Should I enter it or not?"

"You have nothing to lose."

"Right."

"As your mother says, you have nothing to lose now. I see Saint Peregrine around you, which is a symbol of cancer but also a symbol of hope. So definitely take that into consideration," George said.

"Okay. Thank you," Mary answered.

"If you do pass on, come and visit me," George answered.

"You'd better believe it! Okay. Thanks a lot."

Following the reading, Mary and her husband talked and cried. "We said everything we needed to say to each other," her husband recalled.

Using their recording of the reading as a catalyst, they verbalized feelings about her death that each of them had so far largely evaded. They expressed how much they loved and would miss each other. Until this point there had been a good deal of denial about her death, but the reading enabled them to confront it. Mary urged her husband to go on with his life, reminding him that George had assured her that she would be fine and with loved ones on the other side. After Mary shared her feelings and thoughts with her husband, she called in each of her two adult daughters and spoke to them individually. Then the entire family gathered again and continued to talk.

Exactly five months to the day after she spoke with George, Mary passed on. She was at home with her husband by her side. She was forty-five years old.

What seems to be the key to making the transition?

"The most important advice is, Alleviate all fear. One thing I've tried explaining to people is, Pride is called the deadliest of the seven capital sins in Christianity, because from it stem all the other sins, such as greed, hate, and jealousy. Fear is by far the deadliest of the negative vibrations, since it can snowball into twenty or forty different negative vibrations. The best thing to do is to overcome fear of the unknown, fear of how we've been programmed to believe this is what's going to happen after we die, this is what's going to happen here, we're going to go to hell, or whatever. To me, fear is *the* instrument of evil."

•   •   •

How does the other side describe what it's like? Similar to or different from what we have been "programmed" to believe by organized religions of "heaven" and "hell"?

"First, let me say that the other side speaks to me in terms of Catholic words or dogma because they know I understand that. They're always trying to reach to your particular level of intelligence and understanding. Maybe the other side is more accurately described in terms of Einstein's theory of relativity, but those on the other side know I'm a total idiot in that area, so they'd be wasting their breath! To help me to understand and help others to understand, they'll say to me, 'It's like purgatory, but not in the sense of suffering, fire, and all that nonsense.' It is purgatory in the sense that you're still going through growing stages, still trying to progress upward."

When somebody escapes justice here—say, a murderer—does he go to a hot, fiery hell, or to someplace much colder?

"That's interesting. The other side states that they're not in the eternal fire, but it's so hot that it's freezing cold. Again, you're putting yourself there—not that you're condemned there for eternity. You've condemned yourself. You're doing 'time,' so to speak, but you still have the opportunity to change if you want to, if you want to forgive yourself. The most difficult lesson to learn here or hereafter is forgiveness of self. Forgiveness of others can be hard enough, but forgiveness of self is greater. Sooner or later, we have to face ourselves."

We have many divisions among us as human beings. There are Catholics who say that the Jews won't go to their heaven. And there are Fundamentalists who claim that neither Catholics nor Jews are going to go to their heaven. We divide ourselves up by race and religion constantly. When we get to the other side, is there a white heaven, a black heaven, a Moslem heaven, and so on?

"Absolutely not. This division is all physical. You are handled spiritually according to your merit here. I'm not going to get to heaven any faster because I was baptized a Roman Catholic. You're not going to get to heaven any

faster because you were raised Jewish. Think about how
many highly spiritual people were persons of color. Yet
many organized groups would not acknowledge them.
Things like this confirm my belief that when it comes to true
spirituality, most organized religion creates more problems
than it solves. It's as Dr. Pasqual Schievella says in his book
Hey! Is That You, God?: 'In the beginning, Man created
God.' That's what that is to me: man's creation and interpretation of God.''

How and why is prayer so powerful?

"The spirits almost always say to their loved ones, 'You're
not just rattling off repetitive words or prayers; they're very
helpful.' Prayer is like receiving love; it's like receiving a card
in the mail saying, 'I'm thinking about you.' It embraces
them with love, which encourages them to go on, just as you
would support them in whatever they were doing with love
here. That would encourage people to go on with their lives
and to feel good about themselves. It keeps them awake and
flowing. The prayer helps people here because there isn't
anything you wouldn't do for them, especially when they're
suffering. Prayer gives you the opportunity to know that
you're still doing something for them.''

*What does the other side say about our earthly funeral prac-
tices and rituals? If the physical body isn't there, why do we
spend this tremendous amount of money and energy on cas-
kets, flowers, and so on?*

"They say that funerals are for the living, and I do believe
they are. But some people need to be able to look in that
coffin and see the remains, because that signifies the good-
bye, the departing. Most of the time, when the other side
does comment on a funeral or wake, they say, 'Gee, I didn't
know that many people thought that highly of me.' And
they're really impressed by the emotion that's expressed, the
family coming together, the love, the support. Ironically,
tragedy brings people together in a very positive sense. People let down their defenses: they feel emotion, they hug
people, they support, they become spiritual. So in that sense,
yes, funerals and wakes are good. Maybe it's good for the

souls on the other side, to see how much they are loved and missed."

Many times I've heard spirits say through you, "You were just recently at my grave and placed flowers there." So they are aware of it.

"Yes, because it's a physical expression of love, and to them it is important. Here and hereafter, they still need the reassurance that we love one another. When that comes up in a reading, it's always nice to hear the individual soul say, 'My son's disappointed because he never got to say good-bye to me, he didn't make it to the hospital on time before I died.' They often say, 'I'd much rather say hello this way than say good-bye; I'd rather take up where we left off.' "

2

An Evening with George

Nothing about George Anderson's home suggests who he is or what he does. A conventional 1950s-era split-level ranch, its neatly trimmed lawn and pruned hedges blend in with his neighbors'. The town is a typical middle-class Long Island, New York, community, with wide streets, strip malls, high property taxes, and excellent schools—in short, the kind of area where almost anyone would be happy to raise a family.

When people come to George's house to receive a personal reading or take part in a group discernment, they sometimes seem disappointed that it all seems so "normal." Perhaps they were expecting an old Victorian manse with musty velvet drapes or a storefront with a neon sign flashing PSYCHIC.

Each guest is greeted and shown to a small waiting room, the walls of which are adorned with classic movie posters and stills from George's favorite films. Across the foyer is the small, softly lit den where he conducts the readings and discernments. It is paneled in dark wood and simply furnished with a beige sofa, a few chairs, and several small tables. All that distinguishes it from the average family room is a number of religious paintings and symbols—and the corner shrine to Saint Philomena (like Saint Jude, a patron saint of the impossible), to whom George is deeply devoted. For this evening's group discernment, he has arranged two parallel rows of folding chairs the length of the room. Here the subjects will sit while George walks from one to another, as the spirits direct him.

All first-time visitors' faces convey apprehension and hope. Most of them basically understand George's ability, but naturally they still wonder. Perhaps they've come to him because they need to know their loved ones are alive in another dimension, happy and at peace. Others are afraid, worried about what they may or may not hear tonight. Will that special person come through for them? Will their questions be answered? Their faith reaffirmed? For the majority, this will be their first experience with anything psychic, so there is always the natural human fear of the unknown. These are people who, in the words of a young mother who lost her only child, "have had to face death's touch."

Once inside the reading room and in their seats, the twenty or so men and women sit in silence, glancing about, offering one another nods and friendly yet sad smiles. Over the years that George has offered the weekly discernments, he's noticed that each group has its own dynamic. Most of these people will never see one another again, but for this night there is a bond among them. They have come alone or with loved ones, from literally up the street and from the other side of the world, representing every age, faith, and ethnic group.

Although George began the groups to accommodate more people, they have developed into something substantially more than a collection of individuals seeking "psychic readings." They are, in a sense, bereavement support groups in their own right. In traditional bereavement groups, people who have suffered a loss gather for the purpose of sharing their grief and learning to cope. Members search and struggle, talking about and working through their feelings, until they eventually find the strength and the means to move on with their lives.

For many people, bereavement groups and therapy are crucial. George encourages anyone having a particularly difficult time adjusting to a death to seek professional help and peer support. Most important, he does not see what he does as a substitute for such help. But as many people who come to George can attest, sometimes nothing our society is prepared to offer really helps. The well-intentioned words of clergy and psychotherapists strike many as pat. For those whose loved ones pass in brutal or bizarre circumstances, it seems that no one truly understands, and to an extent, they are right.

George views the psychic readings as a beneficial adjunct to other means of coping with bereavement; for some people it is the only way they can resolve their frustrations and fears. Through their communications from the other side, deceased loved ones can prove to the bereaved that they did not die, that they are still part of their lives, and that physical death does not sever the bonds of love and caring. For some, that is all they need to know. But for others, grief refuses to yield because of unresolved issues and questions. Too often, only the person who has passed over can tell us the circumstances of his death—whether or not he suffered, and how he feels about a number of issues.

In the group discernments, participants witness others' readings as well as receive their own personal messages from the other side. Seeing how others cope with death and bereavement can be a cathartic experience, if only because it shows that no one is truly alone, that thinking about a loved one or being depressed isn't crazy or unusual. It's not uncommon for two strangers to be consoling each other by evening's end.

Once everyone is seated, George introduces himself. People are often surprised by how relaxed, soft-spoken, and humorous he is. Some even seem amazed that he dresses casually.

"Ninety-nine percent of the time you're not going to walk out disappointed," he tells them, "but don't have expectations. You must understand that I can't make any guarantees or promises. You may expect to hear from one person on the other side, and another comes through instead. I don't know why some souls get through and others don't. I'm convinced that the spirits see us and pick up our voices, so they have some way of knowing who's here. But I'm not sure to what degree. On the other hand, they may not all be able or ready to come through. We don't know exactly how the ability works. All I can do is go around the room, wherever the other side directs me.

"Don't limit yourself in time and don't block out names or relatives," George continues. "You might hear from whom you least expect. It doesn't matter when they've passed—it could be years ago or even yesterday. There may be relatives or friends of the family who died years before you were born. You may not know them or recognize their names, but you can be pretty sure that they know who you are.

"The best, most dramatic, and for me, most challenging readings, are the ones with emotional connections. If your life is going normally, with no particular crises, the reading may seem quite ordinary. There's really nothing wrong with that; it means your life is progressing smoothly. But your reading may not be terribly exciting.

"Not to sound crass, but I often tell people that if their lives are going swell and few of their loved ones have passed on, don't bother coming to me. They have no need for my services, because what I can tell them, *anybody* can tell them. If I say, 'You're going to change your job,' obviously you're going to do that sooner or later. Obviously you're going to move to a new home sooner or later. Or make investments. To me, it's going to be what I call a fortune-teller's experience. I try to encourage people to come only if there's a need for some sort of spiritual bereavement counseling or help. Also, I strongly encourage you not to come again for a year, so that others who need help can get in."

As the group listens attentively, George explains, "You'll see me scribbling on a pad. Some people call it automatic writing. But I prefer to think of it as a distraction, a form of concentration as I receive messages from the other side. My hand is not under any 'mysterious control.' I'm totally in control. I don't go into a trance. I'll hear a voice or occasionally see a vision. Depending on the person, the discerning goes on for a while. I actually see spirits at times, but my main connection, or communication, is sensing and feeling, or sensing and hearing.

"When the spirits speak to me, it's through the mind, like telepathy, but from the other side, not between you and me. When I see them, they're a spiritual body. Actually, it's so difficult to explain, it would be easier if you could be me for five minutes." Everyone smiles.

"In case you're wondering what my ability feels like, after I pray and ask for protection, as I always do, I feel a little whirring sensation, as if someone flicked on a light switch. Then I sense a presence. I hear the spirits speaking, and I ask, 'If you're in God's light, whom do you go to?' As the discernment begins, I focus and ask, 'Has a male passed?' Once someone can acknowledge the first basic information, the reading has begun.

"Please remember to just say yes or no. Try not to give me any information." George takes a breath. "Okay, I'll just pray silently to myself, to the Blessed Trinity and Saint Philomena, and then we'll begin."

For a few moments after George completes his prayer he sits silently, cocking his head as if listening to someone and making writing motions on the pad on his lap. He rises and approaches a young couple who seem a bit nervous.

"A male close to you passed," he states.

"Yes," the man replies.

"You've lost a brother."

"No, but someone like a brother," the man answered.

"You worked together."

"Yes."

"Your dad, too, has passed."

"Yes," the man says.

"Your dad says this person is like a son to him on the other side," George goes on. "You and this individual were 'partners.'"

"Yes."

"Now, your dad, he was a self-made man on earth."

"Yes."

"The one who's like your brother, he knew his time was coming. He rushed around to get as much done as possible."

"Yes."

"He's a very giving soul."

"Yes."

"He had his money, definitely. He could pay his bills, but he was very giving to others," George says in a relaxed, conversational tone. "You definitely pray for him. He thanks you."

"Yes."

"He was tremendously active and involved with charity."

"Yes."

"He calls to his wife and children. He's very family oriented."

"Yes."

"He knew how to handle money," George emphasizes.

"He knew how to give it away," the man replies with a smile.

"He says he's glad to be relieved of the material pressures." After a slight pause, George says to the man, "A woman has passed. She comes through like a mother."

"Yes."

"Your friend's calling out to his parents. He mentions his dad."

"Yes."

"For the short time he was here, he was very fulfilled."

"Yes, very."

"He was devout to Christ, or to be more exact, an example of Christ. He lived the Gospel."

"Yes."

"I'm seeing the symbol of Saint Vincent de Paul. It's my psychic symbol that he's very giving," George explains. Then he turns to the woman and asks, "Do you take the name John or Joseph? It's a father figure to you."

"Yes, Joseph," she replies.

Then the spirit of the man's father interrupts George's train of thought, and he returns his attention to him. "Your dad was very close to you."

"Yes," the man acknowledges.

"Your dad had a hard life."

"Yes."

"He calls to your mom. She's still living."

"Yes."

"Your friend again: He didn't let this world harden his heart."

"That's true."

"I'm seeing creative symbols, psychically. He was very creative in music or art."

"Yes."

"He played instruments, composed, and wrote."

"Yes."

"Was he famous? Because he says I'd know who he is," George says.

"Yes."

"Did he pass tragically? He says he did."

"Yes, he did."

"Vehicle involved."

"Yes."

"He did concerts."

"Yes."

"He was on his way to work when this happens."

"Yes."

"Did you manage him?"

"Sort of," the man answers.

"He was a singer. He's playing guitar and other instruments," George declares.

"Yes."

"You knew him very well."

"Yes."

"He emphasizes, again, that you two were like brothers."

"Yes."

"He lived on Long Island, he says."

"Yes, he did."

"His passing made the news, he says."

"Yes."

"He passed five, seven, even ten years ago."

"Yes."

"He didn't suffer, he says."

"I don't know; I hope not," the youthful-looking middle-aged man nearly whispers.

"In the back of his mind he knew it was his time," George states, then asks, "Do you take the name William or Bill?"

"Yes, it's my dad."

"Do you take the name Harry?"

"Yes!"

"It's 'your pal,' he says."

"Yes!"

"He was around forty when he passed, he tells me."

"Yes."

"I see him standing in front of you. He's got curly hair, chestnut brown in color, roundish face, clean shaven. He's solidly built."

"Yes."

George has to stifle a laugh. "He says that's why he came in first, because, he says, 'I know how to handle a crowd.' "

"Yes," the man agrees, chuckling fondly as others in the room smile.

"He tells me he died on the Long Island Expressway in Nassau County," George says.

"Yes."

"He's okay and at peace."

"Good."

"Definitely continue to pray for him."

"Yes, I will."

"There's a *mob* of coworkers he calls to."

"Yes."

George, possessor of a wry sense of humor, notes, "He says he's been—pardon the expression—'dying for years to come through,' but he couldn't find a way. He definitely believed in a hereafter."

"Yes."

"He says there's as big a waiting list in heaven as there is here."

"Yes."

"He says something about 'cats.' He's singing something about cats, and playing the guitar. 'Cat's in the cradle.'"

"Yes," the man acknowledges, nodding.

"He seems to know me. He says he's heard of me."

"Yes."

"Is his wife open to this?" George asks. Naturally, not everyone is.

"Yes."

"He's always helping aspiring musicians here and there."

"Yes, he would."

"He's not a churchgoer. To him, God doesn't exist only in four walls on a Sunday morning. He exists all around us, he feels."

"Yes."

"There's a birthday he's around for now."

"Yes, it's his mother's birthday."

"You work in a creative area," George then says to the stranger sitting before him.

"Yes."

"Celebrity status never went to your friend's head. He's very humble."

"Yes."

"His goals here were to help others, entertain others."

"Yes, that's correct."

"I feel very uplifted, radiant, high-spirited with him. He definitely likes to talk," George says with a laugh.

"Yes."

"He says if there was anyone you wanted to hear from tonight, it was he."

"Yes."

"Continue to pray for him."

"Yes, I will."

"There's concern around your father," George says, turning his attention back to the woman. "It's a health concern for his heart. It feels like an irregular heartbeat."

The woman does not answer, and George suggests that the message was meant for the future. "Your grandmother comes through now from the other side."

"Yes, she's passed on," the woman acknowledges.

"There are shamrocks around, psychically. She's Irish."

"Yes."

"Do you take the name Mary?" George inquires.

"Yes, that's my grandmother."

Once again, the gregarious spirit of Harry returns.

"Harry wishes you a happy trip," George says to the man. "It involves business, he says."

"Yes."

"He's well adjusted and as well liked on the other side as he was here. He goes back now," George adds, describing his sense that the spirit is fading or retreating to the other side.

As many during the reading had guessed, and as we confirmed in a later interview, "Harry" was none other than the late singer-songwriter Harry Chapin. One of Long Island's most beloved citizens, he was killed in 1981 at age thirty-eight in a car accident on the Long Island Expressway. As George correctly indicated, Chapin was indeed "on his way to work," en route to a benefit-concert appearance.

In addition to being a successful recording artist, with 1974's Number One "Cat's in the Cradle" among his other hits, Harry was a leader in a wide range of charitable causes and a major benefactor of Long Island arts organizations. Over half the approximately two hundred concert dates he played annually benefited charities. Years before world hunger became a fashionable cause for pop stars, Chapin lobbied tirelessly in Washington and established the World Hunger Year organization, which continues to raise millions each year for the needy. The man for whom George did this reading, Bill Ayres, was Harry's closest friend and partner, and cofounded with him World Hunger Year. I knew Chapin and can vouch that he'd heard of George, for the singer regularly listened to and frequently appeared on radio's *The Joel Martin Show*, on which George made his first public appearances.

Next the other side directs George across the room to a well-dressed couple sitting with a teenage girl.

"A male close to you passed," he says.

"Yes," the man answers.

"A son."

"Yes."

"A grandparent to one of you has also passed. It goes to you." George indicates the man. "It's your grandmother. She's very devout. A real Christian woman."

"Yes."

"Your son passes suddenly. It's a shocking passing. There's no preparation for it, but it's not from a health problem."

The woman speaks up. "That's correct."

"The young male who passed is your brother, and he's younger than you," George says, facing the teenage girl.

"Yes."

"He passed recently."

"Yes," the man acknowledges.

"He says, 'Don't be disappointed in me.' Does that make sense to you?"

"Yes."

"There are brothers and sisters he's calling out to."

"Yes."

"I'm seeing a psychic symbol," George continues. "It's the Sacred Heart of Jesus, a symbol of Jesus's suffering at the Crucifixion. It's often my symbol when someone has taken his own life." It is apparent from the way George frames the question that he knows the answer, psychically, even before it is affirmed. "Did your son take his own life?" he asks.

"Yes," the man replies softly.

"It happened recently. Last year."

"Yes."

"There's no clue whatsoever. . . . There's no apparent reason for why he took his life. He wasn't in any trouble; there was no drug involvement," George—or, rather, the boy—contends.

"That's correct."

"He doesn't even know himself why he did it."

"Yes, we can believe that."

"He was very serious. He took much to heart."

"Yes."

"He's a teenager, about thirteen."

"Yes."

"It happened at home, but it's not actually in the home. Does that make sense to you?"

"Yes."

"There's a vehicle nearby . . . It didn't happen *in* a vehicle, but a vehicle is involved."

"That's correct."

Suddenly George experiences sympathetic pain. "I feel a choking sensation," he says, clutching his throat.

"Yes."

"He tells me he hanged himself."

"Yes."

"I'm seeing a turkey, a psychic clue that this happened around Thanksgiving . . . between Thanksgiving and Christmas."

"Yes."

"Your son hanged himself in the garage, he tells me. That's why I felt a vehicle nearby. That's why a car was there. He's over the car."

"Yes."

"You're Christians. He says to tell you that Jesus did not send him to hell and to please continue praying for him."

The parents glance at each other, then nod to George that they understand. The teenage sister weeps softly, dabbing her tears.

"He's with one grandmother and his great-grandparents on the other side," George says. "He's a good boy. There's nothing wrong with him. It's almost as if he were playing around and it went too far."

"Yes, it's possible."

"But he was in a slump, so to speak, a depression at the holidays," George explains.

"It could be."

"He embraces the sister here," George says, pointing to the teenager. "You two were close."

"Yes."

"He says that at the time he took his life, 'My parents were away.'"

"Yes, that's correct," the boy's father answers.

"He never talked about being depressed. He was very introverted."

"Yes."

"He says, 'Please don't think you've failed me. I don't want you to feel guilty.'" Neither parent responds. A few seconds go by, then George looks up and asks, "Do you take the name Josh, or Joshua?"

"Yes, that's him, our son!" the man replies, his voice choked with emotion.

"It's hard to understand," George continues. "Everything in his life was fine: family, school, friends, church. There's no reason why he did this."

"We agree."

"The only thing is that he was very down and depressed at the holidays, and it went too far."

"It's possible."

"Jesus has been merciful to him. Now he calls to a brother."

"Yes."

"There is a total of three children, including him, he says."

"Yes."

"Wait." George pauses, then looks at the girl. "He's apologizing to you. Did you find him? Because he says you did."

"Yes," she replies, tears streaming down her face.

"You're a very happy family, and there were no outward signs at all of anything wrong."

"That's true."

"He's saying to you"—George indicates the girl—"that he's appearing to you in your dreams. You've been restless in your sleep."

"Yes," she acknowledges, stunned.

"He says that he's disappointed in himself. He's hard on himself on the other side, too. . . . He apologizes to you and asks for prayers. Don't feel Christ has let you down," George urges the family. "I'm psychically seeing the symbol Dorothy and Auntie Em from *The Wizard of Oz.* He doesn't want you to be guilty, angry, or carry bitterness. . . . Your son is very bright and creative. He's a talented boy, there's nothing wrong. 'He's perfect,' if I can use that expression."

"Yes."

"He says his biggest problem in life was himself. But he's coming along, and don't feel you've failed or have let him down."

Once again George pauses, straining to interpret the seemingly random bits of information he's receiving from the other side of the veil. Sometimes it is difficult to decipher what he hears psychically, a situation George describes as similar to a weak or static-plagued telephone connection. At last he asks, "Do you take the name Mark? Or maybe it's Mike?"

"Yes, Mike. That was his best friend," the mother says. Like many first-time subjects, she shakes her head, astounded by George's accuracy. The others in the room watch and listen, likewise astonished.

"Your son is calling out to him," George says. "Now he's speaking to you." Again he focuses on the sister. "He says you feel bad because you didn't keep an eye on him. But he says, 'I want my sister to know that she's not to blame. I made the decision of my own free will.'

"He's going back now," George tells the three of them. "He sends his love to all of you, and he asks you to continue praying for him."

The specificity and accuracy of this particular reading is obvious. The family, who'd traveled hundreds of miles from another state for an audience with George, were emotionally shaken but tremendously relieved by their son's message. Families of suicides frequently bear the additional burden of guilt, perhaps wondering what they could have done to prevent the tragedy. But as Joshua told his parents and sister, there was *nothing* anyone could have done. For survivors, releasing the guilt and anguish is a giant step down the path toward overcoming grief.

Another interesting point about this discernment was the spirit's mentioning that he had appeared in his sister's dreams. This is a form of what we call direct communication, with the spirit initiating the contact. One problem with direct communication, whether it be through dreams, apparitions, or somehow "giving a sign" ("moving" an object, or creating a certain scent, of roses, for example, around the loved one), is that we in the physical state of life don't always realize when we're receiving a true communication. It's human nature to assume that we're imagining or seeing things. With dreams, it's particularly difficult to discern whether we've been contacted by or merely dreamed about the person who's passed. In this instance it seems clear that the girl wasn't "just" dreaming; Joshua had indeed come to comfort her.

Arguments and conflicts with others are, unfortunately, part of life. So what happens when a sudden passing steals away our chance to resolve discord, to say, "I'm sorry"? Loved ones on earth commonly carry the painful burden of that "something" left unfinished or unsaid. Survivors aren't the only ones who feel compelled to settle differences. As the next two readings illustrate, those on the other side experience those same feelings of regret, guilt, and incompleteness. Thus, when a spirit comes through to apologize or to forgive, seemingly unresolvable problems can be put to rest. As one person said, "It's really no different than two people here who've had a quarrel and later made up." Such was the case in this reading, from the same discernment, for a heavyset middle-aged woman.

"There's a female entity present," George begins.

"Yes," the woman answers.

"Your grandmother has passed."

"Yes."

"But your mother is still living."

"Yes."

"Your grandmother is your guardian angel, without a

doubt. She's very devout, spiritual and mystical." When George refers to a spirit as a "guardian angel," he does not mean to suggest the traditional religious image of a pure spirit drifting through clouds in a flowing white gown and matching wings. He doesn't literally see the loved one in that form, he simply uses the term in the sense of a protector looking out for you, caring for you from the other side as she would have here on earth.

"Yes," the subject agrees.

"She likes what's in this room," George adds, motioning at the religious statues and paintings.

"Yes, she would."

"Your father has passed. Recently."

"Yes."

"All four grandparents who've passed come through."

"Yes, all four have passed."

"You took care of your father."

"Yes," the woman replies, wiping away tears.

"He thanks you."

"Yes, I understand," she says.

"He was a very spiritual man."

"Yes."

"Do you think he's mad at you?" George asks.

"Yes," she admits, still crying.

"He says, 'You didn't let me down or abandon me.' Did you have a distancing or a falling-out?"

"Yes."

"He calls to your mother. There's an emotional separation there. Did they split up? It seems they talked about it."

"Yes, they talked about it. After forty years of the marriage, he wanted to walk out, but he didn't do it. They fought a lot," the daughter explains.

"He says his mother-in-law met him on the other side. They were close."

"Yes."

George waits for more information. "His life here was a struggle, he tells me."

"Yes."

"But don't feel you abandoned him or that he's mad at you."

"I'll try," she answers.

"I see Saint Joseph, my psychic symbol of a happy or peaceful death. He says he went to sleep and passed on."

"Yes," the daughter replies. "My father fell accidentally, was knocked unconscious, and died."

"I'm psychically seeing Saint Anthony," George says, smiling. "Your grandmother tells me he was her favorite saint."

"Yes, he was."

"Your dad is calling to your mom. He jokes, 'Tell her I'm waiting over here for her in the boxing ring.' "

The woman laughs. Readings may be emotional experiences for most subjects, but they encompass all human emotions, including, at times, humor.

George's light tone quickly changes, however. "Your father drank," he notes seriously.

"No."

"Or took medicine, then, because I'm getting a light-headed feeling," George explains.

"Yes, he took medicine."

"He's happier in the next stage."

"Yes, I believe that."

"He hands you roses for your birthday." Roses are a common spiritual expression of love or congratulations from the other side. "He also talks about a trip you're involved in."

"Yes, I just came back today."

"He calls to grandchildren."

"Yes."

"He encourages you toward spiritual work."

"Yes, I used to do volunteer work."

"But he's not telling you to go into the convent. Do you understand what he means?" George asks, obviously baffled.

"Yes," his daughter says, laughing. "He was afraid I was going to become a nun."

"Well, your dad is happy and at peace on the other side. He says don't blame yourself for his accident. It wasn't your fault. You need to put your mind at ease."

"I was with him when he fell, when he died," she explains.

"He and your grandmother ask that you pray for them, and they step aside. Your father says, 'Know that I'm always with you.' "

Later that evening as she left the discernment, the woman happily exclaimed, "I can sleep tonight!"

The next subject is an attractive, well-dressed woman in her forties.

"A male close to you passed," George establishes.

"Yes," the woman confirms in a tense tone.

"Your father has passed, that's who it is."

"Yes."

"You two had a poor relationship."

"Yes."

"Your father says you didn't even go to his funeral."

"Yes, that's correct."

"Did he give you the back of his hand, so to speak?" Her response is a bitter yes.

"He definitely looked down on women."

"Yes."

"They were second class to him, and now he apologizes for it." George continues writing. "You're established in your job or career. I'm seeing the psychic symbol of the Virginia Slims cigarettes slogan 'You've come a long way.' " As you can see, the range of symbols used to communicate with, or through, George is remarkably diverse.

"You've reached an understanding in your life," he goes on. "You've overcome many obstacles."

"Yes," the daughter acknowledges.

"Do you teach? Because I'm psychically seeing you in a classroom environment or a school."

"Yes, I'm a teacher and a school administrator."

"Do you write? I see you writing."

"Yes."

"You've been published and will be again."

"Yes."

"You deal with bitterness," George observes. "Your father hopes his apology will help. He talks about the loss of a child—emotionally. I think he means you."

"Yes."

"Are you married now?"

"No."

"But you *were* married."

"Yes."

"You're divorced."

"Yes."

"You've reached a plateau of understanding."

"Yes."

"Your father tells me that he called you by a 'put-down' name. He won't repeat it here, but he says you know what he's talking about, and he apologizes very strongly for it."

"Yes," the woman answers. Thus far she's betrayed little emotion, but now tears fill her eyes.

"The words and put-downs he used did more damage emotionally than if he had physically struck you," George says.

"Yes."

"He admits he used harsh language toward you."

"Yes."

"He says that he can't use that language on the other side, or else 'the entities here will jump all over me.' The name-calling of you was a manifestation of his own inadequacy."

"Yes."

"You don't sleep well," George says with concern. "Your dreams are filled with anxiety."

"Correct."

"He says he hopes his coming through for you will help. . . . He calls to your mom, if you have contact with her."

"Not too much."

"He wants you to bury the hatchet with her," George says, conveying her father's message.

"Yes, all right."

"You're distant also with your brothers and sisters. Your father says he wants to 'mend family.' "

The woman sits silently.

"Forgive and pray for him," George says, explaining that he's repeating the message he heard from her late father.

There is a long pause, then she murmurs, "I forgive him."

"He says you should write about the family problems, about your life. Have you ever thought about doing that?"

"Yes."

"He says he has got to face up to himself, and he's at peace for getting this off his chest," George tells her. "He says,

'Please go on with your life, as happily, as best you can.'
Your father says he knows he's not much of a bargain, but
he wants you to know that he's near you."

A fascinating aspect of group discernments is that when
subjects witness other people's readings and George's accuracy, it validates their own experiences. For the rare person
who persists in believing that George just "got lucky" with
his or her particular reading, seeing him deliver a wealth of
specific details and facts for others inevitably dispels any
lingering doubt. The next two readings, both from the same
group discernment, involve extremely unusual deaths. As
you will see, there is no way George could have "guessed"
or "figured out" the incredible stories behind these passings.

The first subject is a widow from overseas. While residing
with friends on the West Coast, she heard about George and
decided she had to see him.

"A young female has passed, a daughter," George begins.

"Yes," the woman confirms.

"I'm getting pain to my head." Sympathetic pain. "There
was pain to her head."

"Yes."

"She's saying she's hit. A vehicle accident."

"Yes."

"She says, 'The vehicle glides.' "

"Yes."

"Why does she keep saying she's falling? Does that make
any sense?"

"Yes."

"She's hit by a vehicle gliding at a great speed," George
says, straining to interpret logically the psychic symbols and
messages.

"Yes," the woman acknowledges.

"There's terrible pain to her neck, like . . . decapitation!"
George says, rubbing the back of his neck.

"Yes." The woman breaks down, sobbing hysterically.
Once she regains her composure, George continues. "Her
neck was broken."

"Yes."

"She says she passed instantly. She got in the way of it.
She keeps saying, 'I didn't kill myself. I didn't see it.' Is it a

plane?" Before the subject can answer, George declares, "It's a plane!" and shudders. The things he is told often startle him as much as they do his subjects, sometimes more so.

"Yes."

"It's gliding, and then it lands. It's a small private-type plane."

"Yes."

"She says the passing looks horrible, disastrous, a pretty gory sight. It looks like she's signaling or trying to land it, but she's on the ground, not in the plane. She's signaling the plane."

"Yes," the woman confirms through tears.

"She's sixteen years old when she's killed."

"Yes."

"She's calling to her grandparents on earth."

"Yes."

"Your daughter is saying, 'Thank God for letting me come through to tell you I'm fine.' She says her vision was impaired; it was dark."

"Yes."

"She says this happened near her home."

"Yes."

"This happened outside the United States."

"Yes."

"New Zealand."

"Yes."

"She says someone was with her when this happened."

"Yes."

"It looks as though she's running and waving her arms and hands to let the plane know it's too close. But it's too dark, and she's trapped, caught, and the tragedy happens."

"Yes."

"She says, 'The plane didn't even know I was there. It didn't even see me until I walked into it.' Propellers . . . *slicing . . .*" George's voice trails off. " 'Continue to pray for me,' she says. 'I'm all right and at peace.' "

Afterward the woman clarified the unusual story. Her only child was waiting with friends one night to commute by plane within New Zealand. She didn't realize she was too close to a runway when she was killed, precisely as George had described.

• • •

The second reading also involves a young woman.

"A male close to you passed," George says.

"Yes," she answers.

"He's related by blood."

"Yes."

"He says he's your brother."

"Yes."

"He's a young man."

"Yes."

"He appears before me in a tuxedo."

"Yes."

"Now there's a girl, a young woman, standing near him."

"Yes."

"She's wearing a wedding gown."

"Yes."

"They're at a wedding, they tell me . . . *their* wedding!" George exclaims.

"Yes."

"Now, there's a woman passed, also at the wedding."

"Yes."

"It's the mother to one of them."

"Yes."

"Wait!" George knits his brow. "Others are stepping forward now: brothers and sisters, other relatives, and friends. They keep coming. They were all together!"

"Yes."

"They all passed at the same time."

"Yes."

Suddenly George gasps for breath. "I feel as if I can't breathe," he tells his subject. "Does that make sense?"

"Yes."

"It feels very hot."

"Yes."

"I'm psychically seeing flames. Fire."

"Yes."

The tuxedoed young man explains from the other side that he had passed on when fire broke out at the hotel reception hall during his wedding. The flames spread so rapidly that he, his new bride, their families, and friends—the entire wedding party of more than thirty people—perished, trapped by flames and smoke.

George conducts several more readings that evening. Finally, after several hours, the group discernment concludes. Some subjects seem happy, relieved, others disoriented, milling about the room in a daze. It will undoubtedly take some time before this intense experience, as well as its profound implications, sink in. As they each shake George's hand and thank him, there is no question that all are grateful to have come and are deeply comforted by having heard from their loved ones on the other side.

(3)

The Compassionate Friends

"I really hesitate to categorize someone's loss, or grief, because any loved one's passing is painful," George says. "But as anyone who's suffered this can attest, the death of a child is perhaps the most devastating loss one can imagine. You could be in your twenties, thirties, or nineties. Your child could be two months old, or sixty years old; it doesn't matter. When you lose a child, you lose a part of the future. We assume, and hope, that our children will survive us."

On Long Island nineteen-year-old Peggy O'Connor and her brother, twenty-one-year-old Denis, were killed when their car crashed into a raised drawbridge. It was a short drive on the same road Denis took every day to and from his summer job as a beach lifeguard. According to forensic experts, when the vehicle was about one hundred feet from the warning gate, the bridge was down. There was ample time for Denis to stop.

No one knows what happened next.

Inexplicably, the car smashed through the wooden gate and struck the now-vertical bridge. Peggy was killed instantly, and Denis mortally injured. But why? There were no brake skid marks, no witnesses, no evidence of substance abuse, and no mechanical problems with either the car or the gate.

In the several days after the accident, their mother and stepfather, Elaine and Joe Stillwell, hurried between the intensive-care unit where Denis lay with severe head injuries and the funeral parlor where Peggy was being waked. One day after her funeral, Denis was declared clinically dead.

"A lot of people couldn't even come to the second funeral when Denis died," Elaine recalls. "They said they couldn't handle it. They'd just been to Peggy's funeral. Now, that kind of hurt. I thought when people saw other people hurting, they'd jump in. But it didn't work like that with everybody. Some people run away. I had a lot to learn."

Elaine discovered a local chapter of The Compassionate Friends, a national self-help organization for bereaved parents and siblings. After attending several meetings, she and Joe formed a chapter in their town of Rockville Centre, New York. She's since become an authority on the loss of children. "When someone is grieving for children," Elaine says, "they need to know someone cares. And not everyone can do that, because a lot of people hold back. But I've learned that you don't sit back. You go over to the house. We all go to the funeral. We send sympathy cards. You do all those things. But I've learned a step beyond that. I've delivered meals and things like that. It's not just that first week or that first month. It's the continuation.

"I think the people who come to The Compassionate Friends are hurting so badly that anything we can do helps, whether it be giving them a book or just holding their hand. George Anderson," she says, "seems to be the only one that has given them a peace that lasts. All you really want to know is that your children are safe and happy and are watching over you. They are a part of everything that we do.

"Some people cry when they see George. I didn't cry. I smiled. Everything he told me gave me such utter peace, because when my children died in the automobile accident, there were no observers there, and we never knew what the cause was." George relayed to her Peggy's and Denis's message: It was simply an accident.

"George's readings give your heart a chance to heal, and they give you the hope to keep you going, because your lost loved one is safe and waiting for you now," she says. "We have people who've lost a child and want to die and jump in the casket. They literally want to be buried with their child. That's all they talk about. They just want to be with their child.

"I'm helping people right now. I'm not ready to jump in the casket. I've got a few things I've got to take care of. But that's me. Your temperament matters a lot. People say that I'm strong. Maybe it's the sense of faith that I have. When someone asks how many children I have," Elaine adds, "I finally found out how to answer. I say I have three: Annie lives with me at home, and Denis and Peggy live in my heart."

To reach as many bereaved as he can, George often appears at gatherings arranged by various organizations that work with the grieving. One wintry Friday evening George was a special guest of Elaine Stillwell's at a meeting of The Compassionate Friends.

Nearly two hundred people assembled in the auditorium of Rockville Centre's Molloy College that night. Most were from Long Island, other parts of New York, New Jersey, and Connecticut, but others traveled from as far as Pennsylvania and Canada to hear George speak and demonstrate. Elaine talked briefly about who George is and what he does, explaining what a psychic medium is and the various psychic means through which he receives communications. After discussing what they could expect to see during the later demonstrations, Mrs. Stillwell told of her personal experiences with loss, bereavement, and George.

"I believed I'd have to spend the rest of my life searching for pieces of information that might explain the accident," she said. "After meeting with George Anderson three months ago, my heart overflowed with the peace and love of his message. Through him, I found that although Peggy was pinned in the car, she died instantly, suffering no pain. It was just an accident, after all. No one was to blame.

"I also learned that my mother, who died twenty years ago and after whom my daughter was named, welcomed her across. Four days later when Denis died, he was welcomed by Peggy. They both vehemently explained four times that they were grateful to God to die together, and that neither would have wanted to live without the other. That thought comforted me all along, that they were together. But to know they felt that way really helped my heart a lot. I also learned that they were united with a sister they had never known." (George psychically discerned, correctly, that Mrs. Stillwell had suffered a miscarriage years earlier; thus the second sister.)

As Elaine related her story, everyone listened with rapt attention. "George told me my children consider themselves famous, because I joined a bereavement group, put their pictures around, and told everybody about them!" she said. "When they died, I never wanted their names erased. They were my special children. To know they felt famous when all I was doing was answering the telephone and conducting meetings of The Compassionate Friends made me feel pretty good."

She smiled, then continued. "I also found out my children are with my mother in the afterlife. My children told George that they're with Uncle Joe, my father's brother, whom none of us knew, since he had died at the age of twenty-one in 1925. On the light side, we were told that my best friend's dog, which had died only two weeks before, was with them, and that Peggy and Denis were taking care of it over there.

"So as we left George Anderson's that night, we felt very much at peace, knowing that our children were in good hands and were happy together. Let the love and hope that's in this room tonight help you."

Mrs. Stillwell then explained that George would demonstrate for anonymous subjects chosen randomly from numbers placed in a hat. The only restrictions were that the subjects be bereaved parents who'd never had a reading with George before. The numbers selected, Mrs. Stillwell introduced George. He walked onstage to a warm round of applause.

"Even though your children are not in this stage of life, you still think about them, you worry about them, you pray for them," he began. "In my experience, parents of suicides suffer excruciating agony. Parents of children who've been murdered suffer the most anger. Then there's the shock and remorse, even guilt, associated with sudden, tragic deaths and loss from any number of dread diseases. You must remember that even though your children are in the next stage, they're closer to you than you can imagine. They are alive and at peace."

As he does before every psychic reading, George instructed his subjects to answer with only a yes or a no and not to feed him any information. The first subject, a plainly dressed woman who appeared to be in her early fifties, took her place in a metal folding chair facing George on the auditorium stage.

"Your son passed young," George said.

"Yes," she acknowledged.

"His passing was tragic."

"Yes."

"His grandmother is with him, taking care of him on the other side."

The subject nodded.

George observed with a laugh, "Your son is talking fast. He's nervous and anxious. He calls to his father, but they were distant."

"Yes."

"He calls to siblings."

"Yes, I have two other children."

George put his hands to his head, sensing momentarily the pain suffered by the young man at the moment of physical death. "There was pain to his head," he said.

"Yes," the mother confirmed.

"It's an accidental passing, he tells me."

"Yes."

"A vehicle involved."

"Yes."

"But he says he did not suffer prior to his passing."

"Yes, they told me it was instantaneous," the woman answered.

"He went through a bad time prior to his passing, he says. He was out of sorts, anxious, and hot tempered," George stated.

"Yes, he'd had an argument with his girlfriend."

"Your son was out socially at the time."

"Yes, out with his girlfriend."

"She survived," George said.

"Yes."

"Your son says it was an accident. It's not her fault. Don't blame her. You do, but it's not her fault." The woman nodded that she understood. "Now your father is coming through to admit that he kind of abandoned you. He passed when you were young?"

"Yes, he did."

"Because he says now he's a guardian angel to you. Your son," George continued, "is calming down. He says your life is getting back together. The 1990s will be better for you than the late 1980s were. Now there's another male, another loss. Do you take the name Frank?"

"Yes."

"He's passed on, and he's with your son. They're together on the other side. Frank was a friend of the family's."

"Yes."

"But he says you and he went out socially, because there's a fondness from him to you."

The audience laughed, and the woman smiled and blushed. After several more minutes George concluded by saying, "Your son thanks you for your prayers, and he and the others are going back now."

Next came a married couple and their daughter, a young woman in her early twenties.

"Your son passed," George began.

"Yes," the woman verified.

"He passed young."

"Yes."

"And tragically."

"Yes."

"But he passed from an illness."

"Yes."

"He says he suffered in silence."

"Yes."

"But now he can talk about it. The illness affected his blood and breathing."

"Yes."

"He says he knew he was going to pass on."

"Yes."

"There's fluid, hoarseness in his breathing. His back is affected. There's a heaviness in his back."

"Yes."

"He says there's treatment, but no cure."

"That's correct, George."

"He was on oxygen."

"Yes."

"It's a serious illness, like cancer."

"Yes, cancer."

"His glands are affected. Lymphatic cancer."

"Yes."

"I'm psychically seeing the last scene from [the film] *Terms of Endearment* as my clue," George explained. The reading lasted for several more minutes, concluding with George reminding the woman that her son asked that she "dust off her rosary beads" and pray for him. Here is yet another example of George receiving a message in terms he would understand. Spirits frequently entreat us to use rosary beads or to recite a specific prayer, such as the Catholic novena, a devotion consisting of nine days of devout prayer.

Is George espousing or promoting Roman Catholicism over all other organized religions—or saying that subjects can pray only with rosary beads? Absolutely not. This seems to be another instance in which the spirits convey to him an image they know that he will comprehend, tapping into his mental vocabulary of images, words, and associations. As it happens, George was raised a Catholic. Had he been Jewish, the other side might have shown him something signifying the Kaddish, the Hebrew prayer for the dead.

"You lost a son," George told the next person facing him, a woman.

"Yes," she answered.

"You were close to him, he says. He's very family oriented, friendly, outgoing, sociable."

"Yes."

"He says you took care of him, you didn't fail him, and he thanks you. There's no uncertainty about that," George said.

The mother nodded and smiled slightly.

"His illness affected his blood or blood cells."

"Yes."

"It's like cancer."

"Yes."

"He's very close to his dad."

"Yes," she agreed.

"His dad is suffering his grief inside."

"Yes."

"Do you take the name Paul?"

"Yes, my cousin, from many years ago."

"Paul passed young, too," George said. "He's telling me that he died of exactly the same thing your son did."

"Yes, they both died of the same kind of cancer," the astonished woman acknowledged.

"Your son says Paul was the one who crossed him over. Now your son is touching you on the stomach. You have stomach trouble, he says."

"Yes! That's amazing!" the woman exclaimed.

"They're sharp, ulcerlike pains."

"Yes."

"Watch your diet. It's stress or nerves."

"Yes, I understand."

"Your dad is coming through. He says he could have been closer. He was there, but he wasn't."

"Exactly."

"He wasn't the kind to apologize."

"Exactly."

"Well, he does apologize now. Your dad says he crossed your son over to make up for it."

The next subject was a man in his forties.

"Two males close to you passed," George said.

"Yes," the man answered.

"You lost a son, that's one of them."

"Yes."

"Your dad has passed. That's one of them."

"Yes."

"I hear a foreign language in the background," George observed.

"Yes," the man acknowledged.

"It's German sounding."

"Yes," he replied, "it's Yiddish."

"Your son was in his early teens, thirteen or fourteen, when he passed."

"Yes."

"Tragic passing."

"Yes."

"The two of you, you and your son, were close."

"Yes."

"He shows me a vehicle accident."

"Yes."

George chuckled. "He's a talkative little guy."

"Yes," the man answered, mouth widening in a smile.

"An uncle has passed."

"No."

"Are you sure?" George asked.

The man thought a moment. "Oh, you're right," he said. The audience, attentive throughout the demonstration, laughed. It's not uncommon for subjects to focus so intensely on hearing from a particular person, they "blank out" on other names and facts.

George continued. "Do you take the name Andy?"

"Yes, that's my son," the man confirmed happily.

"But there's another Andrew who's passed on," George insisted.

"Yes."

"That's the uncle I mentioned before who'd passed on."

"Yes!"

The circumstances of the fatal accident were then communicated to George. "Your son is speeding or going fast at the time of his passing," he said to the father.

"Yes, going fast; not speeding."

"He says it's a bicycle or wheeled vehicle."

"Yes."

"I psychically see an automobile accident. He's going on a bike, and he's hit by a car," George said.

"Yes," the man answered.

"That car was going at a high speed."

"Yes."

"He says you pray for him, but you could do it a little more frequently."

"I guess," the father admitted sheepishly.

"Your son says he's okay and at peace. He didn't suffer. Your Uncle Andy is his guardian angel on the other side and helped him."

Now another man took the seat opposite George. He appeared to be in his early forties.

"A female close to you has passed," George said.

"Yes," the man acknowledged.

"Mother or grandmother."

"My grandmother."

"She spoke a foreign language."

"Yes."

"It sounds like Italian or Spanish."

"Yes, Spanish."

"She comes to you like a mother figure."

"Did you grow up with her?" George asked.

"Yes, I did."

"You lost a child."

"Yes."

"You lost children. Twice. One was a miscarriage."

"Yes."

"You lost a son."

"Yes."

"He calls to his mother."

"Yes."

"It's a tragic passing," George said.

"Yes," the man answered.

"Accidental, a vehicle involved."

"Yes."

"He mentions he was about to go to college."

"Yes, his first semester."

"He was hit by a vehicle."

"Yes."

"I see his spirit appear to me. He was tall—five-feet-eleven or six feet."

"Yes."

"He calls to Joe."

"Yes."

"He was a friend of your son, I'm being told."

"Yes."

"Your dad passed."

"Yes."

"He's with your son."

"Oh, okay."

"Do you take the name George, or Jorge?"

"Yes, my brother. He's living," the man said.

"Your mom is living."

"Yes."

"Because your dad says, from the other side, that there's trouble with her legs."

"Yes."

"Your dad was very forceful, very strong willed."

"Yes."

"Your son says his grandfather is keeping him in line."

The man smiled, and the audience laughed.

Now George psychically heard music. "Your son played an instrument," he said.

"Yes, the guitar."

"Your son has a crazy sense of humor. He's joking with me from the other side."

"Yes."

"He says to his mom, your wife, that she has back trouble."

"Yes, she does."

Moments later, George said the spirit of the young man was fading and going back.

The final demonstration was for a family that had traveled to Long Island from Ontario, Canada. George sat facing an older man and woman, Peter and Sheila. Between them was a young woman in her twenties named Leslie. The bulk of the reading came from Leslie's late husband, Mark, Peter and Sheila's son.

"There are a number of people," George began. "A male close to the three of you passed on."

"Yes," Sheila answered.

"Your dad passed over."

"Yes."

"Okay, just say yes to confirm he's correct, because there's someone around who claims to be *your* [Peter's] father. That's one. Your father passed before [Sheila's father]. The reason I want to establish that," George explained, "is because your son claims your dad came to meet him when he crossed over. I wanted to make sure he was telling me the right information."

After a brief pause, George addressed Leslie. "Just answer: Your husband passed on?" She nodded. "Oh, are you their daughter-in-*law?*" She nodded again.

"Oh, I thought you were their daughter. Their son is your husband. [I was confused] because he keeps saying to me, 'That's my wife,' and I'm saying to myself, *You're married to your sister?* And as I'm sitting here listening, he says, 'No, no, no, that's not their daughter,' and . . . I just realized he's probably trying to tell me that's their daughter-in-law." To the spirit, George said, "Sorry!" then continued.

"Did he pass on not that long ago? Nineteen eighty-nine? He claims, 'last year,' and I almost said nineteen eighty-eight. Then I realized we're in nineteen ninety now. [The reading took place on January 12 of that year.] Just say yes or no: a shocking passing . . . Wow!" George yelped. "I feel . . . the reaction is a slap in the face! I don't think I'll have to question this symbol: car accident? He claims it was a vehicle accident. He's driving? I feel as though I'm driving."

"Yes."

"Your father passed on also," George said again to Sheila. "I see *another* man appear behind you. You have other children, true?"

"Yes."

To Leslie, George remarked, "You were not married that long? Because I feel like you're just married. You have no children, true?"

"No."

"I hear a name: maybe André . . . Andrea . . . It's probably *Alice.* Your son was saying what sounds like Alison or Alice was with him, and I couldn't tell." Alice was Mark's maternal grandmother. "Did she go before him? He says she was there to meet him when he came over. Did she live with you?" George asked.

"He was very close to her," Sheila answered.

"He says that if there was anybody he knew who passed over, it was she, because he grew up with her, so to speak. That's why she was there to cross him over. Your mom a very spiritual woman?"

"In her own way, I guess," Sheila said.

"Very spiritual in her own way," said George, "definitely a very strong motherly vibration. I mean, like the perfect mother. He seems to feel she had a great influence on him, growing up."

"That's for sure."

"Did he collide with another vehicle?"

"The other vehicle hit him," Mark's mother clarified.

"Oh, that's what I mean. Like, he didn't collide with a tree or something, there's a collision with another vehicle. That's what I'm getting at, because he says he collides with another vehicle. Whether a car hits him or not, it's classed as another vehicle. Your mother keeps saying 'Mark' is with her."

"My God!" Sheila cried. "That's him! Does he say why it happened?" she asked.

"It's an accident. The party that hit him lost control of the vehicle. . . . Were they drunk or something?"

"Crossed the median," Sheila explained.

"Because it doesn't seem as though they're paying attention to what they're doing, and that's what causes it."

Leslie wanted to know if her husband suffered.

"No," George replied confidently, "he says he passed instantaneously. Was he hit broadside? Because I feel as if I'm being hit on the side."

"Yes," said Peter.

"He says at first he didn't realize that he had died, as we understand it. Then that's when your mother came to him. He thought he was dreaming at first."

"We were told that he was not instantaneously killed," Mark's father remarked.

"He says he didn't suffer," George insisted, "so I'm going to have to take it."

"He was brain dead at the scene," Peter added.

"He says, 'I passed on instantaneously, so there was no suffering.' . . . Is there a Margaret passed on?"

"My grandmother," Sheila responded.

"She says she's with him also."

"Is there an anniversary approaching?"

"Just passed," Leslie answered.

"Because he keeps wishing you 'Happy Anniversary.' He'd have to mean his wedding anniversary, because he directed it right at you. Did he have a pleasant but forceful way?" George wanted to know. "He said to me, 'For once, don't argue with anybody,' and he told me what to do."

"Sounds like him," his mother concurred.

"He's very polite about it, but forceful. It's as if he knew I'd shake my head."

"Fits him to a T," Sheila said.

"The thing is, when he said that you [Leslie] were his wife, and I said, 'Wait a minute, that's their daughter, how can that be your wife?' he said, 'Don't argue with me this time.' "

"Do you see him?" Sheila asked anxiously.

"I don't see him, but I can feel him in the room," George explained. "I see him through the feel. Now, he didn't know Margaret, true?"

"She was gone before him," Sheila said.

"Because he says she's there with him, too. He claims he lives with your mother over there. Did she speak with an accent or something?"

"No, Peter's mother did," Sheila answered.

"No? Wait: You're . . . She was Canadian, yes?"

"Yes."

"Okay. She doesn't sound as though she's from *New Yawk*. That's why when you said no, I thought, *Wait a minute; she doesn't sound local*. To me, she sounds as though she has an accent. . . .

"Was he involved with his work, either going or coming home? He keeps telling me his work was involved. Either he was going to work or coming home from work, and I can't tell which one. . . . Both of your parents passed over, too?" George asked Peter.

"Yes."

"Both of them are there with your son. . . . Did it happen around Toronto? I keep feeling as if I'm in the Toronto area."

"Yes."

"Needless to ask, you do pray for him, yes? He thanks you for the prayers and also asks you to please continue." George turned to Leslie.

"Did you light a candle for him or something? Are you a Catholic? Because he says you lit a candle for him in church—it must have been a Catholic church—and he thanks you for the light that was sent through the candles." Leslie was stunned. She'd told no one of having done this, not even her in-laws.

"Your husband states, and your son says to you, 'This is the most terrible blow of your lives, but you must still go on with your lives.' That's something you have to decide at your own pace. He says he's happy and at peace over there. One thing about him, he's very adaptable and conscientious, and he had to go on there. And you have to go on here."

Facing Peter, George asked, "Now, you said your first name is Peter?"

"I didn't say it, but it is!"

"Oh, I thought you did. I know I heard it. Well, if I'm not hearing it from one of you, I must be hearing it from there, because I heard somebody say 'Peter.' . . . Did he always speak his mind? He was an outspoken kind of guy, yes? Was he a very honest type of guy?"

"Very honest," said Leslie.

"He does admit that he felt a little cheated at first when he got over there. He admits all this isn't fair. 'I was a success, I was doing so well, everything was going well, and now look what's happened.' So your mom had to try to calm him down and help him adjust to a new life. Although he was brain dead at the scene, he wasn't technically dead yet, but even if he could come back, he would be a vegetable. He wouldn't want to come back under those circumstances. He says to me he had a choice."

"He had a choice?" asked Leslie, puzzled.

"He realizes he could have come back to the body," George explained, "but it could not sustain him. So the choice was that he'd have to pass on, because he realized he'd be brain dead, and he couldn't live like that. He knows it would be much better to go on to the next stage in life and be around spiritually rather than to be around as a vegetable. He says he always made his choices well in life. You're his perfect example," George said, looking at Leslie. "Does the name Laura or Leslie mean anything?"

"I'm Leslie!" she answered.

"I'm glad I didn't block it out, for once. He doesn't like to be argued with, because I couldn't tell if he said Laura or Leslie. . . . He says he has to go back," said George. "God is calling him back again. Though you miss him, try to go on with your lives, he states."

"Is there any chance of asking him a question, or getting a reaction to something?" Peter asked.

"You can try."

"After the accident, we undertook something," the father said cryptically. "The question is, Was that something beneficial to him in the next life?"

"Was it spiritual? You gave . . . I feel it's charitable. I keep seeing the symbol of charity in front of you. That's why I said it's spiritual. . . . It's not that you sat down and said a special prayer, but it's giving, it's charitable."

"Charitable in that it benefited other people," Peter said.

"Yes, exactly. It's charitable in every sense. It's like one good work."

George was able to do readings for only a handful of audience members that night. But even to those not selected, he'd brought comfort and hope as well as a new perspective on life and death. The subjects who shared their readings publicly made it possible for others to see that the contacts are real, the experience genuine and not at all "spooky," as some people fear.

These readings for The Compassionate Friends were largely typical in that the subjects left that evening knowing their loved ones were safe and still cared for them. In each instance, a certain nagging question or doubt was resolved. But in and of themselves, these answers cannot expedite the grieving process. The young widow Leslie, for example, will surely not miss her husband any less because she's heard from him. Knowing he calls out to her from the other side cannot make her life here what it was before he passed over. However, there is an element of comfort, a reassurance that our faith needn't be blind, which many people find helps them to cope a little better.

As we noted in this book's introduction, not every reading has a happy ending. Grief is a personal, unique experience for each of us. In the following story, a man's vow to avenge his daughter's murder remains firm despite her repeated pleas for him to forgive.

Ten-year-old Lorraine Pacifico came from a family all too typical of today's American households. Her parents were divorced, with her father, Peter, having remarried and moved to another town, about forty miles away. The girl lived with her mother, Vivian, and two older brothers on Staten Island, a mostly middle-class borough of New York City. Their spacious attached house sat on a quiet, tree-lined street where everyone knows his neighbors. Lorraine's parents, like most Staten Islanders, were proud of the community feeling that made it seem more like a small town than a piece of urban sprawl.

"Loving and carefree," is how Peter Pacifico describes his little girl, smiling. "A delight." With long, flowing brown hair and luminous brown eyes, Lorraine was petite, even dainty. Few who saw her would guess that she was extremely athletic and, even at her young age, an accomplished swimmer.

Like any father, Peter loved all three of his children, yet he felt his relationship with Lorraine was special. She was always, he often said, "my baby." After Peter married his second wife, Stacey, and moved to Long Island, he made every effort to maintain that closeness with his daughter. Every Saturday, he drove to Staten Island to fetch Lorraine, who spent the night at his new home. Then the next morning he returned her to her mother.

Sunday morning, July 6, father and daughter drove back to Staten Island, happily making tentative plans for how to spend their next day together. When they pulled up in front of Vivian's, Lorraine gave Peter a kiss and shouted, "Bye, Daddy!" before skipping up the sidewalk and disappearing into the house. Later that night he spoke to her on the phone. "She told me what a good time she'd had," Peter recalls. "Then Vivian got on the phone and we argued about some things, like my visitation rights."

The next afternoon Peter called the house again for his daughter. One of his sons answered the phone. "Lorraine's not here," he said. "She probably went around the corner to play or to the train station to meet Mommy."

"All right," Peter said. "Just have her call me."

Peter's phone was silent until about 6:30 that evening when Vivian called, angrily demanding, "Do you have the baby?"

Peter, a self-confessed hothead, snapped, "Don't bust my chops!" and angrily slammed down the receiver. Overhearing him, Stacey suggested, "Maybe you should call back, Peter. It sounds serious. Vivian wouldn't just say something like that for no reason."

"When I called Vivian again, she was frantic," Peter says. "She couldn't find Lorraine. I told her to go to the train station and look around. But by then Vivian and the boys had combed the neighborhood. Every fifteen minutes I'd call and ask, 'Any news?' but there wasn't. Even I was beginning to panic. It wasn't like Lorraine to take off and not tell anyone where she was. After about an hour, I suggested they ask their next-door neighbors, a cop named Tom and his wife, Donna, for help. Tom immediately went out looking for my baby, but there was nothing, and the police were notified. Lorraine was missing."

Racing from Long Island to Staten Island, "I worried that she'd run away from home because she'd heard her mother and me fighting on the phone," Peter says. "Maybe she'd become upset and had taken the train out to see me. I kept turning over in my mind every conceivable possibility and some that were pretty farfetched. We never thought for a moment that anything else might have happened to her, or that she wouldn't turn up okay."

When Lorraine had been missing for two days, a police officer friend sadly advised Peter, "Hope for the best but expect the worst." On July 10, four days after the girl's disappearance, the worst came.

"When the detectives came up the steps, I knew," Peter recalls, his voice cracking at the memory. "They told me, 'We found her. It's bad news, Mr. Pacifico.'

" 'No! No! Don't tell me!' I screamed. But one cop said, 'She's deceased.'

" 'Where is she?' I demanded. At that moment Vivian came running out of the house screaming, 'No! No!' All I wanted to know was where Lorraine was. They said she was at the train station, so I started running up the street. Soon I could see the police and the body bag. I was chasing the van after they put the bag in, because I wanted to see my daughter. I screamed for them to stop, but the van just kept going. Then I collapsed in the street.

"Later I had to identify my daughter's body. She looked discolored, a bluish-black color. Her hair was sticking straight up. When they first brought her out, I couldn't make the identification. I started swinging my arms and shouting, 'That's not my daughter! That's not my daughter!' But then I saw the other side of her face, and it was beautiful. Still, we had to have a closed casket."

Normally the train station near Vivian Pacifico's home is

congested with commuters at all hours, yet no one in the area saw Lorraine there the day she was murdered. Police speculate that she was abducted, assaulted, and perhaps even killed in the few moments immediately after a train emptied and the passengers all scurried to the parking lot.

For Peter, much about his daughter's last moments will always remain a mystery. "We think that when she saw him [the killer] on the station platform, she tried to run away but was trapped," he theorizes. "They found his pubic hairs on her thigh, so we know he tried to rape her. But he didn't succeed. In view of what happened, it seems a small thing, but I thank God for that."

As Lorraine struggled to break away, the killer picked up a large rock and smashed her in the head repeatedly. The medical examiner ruled the official cause of death was a fractured skull and multiple contusions. "I wanted to know if my daughter suffered," Peter says. "The medical examiner told me that after the first blow to her head, she didn't feel anything."

Over the next week the police combed the area for clues leading to Lorraine's killer. They soon focused their investigation on a twenty-year-old neighborhood youth named Keith, who, when questioned, offered inconsistent, contradictory information about his whereabouts at the time of Lorraine's murder. He denied having been at the train station that day, which immediately aroused suspicion, since several people recalled seeing him there. Also, many of those witnesses mentioned that he was acting strangely, as if drunk. Police later determined that Keith had been drinking alcohol and taking Quaaludes, an illegal sedative.

Two days after Lorraine was buried, Keith was arrested and charged with murder. He confessed orally, in writing, and on videotape to killing the girl. Why would anyone commit such a horrendous, senseless crime?

Keith pleaded guilty to murder and was sentenced to twenty years to life in prison. There was no trial. While this no doubt spared the Pacificos the agony of having to relive the tragedy and hear gruesome medical testimony, it denied them a sense of closure, a way to begin putting it all behind them. Peter, unfortunately, still has yet to reach that stage.

"The day Keith was in court to be sentenced," he remembers, "I lunged at him, but the court officers stopped me. I got within six inches of him, though, and I looked into his eyes. I said, 'My daughter is dead, but remember, what you did to her, I can do to you!' He didn't say anything. He just turned away. Then they threw me out of court.

"For the next six months I lay in bed. I mean, I *lived* in my bed. I wanted to die. The only times I left the house were when I'd go every day to the killer's house. I'd sit outside in my car with my gun fully exposed on the dashboard. I'd wait for his family to put on the lights in the house. I knew they would see me. Then the police would come and chase me away. Of course, I hid the gun then. Finally, one of the cops said, 'If you come again, we're going to have to arrest you.' I answered, 'Good. Put me in with my daughter's killer!'

"I went to Lorraine's grave every day. After I finally went back to work, I thought the New York City Transit Authority was going to fire me because I was taking off so many days." Peter used to pick up youngsters dressed in blue-plaid parochial-school uniforms that reminded him of his daughter. "I'd be driving the bus," he reflects, "and there would be tears running down my face. One time I got to the end of the line, and I called my boss and said, 'I can't drive the bus. I just can't. I can't do it.' Fortunately, the guys I worked with understood and covered for me a lot. My life was falling apart."

A full year after the tragedy, "I was still having a lot of trouble sleeping, and one night Stacey was watching George Anderson on television. I was lying in bed, just listening. I was intrigued, but my first thought was, *This guy is full of crap.* I figured, either he's a great con man or he's legit. But I got up and I listened. I heard people calling him on the phone, and him telling them all about their dead relatives. It's hard to explain exactly how I felt then. I wanted to believe it, but I didn't.

"Still, I took down the phone number, and the next day I called him. When I finally got through, the only information I gave to whoever answered his phone was my name, Pete. I was given an appointment for the following week. In the meantime, I called a friend who's a detective and asked if there was any way in the world George could get court records or any kind of information about me. He said, 'With just a first name? Peter, come on. No way.'

"Even up to the moment I was in the waiting room, I refused to believe it. Someone said, 'I hope George is good tonight,' and before I knew it, I said, 'This is all bull!' Stacey calmed me down. 'You're here, Pete. Let's see what happens.' "

Then during that evening's group discernment, George walked over to Peter's chair.

"Somebody here lost a child?" he asked.

"Yes," Peter answered.

"A female."

"Yes."

"Then it goes to you. She's very young."

"Yes."

"She gives me the impression that she passed on between the ages of seven and ten."

"Yes."

"She passed on within the last three years."

"Yes."

"Well, you know who's near you. It's your daughter."

"Yes."

"Did she pass very unhappily?"

"Yes."

"Was there violence involved?"

"Yes."

"Was she murdered?" George asked.

"Yes."

"Okay. This is not your daughter's name, but does the name Rose mean anything to you?"

"Yes."

"She's passed on."

"Yes."

"She's with your daughter. Did she pass on before your daughter?"

"Yes."

"Because Rose says, 'I was here to meet your daughter when she came over.' Rose is related to you."

"Yes."

"She's a mother or grandmother?"

"An aunt," Peter explained.

"That's enough," George said.

"Yes, she was like a mother," Peter offered.

"Oh. I couldn't understand why I was getting a strong mother vibration with her. Did she live in your home when you were growing up? Did she have anything to do with raising you, so to speak? Or did she have an influence on you when you were growing up or was she around you a great deal?"

"We lived with them for a while."

"Okay. Because she's pushing stronger on the mother vibration than on the aunt vibration. She's a very warm woman, an affectionate person. She says to me that your daughter is present. Your daughter is here, but your aunt has more experience on the other side in getting communications across. Was she very religious?"

"Yes."

"That's helping her tremendously. She's giving me the sign that she's a woman of great faith."

"Yes."

"Did this tragedy to your daughter happen in warmer weather?"

"Yes."

"Because she says we're not too long after the anniversary of this. Your daughter is a very attractive child."

"Yes."

"I keep seeing—she looks like an angel—very, very attractive. Was she strangled?"

"No."

"Something is injured in her throat," George said.

"Not that I know of," Peter answered.

"Anything involving the throat that involves your aunt?"

"No."

"Can anybody take that at all?"

No one in the room acknowledged George's query. However, from time to time during readings, George will psychically sense a word, name, or circumstance that cannot be readily interpreted or confirmed. Nevertheless, when George remains insistent about something, he is usually proven correct at some point.

"It's too strong," he said. "It's insisting. I'll block it. . . . Your daughter has been found."

"Yes."

"The body has been found. Was she found near water or a bridge?" George asked.

"Not water. A bridge," Peter confirmed.

"Maybe it's just a symbol. Does Christmas mean anything with her?"

"We used to have a saying—"

George put a finger to his lips. "No, don't tell me. Let me leave it, because she's just commenting that Christmas and her mean something, and you'll understand, undoubtedly. She called you Daddy, I assume. Right?"

"Yes." Peter had to blink back tears.

"Do you have other children?"

"Yes."

"She calls out to brothers. At least two. Two brothers. You have two sons."

"Yes."

"It's like a greeting, more or less. She's saying hello. Were you called by a nickname? Your aunt seems to be calling you by another name. I can't hear it, but I can feel it. Did your aunt speak another language?"

"Yes."

"Italian."

"Yes."

"Would the nickname be said in that language?"

"Yes."

"That's what I'm hearing," George explained.

"Yes, yes."

"I'm hearing it in Italian. . . . Did your daughter have very striking eyes? I keep seeing eyes in front of me. They're on the child's face."

"Beautiful eyes."

"Her death was not here [on Long Island]. I go away from this area."

"Yes."

"But I'm still in New York State."

"Yes."

"Okay. I don't know if I'm seeing the symbol or the name. Does the name Rosario mean anything to you?"

"Yes."

"Passed on?"

"No."

"Living. Okay. I'm getting the name from your aunt and your daughter."

"Yes."

"Does he know your aunt?"

"It's me. It's my middle name," Peter explained.

"Oh! Your aunt was showing me the rosary as a clue, so I would take it. Were you ever called by that name?"

"Never."

"Your aunt is a very patient woman."

"Yes."

"Because she's not rushing me. She's taking her time," George said. "Every now and then she gives me a breather and then she starts again. Did she have any trouble with her legs?"

"Yes."

"Not anything serious."

"No. It was near the end of her life."

"She's big with the rosary. I keep seeing rosary beads."

"Yes."

"I mean continually."

"Yes, continually. All through her life. We couldn't curse in front of her, at all."

"I'd better watch my language now, or she'll hit me," George joked.

"Yes. Because if she hits you, I'm going to feel the pain, too," Peter replied, returning the humor. Everyone else at the discernment laughed.

"Was your aunt married?" George asked.

"Yes," Peter answered.

"Her husband passed on."

"Yes."

"He passed before she did."

"Yes."

"She's in black for a long time."

"Yes."

"Because I see her in black. Not that she's in sorrow or anything. It's just a clue."

"Yes, yes."

"Who's Petey?"

"Me."

"Did she call you that? Or were you ever called that?"

"Yes."

George paused momentarily, rapidly writing on a pad several words he heard psychically.

"I keep seeing Christmas symbols around you. Without telling me . . . they're trying to tell me something. I want to let them tell me. I see a wreath in front of me. I see a Christmas tree."

"Yes."

"Does the name Viv mean anything to you?"

"Yes."

"Passed on or—"

"No."

"On earth."

"Yes."

"Again, these two people would know her, your aunt and your daughter."

"Yes, yes. Definitely. It's my daughter's mother."

"Because your aunt and daughter call out to her."

"Yes."

"Is she open to this?"

"What do you mean, George?"

"Could you tell her about this experience?"

"Yes. Sure."

"Okay. Because your daughter says, 'Please tell Mommy you've heard from me.' Without telling me: Are we near an immediate family member's birthday?"

"Uh . . ."

"Just say yes or no. I just want to interpret the symbol. Are we near an anniversary?"

"Yes."

"Is it a wedding anniversary?"

"Yes. Not mine."

"It doesn't matter. It's someone in your immediate family. Your daughter says, 'You ask the big question: *Why?* '"

"Always. 'If' and 'Why.' George," Peter implored, "don't hold anything back."

"Okay."

"Good."

"Is your daughter's name Holly?"

"No."

"Does Christmas holly mean anything to you? Again, there are all these Christmas symbols," George said.

"Yes, Christmas."

"It means something with your daughter."

"Yes."

"There's something special. That's what I'm saying."

Peter explained: "My daughter used to say, 'Every time I see my Daddy it's Christmas.' It's because I'd always bring her a toy. Every Friday."

"Because she keeps putting all Christmas symbols around you. I didn't know, and then I realized [seeing] Christmas holly, I could be getting a name."

"Every Friday was Christmas," Peter said sadly.

"Okay."

"George? Can I interrupt?"

"Yes, as long as you don't—"

"George, when you were going back to Petey? Petey was also my father, my Aunt Rose's brother."

"Is he passed on?"

"No."

"Okay," George said.

"That's my father. He's alive."

"Well, she still points it more toward you."

"All right," Peter answered.

Here is an example of George holding fast to the message he has been given. He insists the communications go to the subject rather than to anyone else. It is an important point that George will not be swayed when he is certain he has psychically received a specific name, relationship, or detail. Psychics are often criticized for bending their responses in the direction of a subject's acknowledgments. George does not do that.

"Is there a health problem around [the other] Peter, at all?" George inquired.

"Not that I know of."

"Is there any trouble in his chest? Is he the type that wouldn't say anything?"

"Yes, that's correct."

"Because according to your daughter, there is trouble in the chest."

"There are so many Peters in my family."

"This is your father," George stated firmly.

"Yes."

"The message comes from your daughter."

"Right, right."

"Did she call him Poppa?"

"Yes."

"Because she keeps saying to me, 'There's trouble in Poppa's chest.' "

"Yes, yes."

"Has he had a heart attack?"

"Yes."

"More than one, or just one?"

"Yes, one big one."

"Okay. Because I'm getting more than one, but not that serious. In any case, is he supposed to be on any special kind of diet?"

"Yes."

"You might as well knock your head against the wall."

"You got it!" Peter acknowledged.

"I don't know if your father's open to this. Your daughter says to tell Poppa to listen to what he's being told," George explained.

"Yes."

"Much as she'd like to have him there with her—"

"How do you see her, George?" Peter interrupted.

"I'm not seeing," he explained, "I'm feeling. It's whatever channel that's the strongest, that's what they'll come in on. Clairsenses, or psychically perceived feeling, always seems to be the strongest. Once in a while clairvoyance, the psychic sight will open up, and you can see.

"But she warns that Poppa should be on the alert. This is not a forecast that he will have a massive heart attack and pass on, it's just a warning. She's seeing ahead, and it's as though it's her first mission of mercy. She's able to come through with it, like a child learning how to read."

"Yes."

"She's very excited about getting [the message] through.

That's why when you were saying no, she kept insisting and saying that you were wrong and she was right. . . . She just kept saying to me, 'Keep asking. Don't leave it.' Do you know Dominick?"

"Passed on?"

"Yes. It seems to push toward you. Think. Go back."

"There have been a few passings since Lorraine, but that's the wrong name."

"Ooops, you slipped," George kidded Peter. "You gave me her name. Well, it doesn't matter. She's come through already. No, the name Dominick goes to you. I'll just ask you to keep it in mind."

"I have a friend . . ."

"No, this one's definitely passed on. He's insisting he's over there now. Does the name Michael mean anything to you?"

"Yes," Peter verified.

"Passed on or—"

"No."

"Living."

"Yes."

"Would your daughter know him?"

"Yes."

"Is it a son?"

"No."

"Wait a second; I'm getting a son vibration again. Would you understand why? Without telling me: Is it your brother? She keeps saying, 'Son. Son.' I don't know what she means."

"He's a very close friend," Peter explained. "Very close."

"He's like a brother," George said.

"Oh, yes."

"That's what she means! Because she said, 'son' and then she said, 'brother,' and I didn't understand. I thought she meant your brother by blood. Does he believe in this?"

"Yes, yes."

"She says, 'Please tell him you've heard from me.' It seems that your Aunt Rose has been of tremendous help to her over there. They seem to come in together. She watches over her on the other side."

"George, can I ask you a question?" Peter asked. "My daughter never knew Michael."

"She knows of him over there. This is your proof that she would be like a little guardian angel to you, because she seems to know what's going on around you."

"Oh I see. Michael's not passed on."

"No, no. He's here on earth, and she's acknowledging that to you. She sends greetings to him."

"Oh, okay."

"Did somebody ever refer to your daughter as 'a little treasure,' or something?"

"Yes," Peter confirmed.

"Because your aunt says to me how lucky she is to have her as a little treasure over there, but she says it means something besides her saying it. You know that it means something specific."

"Yes."

"Did your daughter pass on in New York State, but on an island?"

"Yes," Peter confirmed.

"Oh: Richmond. Staten Island!"

"Yes."

"Did you ever call her Lori?"

"Yes."

"I'm glad she did that, because I know you said her name before, but now she comes in and says, 'This is Lori.' Your aunt is back with her again, because she's going to take her back over, beyond the veil. She says a very big lesson for you to learn—*a very big lesson*—is love and forgiveness. She keeps saying, 'Forgiveness for the killer and love for the killer.' "

Upon hearing this, Peter erupted, shouting, "No, no, no!"

"I hate when they give me messages like that," George admitted.

"That will never happen!" Peter vowed bitterly.

"Well, that's what she says. That's the reason why. 'It's part of the soul's growth,' she says. A very big lesson in love and forgiveness. She says, 'You think about it, Daddy. You think about it.' They're gone now," George told Peter. "They're cut."

Reflecting on that first reading with George, Peter says, "The things that confirmed it for me were what Lorraine said about Christmas and when George said Rosario, which is my middle name. Also, an aunt who'd died of throat cancer came through, and George gave me the name Lori. There's a sign in my house for her that reads 'Lori.' "

Peter has returned to George annually for subsequent readings. In one, George described what Lorraine was buried in. He saw a white dress *and* a blue dress. That might sound contradictory, but George insisted he saw both. Peter later explained that he was correct on both counts. Because Lorraine's white communion dress no longer fit her, it was buried in the coffin with her. She was laid to rest in a blue frock.

Another time Peter was considering moving to the West Coast. The only thing holding him back was realizing he wouldn't be able to visit his daughter's grave as often. Aware of her father's quandary, Lorraine told George to tell her father, "Daddy, you don't have to come to the grave. I'm in your heart. I'm around you." Peter also learned that Lorraine was among relatives who had predeceased her, some even before she was born. Peter's Uncle Michael, whom George accurately determined was a paraplegic, an Aunt Carmela, and a pet dog have also appeared.

Around the time of Lorraine's death, a friend of Peter's met a woman named Helen whose daughter had also been murdered. "I was very intrigued to talk to her," Peter says. "I had questions, like, How do you deal with this? How do you get by? What can I do to keep from staying in bed all day? Helen told me, 'You've got to live it day by day. You're never going to get over it.' She was very up-front, but her attitude was actually worse than mine. I was so mad at God. I broke many a crucifix and religious statue, yet the next day I'd still get on my knees and pray. Even Lorraine could see this. A lot of times she's said to me through George, 'Daddy, you'll say a hundred rosaries, then when you get to the hundred and first, you'll say, "To heck with all this." ' She was right!

"Anyway, I knew that I had to bring Helen to George so that she could have the same peace of mind I have, knowing her child is in a safe place."

George began his reading for Peter and Helen by exclaiming, "Peter, don't tell me you've lost another child!"

"No."

"Because Lorraine is here with another child," George insisted. "She has her by the hand. And Lorraine is telling me that this other child has a name similar to hers. It starts with an *L*. Who's Lisa?"

Startled, Helen looked at Peter in amazement. Despite all their talks, she had never told him her daughter's name.

"Who is Lou? Do you know Lou?"

"Y-Yes," Helen stammered.

"Lou is sorry for the hard time he gave you and your mother," George said. Only later did Helen tell Peter that Lou was her alcoholic father.

"I was always reluctant to bring anyone to George, because everyone's so skeptical," Peter recalls. "But I knew how much it could help. And I've never walked out with somebody who hasn't hugged or kissed me because of the reading they got from George."

Yet despite all the comfort the readings have brought Peter, neither the experience itself nor Lorraine's pleas from the other side have changed his feelings of rage and vengeance toward her killer. "Each time my daughter comes through, she says, 'Daddy, forgive.' But I can't. It's not just about *my* revenge. It's also to show this damned system that you can't murder somebody and get away with it. Now, I know that people will say that the kid didn't get away with it, because he went to jail. But that's not good enough for me.

"I once told George that if I were standing before God Almighty—and we'll all have to stand there one day—and God said, 'Your daughter is in room one, but her murderer is in room two. You can go in room one with Lorraine and have eternal peace, or take him, the murderer,' I'd take him. Because I know through George that my daughter is at peace now and will always be. I would give up being with her to get the SOB for what he's done to her and my family here on earth.

"I know there are people who go to bereavement support groups. I've never been to one; it's not for me. I know a man whose son was brutally murdered. I've seen him on TV. He's always so calm and low-key. So he lives with it his way, and I live with it mine.

"Is it better to forgive? Should we forgive?" Peter asks.

"Lorraine wants me to forgive. I've thought about forgiving, and maybe it's for others. But not for me. I brought to George a woman whose son, a cop, was murdered. Her husband is very pious and calm about it, but not her. She always says, 'I'm gonna kill those bastards!' And my advice to her? Let her do what she wants. That's what *I* intend to do.

"There's nowhere that my daughter's killer can hide. There isn't a place on earth that I won't find him. I often think that if I hadn't been married to Stacey when Lorraine was killed, I'd have gone to Staten Island, killed the murderer, then blown my own brains out. But I can't live knowing he'll be out walking the streets someday. I fully intend to kill him. I know I'm never going to get away with murder; no one should. But I'll be an old man, and, I don't care, I'll go to jail. I don't worry about me or my life, but every night I pray that thousands of other kids won't be hurt or killed. What's the state doing to protect them right now? Not enough. And what happens to these guys when and if they're caught? What good is the punishment if these guys are living, and our children are dead?"

George has often been warned by the other side to keep his emotions out of the readings as much as possible. When he relays the messages, he does so without "editorializing" or offering his own opinions. But, as you can imagine, it's extremely difficult to remain detached when faced with a situation as painful and as emotionally charged as this.

"Nothing can change the reality of what happened," George says. "You have anger because that's part of the bereavement process. You have to have your grief. Yes, the other side says forgiveness is greater, and love more powerful than hatred. It's an important spiritual lesson to learn. But it's also a very hard one.

"Peter says he can't forgive. How can I convince him to? I can't. His daughter can suggest it. She can say it. She can advise it. But even she can't force it on him. And neither can God. At least Peter knows she's at peace. He knows his daughter is alive somewhere else with other relatives and loved ones, and that she's growing spiritually and is okay. No more harm can ever come to her. That's the one consolation he can have out of this horrible experience.

"As for Peter wanting to kill his daughter's murderer, of course I tell him that two wrongs don't make a right. But," George adds sympathetically, "I'm not in his shoes."

At least Peter's rage has a target. And at least he can take a small measure of satisfaction knowing that his daughter's killer was caught, tried, and brought to justice, regardless of how lacking he finds it. Imagine the agony, then, of Bonnie, who will probably never see her daughter's murderers brought to justice. In fact, she will probably never even learn their identity.

Pamela was a twenty-year-old Boston University psychology major studying in London for a semester. On the morning of December 21, 1988, she called her mother back in the States, as she often did, to say how she couldn't wait to see her. "I told her to have a safe trip," Bonnie recalls, "and that was the last time we spoke." Pamela then boarded Pan American World Airways flight 103, bound for New York City.

Later that afternoon Bonnie listened speechlessly as a TV newscaster reported tersely that Pan Am flight 103 had crashed in Scotland. As she and the rest of the world would soon learn, the plane had been blasted out of the sky by a Palestinian terrorist bomb, killing all 270 aboard. Eleven people on the ground also died from the flaming debris that rained down on the tranquil village of Lockerbie.

"There are no words to describe the crash," Pamela's mother says. "I still cannot believe my daughter isn't coming back to me. She was so much a part of my life. The loss and heartache and pain just go on and on, every minute of the day. It's indescribable. It's a heartache you just can't begin to imagine. Pam touched lives," she reflects both proudly and sadly. "If you were with her for even an hour, you wouldn't forget her. She gave and asked for nothing in return."

In Bonnie's reading with George, he psychically heard what he described as "a huge . . . loud . . . explosion!" and sensed her daughter "falling." He also psychically saw fire, smoke, and an accident of some kind. As the reading progressed, the young woman's spirit confirmed to him, "It was a definite terrorist attack, and a bomb had been brought aboard."

Then George told the grieving mother that her daughter's spirit said, "Marc is with me." After the reading, Bonnie clarified for us that Marc Tager was a handsome twenty-two-year-old Englishman, also a passenger on Pam Am 103. He and Pamela had met, she said, "on line, checking in for the flight" and were instantly attracted to each other. "Apparently, he called his father [from the airport] to say that he'd met this fabulous-looking American girl and had arranged to sit next to her." In the aftermath of the crash, a seating chart confirmed that the two had been sitting side by side.

Now, from the other side, Marc said, in what George correctly discerned was a British accent, "I still have a crush on [Pamela] in the next stage." When the dead woman's spirit called out to a beau, she added jokingly, "Don't tell him Marc has a crush on me!"

For reasons that are still unclear and illustrative of the perplexing—and sometimes frustrating—psychic-mediumistic process, George psychically saw the letters *M* (the clue was M&M's candies) and *A* as parts of Pamela's name. Although he had accurately heard her call her mother by name, he had uncharacteristic difficulty deciphering the third letter, *P,* so could not give her name, though he did give Marc's.

Much to Bonnie's relief, George told her that although Pamela had sustained numerous internal injuries in the explosion and crash, she did not suffer. "She went quickly," he said, "from one moment to the next. They didn't know what hit them. Your daughter knows her remains were found. She's fine now in the spiritual body. Don't feel that her life has been snuffed out. She continues in the next stage. It's a tragedy that you have to live with," he said sympathetically, "but know that she's all right and at peace."

Suddenly Marc came back in. "Tell my parents you've heard from me," he asked Bonnie, through George. She later told George and me that since the tragedy she and Marc's mother and father had come to know one another, sharing their sorrow in transatlantic phone calls and letters. Bonnie assured George—rather, Marc—that she would telephone his parents immediately and relay his message.

In the course of the reading, George explained that the fanatic Moslem terrorists behind the bombing "may think they were right in their actions, but they will have to pay for what they did when they get to the next stage. They broke God's law." Pamela also added ominously, "Watch that part of the world, the Middle East. That's where the next war could take place."

The young woman tried to comfort her mother by saying, "Think of it like I'm away at school, and this [the reading] is like the phone calls I used to make to you."

The Wolf in Sheep's Clothing

Sam and Jeannie Clarke were up before sunrise, going through their weekday routine. It was early February, and the weather was unseasonably mild for that part of the country. The sky, however, was dark and ominous, with showers predicted.

As Sam, a civil engineer, prepared to leave for his office, and Jeannie gathered her things for the short drive to the manufacturing plant where she worked as a secretary, they chatted with their eldest child, sixteen-year-old Becky. It was a family tradition to give her younger brother, Billy, "his space." Usually sociable and affable, in the morning the fourteen-year-old could be described only as grumpy. In this and many other ways, he was a bundle of contradictions, or, as Jeannie often said with a sigh, "a typical teenager."

While the rest of the family bustled around the house, Billy stayed in his room. He'd recently insisted on having his own bedroom rather than share with his younger brother, Daryl. With a TV, stereo, a cache of video games, books on music and fishing, and dozens of heavy-metal rock albums, tapes, and magazines, the room was Billy's private domain. Its walls were papered with posters of his favorite metal stars, such as Motley Crue and Alice Cooper. To some in this rural community, heavy metal was anathema, a corruptive, nefarious influence. The Clarkes saw nothing wrong with Billy's intense interest in the music and its theatrical personalities. As far as they were concerned, heavy metal was to Billy and his peers what Elvis Presley and the Rolling Stones had been to earlier generations: an expression of independence and rebellion.

Billy rose each morning when his alarm clock sounded at 5:30 A.M. He showered, then spent what seemed to his family like hours standing before the mirror styling his long, wavy brown hair. Tall for his age and good-looking, Billy had become increasingly self-conscious about his appearance, his friends, and girls. The Clarkes were relatively new in the community, and Billy wanted desperately to fit in. This morning he dressed for school in his usual neatly pressed blue jeans, a new pair of white sneakers, and a T-shirt bearing the name of a favorite rock group.

This morning, like every morning, as he and his wife left for work, Sam told Billy, "I love you. Have a good day at school today."

"I love you, too," Billy replied.

The Clarkes both felt they had been blessed, raising three children in what seemed like an ideal environment, a hamlet of fewer than three thousand. They lived in a sprawling, modern one-story brick house that was set back a distance from the road on a heavily wooded two-acre lot. Out in back of the Clarkes' home, beyond the pine, willow, maple, and oak trees, ran a stream.

Billy ambled into the kitchen for his usual breakfast: a scrambled-egg sandwich with mayonnaise and American cheese. Becky, meanwhile, was elsewhere in the house, listening to her Walkman. At around 6:45 she glanced at her watch and realized the school bus would be pulling up outside any minute. She went to remind Billy and found her younger brother standing in the hallway outside his parents' bedroom.

"How long before we have to catch the bus?" Billy asked casually.

"Just about five minutes, that's all."

Becky hurriedly collected her schoolbooks and put away her Walkman, returning to the hallway to meet Billy, but he wasn't there. "Billy! Come on! Let's go!" Becky called, patrolling the house. She poked her head into Sam and Jeannie's room. Still no sign of Billy.

"Billy, *come on*!" Becky said, exasperated. "We'll be late for—" She stopped, noticing the light illuminating the carpeting around her father's closet door. "So that's where you are! Fooling around, huh?" Billy loved to play practical jokes and was hiding in the closet, she figured.

"Billy, will you please stop goofin' around!" Becky

grabbed the doorknob and pulled open the door. There was Billy, standing—leaning, it seemed—up against his father's clothes. All of a sudden the boy fell forward, landing with a heavy thud on the plush blue carpet. At first Becky didn't notice the widening crimson pool around her brother as she knelt beside him. Then she saw the blood, which literally poured like water from one side of Billy's head and neck, ran down his shoulder and the length of his body until his blue jeans were soaked red. The wounded boy appeared to be unconscious and was convulsing violently.

Becky was dumbstruck, unable to put the pieces together. Until she saw the gun. She ran to the phone and dialed 911. "My brother shot himself!" she cried. "He needs help!" She hung up and quickly called her parents at work. Neither will ever forget that frantic call: "Hurry home! I think Billy shot himself!"

Sam sped home, making the eight-minute trip in less than two. Pulling up, he ran into the house, screaming, "Becky! Becky!"

"I'm here, Dad!" When Sam saw Billy lying unconscious in his own blood, cradled gently in his terrified sister's arms, he fell to his knees. "Oh my God! Billy!"

His son's eyes were closed, and he was making gurgling sounds. Sam had the presence of mind to lift Billy's shattered head so that he wouldn't choke, but he couldn't summon the strength to move. Somewhere inside, Sam instinctively knew it was too late.

Only after the paramedics arrived did Sam notice anything about the scene. "My God, where's all the blood coming from?" As the emergency workers swiftly checked for vital signs, Sam caught sight of the grisly wound, behind and above his son's right ear. Averting his eyes, he saw the gun: a .22-caliber pistol he'd bought for hunting and protection. He always kept it on a closet shelf, safely out of reach. Or so he'd thought.

Within minutes Jeannie had pulled up the drive just in time to see the paramedics carrying Billy to the ambulance. Her husband tried restraining her, but once she saw her boy bleeding and thrashing on the gurney, she screamed, "Billy! Billy! Don't tell me he's dead!"

Over the paramedics' objections, Jeannie rode with them

and Billy to the hospital, while Sam followed in his pickup truck. Becky, still stunned, remained at home. She'd barely begun to comprehend what had happened when the police arrived. Two detectives brusquely questioned her about her brother, seemingly oblivious of the young girl's shock and distress.

Becky recounted the morning's events as best she could. The detectives took notes and combed the house for clues. Next they drove to the hospital, where they questioned both parents, but especially Sam, and especially about the gun. Once he'd numbly answered each question, the police left the Clarkes to their agonizing vigil. Becky later joined them, still wearing shoes caked with her brother's blood.

Billy's prognosis was gloomy. A doctor told the family that the bullet had destroyed much of his brain. That evening at 8:02, he died. The county medical examiner ruled his death a suicide by self-inflicted gunshot wound.

Today suicide is the second-leading cause of death for young Americans between the ages of fifteen and twenty-four. Each year over six thousand young people choose to end their lives, and according to a federal Centers for Disease Control study, one third of all eighth- and tenth-grade students admit they have contemplated suicide. For reasons experts don't fully understand, the teenage suicide rate has increased approximately 150 percent over the past few years.

Suicides' loved ones face unique problems in bereavement. Not only is there the shock of the death itself, but the endless wondering and, for many, guilt. What could they have done to prevent the suicide? Were there signs, clues, indications they overlooked? Would things have turned out differently if only they'd spent more time together? Talked more? Gotten along better? Because our society views children as products of their family, parents of suicides are often overwhelmed by feelings of inadequacy and failure. Naturally they may feel the same way regarding other problems, but as long as a child is alive, there is always hope of change and reconciliation. Suicides end that possibility forever.

The night Billy passed, Mr. Clarke searched every inch of his room for clues explaining why his son took his life. He listened carefully to every cassette tape Billy owned, hoping desperately to hear a message the boy had perhaps recorded. Or to hear *something*. But the tapes provided no answers, just the rock music Billy loved.

Three days after Billy's death, the police returned to again search all three children's rooms, looking, they said, for physical evidence. A detective specifically requested Billy's junior-high–school yearbook and tapes of his favorite music. Almost all the tapes the couple handed over were of rock; only a few, those by singer Ozzy Osbourne and Motley Crue, would be considered heavy metal, characterized by a furious musical attack and fanciful, often Gothic imagery.

Both parents thought this was strange, but a detective explained that the police learned from unnamed sources that one of Billy's tapes contained a song called "Suicide Solution" and that he'd recently listened to it repeatedly for five hours. Ironically, while many misinformed critics claim this Ozzy Osbourne composition glorifies taking one's own life, it is in fact a plea to listeners *not* to kill themselves with drugs and alcohol. Suicide solves nothing, it clearly asserts.

The police, like most adults not advocates of this controversial music—and inexplicably anxious to close the case—didn't much care to interpret the lyrics properly. Nor were they terribly interested in probing other possible causes for the boy's self-inflicted death. Not even after their search turned up no copy of the "killer" song.

As they were leaving, one cop turned to Jeannie and said bluntly, "We think your son had some involvement in the occult or devil worship."

His mother was struck dumb with rage. "You're crazy!" she spluttered. It was clear, however, that the police believed a link existed between Billy's favorite music and satanism.

But is there really? Yes, heavy metal employs so-called satanic imagery, but so do any number of hit horror films. And yes, some metal groups do espouse satanism, but these comprise a literal handful of obscure underground groups whose independently produced and distributed recordings are hard to find in record stores. Billy's family found no such works in his music collection.

There are some well-known cases in which parents of suicides charge that a certain song "drove" their kids to kill themselves. The obvious question is, What type of person could be so easily persuaded to take his or her life? In the most publicized case, the parents of two Nevada men (ages eighteen and twenty) sued the veteran British act Judas Priest over a song they claimed led the two young adults to shoot themselves in 1985. One expired within days; the other survived with disfiguring facial injuries only to die a few years later in a psychiatric ward where he was being treated for suicidal depression and long-term drug abuse. The two, both high-school dropouts and heavy drug abusers, had been victims of household alcoholism and violence since early childhood. So to lay the entire blame for their suicide pact on the chance appearance of the words "Do it" (Do what?) on a record—audible only if the record were played *backwards,* and, in fact, an inadvertent combination of sounds—is patently absurd. But this 1990 case, in which the judge found the group not liable for the men's deaths, demonstrated how the music has been made a scapegoat for larger problems.

The police briefly considered Becky a suspect in Billy's death, which the Clarkes found painful and irresponsible. In addition, two other flimsy suicide theories were raised: that Billy was distraught over an unrequited crush on a girl named Meredith Walker, his friend Brandon Cooper's steady date; or that he feared his parents' reaction to an anticipated poor report card. They all seemed absurd, Jeannie thought, and yet the adolescent ego is so fragile. Maybe in a moment of weakness . . .

Her mind returned to the police's contention of devil worship. Most parents would automatically reject that as preposterous, but not in their town. As Mrs. Clarke had heard on the news and read in the papers, there was plenty of evidence that beneath the area's suburban veneer lurked an underworld of the disenfranchised: bigots, religious zealots, bogus faith healers, white supremacists, and satanists. In her grief, Jeannie mentally ran down a list of people close to Billy whose influence was strong. For some reason she could not articulate, she kept thinking about Brandon. Did the teenager, a year older than Billy, kill him? Anything was possible. Furthermore, Brandon was the only one of their son's friends who could come and go freely from the Clarke home without their imposing German shepherd, King, barking.

Over two hundred people attended Billy's funeral. The fourteen-year-old was laid to rest not in the traditional dress suit but in his beloved jeans, T-shirt, and sneakers. Everyone who knew the Clarkes was touched by the tragedy, but none so much as Brandon Cooper, Meredith Walker, and Seth Weber, another close friend and classmate.

Brandon told friends he was "torn to pieces" over Billy's death, yet Sam couldn't help noticing that he, and many of his son's friends, acted . . . well, oddly unemotional. Both Brandon and Meredith, a pretty thirteen-year-old with piercing blue eyes and sparkling blond hair, seemed *proud* of the dead boy for having killed himself. Sam, overhearing their whispers, shook his head in disbelief. He recalled Billy's confiding to his mother the night before his death that Meredith had confessed thoughts of suicide herself.

Shortly after the funeral Jeannie had a vivid dream. "Billy was on the bed," she recalled. "I asked him, 'Can you tell Mommy why you did it?' Billy answered no in a soft, sweet voice, slowly shaking his head. 'Were you mad at Mommy and Daddy?' I asked him. 'No,' Billy said, again slowly shaking his head. 'Did your friend Brandon do this?' I asked. 'No,' he answered. Then I woke up."

Still, Mrs. Clarke continued to suspect Brandon of some involvement. When police returned Billy's yearbook, they informed Sam that someone had scrawled the word *Mine* over Meredith's picture. They admitted the handwriting wasn't Billy's but were unable to say whose it was. The obvious possibility was Brandon, her possessive boyfriend. If he didn't actually kill her son, Jeannie was certain he had some idea why Billy might have committed suicide. Yet the police never interviewed him; his parents, it seems, forbade it. The two boys were as close as brothers, with Brandon the stronger personality. He led, Billy followed.

One day Brandon's mother, Arlene, approached Jeannie and said cryptically, "I might as well tell you this: I gave the police a book. They asked me for it, but it doesn't really have anything in it."

A book? Jeannie didn't have the slightest clue what Arlene was talking about. She and her husband later learned that the cover of this book—which the police refused to show them—depicted a goat's head, a common satanic symbol. By now she'd heard the rumors around town and read in the local newspapers the vague speculation that Billy's death was related to "something satanic," leaving her and Sam even more tormented.

Satanic cults are a growing and insidious phenomenon in America today. Documented cases have been reported in virtually every part of the country, as well as in Canada, Mexico, Europe, and Australia. In April 1989 thirteen mutilated bodies were found in the Mexican border town of Matamoros. The victims, including a Texas college student, had been "ritualistically tortured and murdered," leading experts to conclude that not only satanism but also cannibalism was involved. Later arrested were ringleader Adolfo Constanzo and Sara Aldrete, the latter a popular college student by day and reputedly a ritualistic killer by night.

According to a 1990 ABC-TV poll, two thirds of all Americans believe in the existence of the Devil, and half of them feel that Satan has touched their lives personally in some way. Of course, belief in Satan, the personification of evil, is as old as mankind. "Be sober, be watchful, for your adversary the Devil, as a roaring lion, goes about seeking someone to devour," the New Testament warns.

The Roman Catholic Church takes the growth of satanism seriously enough that New York City's Cardinal John O'Connor made front-page news in 1990 when he announced that the Church had performed two exorcisms, rituals to expel evil or demonic spirits, in the area.

With its exotic paraphernalia, rejection of mainstream Judeo-Christian values, and promise to empower followers, satanism appeals to vulnerable, insecure adolescents like Billy for obvious reasons. Dr. Stephen Kaplan, an expert on the paranormal and the occult, notes, "Teenagers are lured by curiosity, experimentation, and the promise of power through Satan worship. Many youngsters obviously don't recognize the dangers associated with satanism. After all, satanists tell their followers they won't even really die, because their cohorts will resurrect them."

Exact statistics on satanism are understandably elusive, for it is a netherworld with its own language, symbols, books, rituals, and holidays. It's important to point out, however, that not all kids attracted to devil worship are really practicing satanists. The subject matter is forbidden and fascinating, which is all the recommendation most youngsters need. For kids who feel disenfranchised and compelled to rebel against the status quo, claiming an interest in satanism, no matter how casual, carries a certain panache unequaled by bizarre hairstyles and wardrobe, sex and drugs, or dropping out of school.

A minority of kids, however, do inadvertently cross paths with real and very dangerous satanic cults. Whether or not these worshipers actually do contact and wield the power of Satan is irrelevant. That they are willing to commit acts of evil, whether in the name of Satan or not, is what's truly frightening.

The desperate need to find out why Billy killed himself mushroomed into an obsession. Neither Sam nor Jeannie Clarke returned to work for weeks. Becky and Daryl, too, were devastated, dreading going back to school for fear that classmates would ask about Billy. Becky had lost not only her brother, but her best friend. Sam pored over volumes on devil worship, then searched Billy's room for anything remotely related to the occult: candles, matches, hair, pictures of goat heads. He was shocked at how the local public and school libraries' shelves contained many books seeming to promote satanism, full of purportedly genuine rituals and spells. The only evidence of devil worship the Clarkes came across were the five-pointed stars, or pentagrams, the boy doodled on his school notebooks.

In the aftermath of Billy's death, the Clarkes were left more alone than ever. Suddenly neighbors stopped calling, and even close friends acted distant. Did someone know something? Was someone hiding something? Did people truly believe that Billy was involved in satanism?

When the police abruptly closed the case three months later without having arrived at a firm conclusion, Sam and Jeannie felt they had no choice but to pursue the matter on their own. They tried to confirm widespread rumors that a local family was involved in the darker side of the occult, and attempted to find the locations where cults were alleged to conduct services. Their efforts were thwarted at every turn by uncooperative law-enforcement officials, school administrators—even the minister of a church that Billy had attended with Brandon. With the start of the next school year, Brandon was sent to a private Christian school that Billy had previously attended.

Sam and Jeannie were so overwhelmed with grief and loneliness, they seriously considered suicide themselves. They'd nearly given up hope of finding peace of mind until one day in 1988 when they caught George Anderson on a national talk show, discussing life after death and demonstrating live his psychic gift for communicating with those on the other side by giving personal readings to audience members. Neither parent believed in psychic phenomena or the paranormal, but just the same they took down George's name and the title of a new book about him, *We Don't Die.*

Both read the book and decided at once to try contacting George. Perhaps through the psychic medium Billy could explain why he took his own life—*if* he took his own life. Writing to George, care of me, was completely out of character for them, but by now the Clarkes were convinced this was the only way they would ever learn the truth.

Dear Mr. Martin,

I know that you probably receive many letters similar to mine which ask for your help in contacting George Anderson. My wife Jeannie and I lost our youngest son, Billy Edward, on February 3, 1988. I believe Billy committed suicide, but I am not totally convinced. Jeannie cannot accept that Billy intentionally took his life. Billy was fourteen.

Jeannie and I just finished reading *We Don't Die.* The book gave us much comfort. I have been contemplating suicide regularly since Billy's death, and I was just sorting out which way to complete the act without messing it up. I am Christian, a good person, a loving parent, just like my wife Jeannie. We have another loving son, Daryl, who is thirteen, and a daughter, Becky, sixteen. None of this mattered. I was still going to kill myself until I read your book. Thank you.

Sam went on to request a reading with George, among other reasons, so that "maybe more unnecessary deaths can be prevented. If we cannot find out why, then we will have the satisfaction of knowing that we tried. Please help us if you can." The letter was signed "Sam and Jeannie Clarke."

George and I were taping our cable-TV series, *Psychic Channels*, that day. After reading the letter, I slipped it back into its large brown mailer, which contained some other papers I didn't have time to look at. I then placed that inside a larger brown manila envelope and sealed it. During a break, I mentioned to George that I had an interesting piece of mail for him, fully expecting him to say that he'd look at it later.

Instead he asked me for it, placed it, unopened, on his lap, and performed what is called a psychometric reading. He'd done this before, but with the subject present, an important distinction. Like a blind person reading Braille, he ran his hands across the envelope, eyes closed. Then he gazed toward a far corner of the studio.

"Does this have anything to do with something in the country?" he asked.

"Yes," I replied. "How do you know that, George?"

"Because I see it psychically. I just saw a license plate of a midwestern state."

My wife and producer, Chris, and our associate, Elise, grabbed pads and pens and started taking notes. We knew this was something special, even for George.

"Does this involve a child?" he asked.

"Yes," I replied.

"I think it's a youngster. That's the feeling I'm getting. It's a young boy. He's nice-looking. He's either in his teens or very close to it. He passes tragically."

"I believe so."

"It's strange. I feel he was forced to kill himself. He was drawn into something and couldn't get out of it." George shuddered. "There's something very evil. His parents couldn't help him. There was nothing they could do. They can't blame themselves, but they do. I see pentagrams, five-pointed stars. There's what I would call noisy music and devil worship."

"Really?" I exclaimed.

"Yes. Devil worship. Evil. He's saying he killed himself, but *they* pulled the trigger. It was more like murder than suicide in that this young boy was forced to do it, forced to take his own life. I psychically hear a gunshot. He shot himself in the head?"

Of course I couldn't verify that then, but George continued. "The boy is telling me this was his choice, but he was trying to protect other members of his family. Now I'm being told that people involved with a Christian church did this to him. I'm seeing a psychic symbol of devil worship behind a cross." After a brief pause, George repeated emphatically, "They forced him to kill himself. He was being used in a satanic cult." George looked up at me, obviously troubled. "Can you confirm any of this?"

"No," I replied. "I've never spoken to the people. The letter they sent didn't say very much. But I'll call them."

George shrugged. "Well, I am seeing a wolf in sheep's clothing. But he's so excited, I can't get him to slow down and tell me further what it means. I think it's from a quote from the Bible. Maybe you could ask his parents? Because he's calling to them and, I think, to a sister. There are people he's trying to protect." George fell silent, cocking his head and listening to the voice he heard clairaudiently.

"This boy says his sister is being accused of this, but she had nothing to do with it. Someone in the family found him. Again, he was forced into suicide. He says he didn't know any other way out. He was threatened, and he felt he had to take his own life before someone else did. There's some kind of scandal involved. Something sexual. Drugs, also. The boy's parents are turned off by the church." George's last remark was interesting, for as we later learned, the Clarkes were not strict churchgoers, further alienating them from their neighbors.

Still running his hands over the envelope, George went on. "It's in the country, as I said. It's very nice. He had posters of celebrities of some kind in his room. Someone introduced him to something that leads to suicide. Whoever it was, he met him or her in school. His parents don't know, and someone threatens to blow the whistle on him. It's like the board game *Clue*. There are many people involved. At least ten.

"There was also someone who wanted to use him sexually. There's pornography involved. There's a cover-up. The young boy is warning his family to be careful. If they try to investigate this privately, be very careful. If they expose it, they'll be in danger. In fact, the boy is saying the family should move. He says his grandfather—I think it's his father's father—met him on the other side."

Just then the show's director called us back to work. "If the parents wish to talk to me," George said as we took our places on the set, "let me know." I never offered to show George the envelope's contents, nor did he ask to see them before or after the stunning psychometric reading.

That evening I called the Clarkes and told them what had happened when I gave George their letter. Their reactions were guarded, as if they no longer knew whom to trust. Still, they were clearly happy I'd called. "I can read you the notes of what George told us," I said, "and you can see if any of his messages fit. I have no way of knowing if any of this is true. You didn't tell me much in your letter."

"Yes, I know," Sam replied. "We purposely told you so little."

Before we began, I told the couple that George would gladly see them should they ever come to New York. Therefore I asked them not to provide me with any new information, so that if they were to have a reading in the future, they'd know for certain that the messages were coming through George from Billy and not as a result of something I might have told him.

As I proceeded to relate my notes, Sam and Jeannie mostly listened, acknowledging information in flat, emotionless voices. I wondered if perhaps George had been totally off the mark. "Is this accurate?" I asked at midpoint. Warily, Sam answered, "Yes."

When I came to the expression George had used, "the wolf in sheep's clothing," Jeannie gasped, "Oh my God! Did George say who it is?"

"No, he didn't. Does that expression mean something?"

"Yes," said Sam, but he wouldn't elaborate. It wasn't

until many months later that we learned Billy had written those words over a yearbook photograph of a schoolteacher, a principal player in this macabre mystery.

Between the time of my conversation with the Clarkes and their private reading with George months later, several strange events reinforced the family's suspicion that satanism contributed to Billy's death. For months following his funeral, they received countless anonymous hang-up calls. Dozens of times, Jeannie, Sam, and Becky noticed they were being followed by unfamiliar vehicles for miles; in several instances, the drivers parked at the foot of their driveway, then drove away. They heard reports of satanic desecrations of headstones in a local cemetery. The following autumn, the rumor that a blond, blue-eyed child would be kidnapped and sacrificed was taken seriously enough that many parents kept their children home from school on Halloween. Similarly, in a nearby town, parents stopped sending their kids to a particular school after widespread reports of satanic activity among certain students began circulating.

There was yet more: A wrecked pickup truck was found near the Clarkes' home, reportedly filled with what authorities described as "satanic materials." And in a neighboring county, a cow was found surgically slaughtered, a method of killing consistent with satanic animal sacrifice and ritual. Most horrifying: the discovery of a baby's corpse near their home.

In desperation, the Clarkes brought in a private investigator who'd heard their story and volunteered his time. When he tried to question students and administrators at Billy's school, the teacher whose picture Billy captioned "the Wolf in Sheep's Clothing" threatened him and ran him off the grounds. Later the P.I. discovered an abandoned barn, its walls covered with various satanic symbols. When he brought a local police officer out to see it, he was shocked to hear the cop explain the five-pointed pentagrams thusly: "Those are just Jewish stars. Must be Jews worshiping around here." Never mind that the Jewish Star of David has six points and Jews aren't known to frequent abandoned barns. Clearly, the investigator's presence was not welcome, and he felt sufficiently unnerved by several other encounters to drop the case and quickly leave town.

"This part of the country is like a Venus's-flytrap," Sam Clarke told me. "It looks innocent, but it can be deadly. In truth my picture-perfect little town was nothing short of a cross between *In the Heat of the Night* and *Rosemary's Baby.*"

Nearly a year after their son's death, in January 1989, Sam and Jeannie Clarke came to George's for their long-awaited reading. George greeted them warmly, feeling that in some sense he knew them. They took seats opposite him and set up their tape recorder.

"You didn't lose a sister, did you?" he began.

"Not that I'm aware of," Jeannie replied.

"Okay. Did you lose a female friend?"

Jeannie didn't answer, deep in thought.

"That's all right," said George. "I'm not going to push it, but there's definitely a female presence around that claims to be a young friend who passed on."

"I don't know of anyone," she said.

"Did anybody else pass on who went to the same school as Billy did? A female?"

"Yes!" Mrs. Clarke exclaimed. "A little girl."

"That's who it is, then. After I said it, she kept walking around you, then stopped near you. She said something about, 'Ask her about the female friend.' I took it as some sort of kinship or fellowship. That's what made me say 'sister.' . . . Then she started talking about going to school and said, 'Wait a minute, think further. Ask her if I went to school with Billy.' "

"She's with Billy," Jeannie remarked, pleased.

"Did she pass on in elementary school?"

"Yes."

"Was she around his age?"

"Yes."

"She passed on before he did."

"Yes."

"She also claims that she was there to meet Billy when he came over. I wouldn't say they were bosom buddies, but they were friends."

Jeannie confirmed that was true.

"She says she was trying to help him from the other side,

like a guardian angel, because she saw the distress he was going through. She said she saw 'what the road was leading to.' That's how she puts it. She says she was trying to help him, and she was with him when he took his own life."

George resumed writing notes on his pad, something he does during unusually difficult or complex readings. "Was your son involved with a lot of adults?"

"Possibly."

"She says she greeted him when he came over because he wouldn't trust adults. It was as if he were afraid of being tricked. So there must have been some sort of experience here on earth in which he felt tricked by an adult. But not by you," George stressed. "She doesn't mean you."

"No." Jeannie sounded relieved.

"Whoever or whatever [it was here], he was afraid somebody was tricking him, so he backed off. This girl came forward, and he had more trust in her because he remembered her. She led him through and helped him out. . . . Something here on earth grossly disappointed him, is what she tells me. Now, he was involved with a church of some sort."

"He had gone to church," Jeannie answered.

"Okay. Was somebody playing the role of being very spiritual to him?"

"Yes."

"Because somebody seems to be—I keep seeing, again, the wolf in sheep's clothing. I remember clearly when I held the envelope. Somebody's pretending to be your minister or to be spiritual, and he's not. It's definitely a male."

"Oh, it's a male," said Jeannie.

"There could be a wife involved also. There's both male and female. The cover is excellent, because you would less expect it in a female than you would in a male. . . . Were they a minister team?"

"No, no . . ."

"Now, wait a minute. This female you're thinking of: Was her husband involved?"

"If it's who I'm thinking of, it's man and wife."

"It's a team," George said firmly. "Maybe not a minister team, but in any case, they're preaching."

"I may be wrong in who I think it is," said Jeannie.

"He says to me, 'It's definitely a female and a male involved,'" George insisted.

"Will Billy give you any names?" Jeannie asked.

"Yes, that's what I'm hoping. I'm not going to rush anything. He doesn't want to talk about it, so the girl talked about it. . . . I won't block anything out, but you may not be able to verify this. Is there—was there—any sexual involvement, do you think?"

Jeannie answered sadly, "I think there's a possibility."

"According to this little girl, there's definitely something sexual going on. It could have been homosexual, it could have been heterosexual. I keep seeing the symbol that your son was tricked, and that's where the anguish comes from. I keep seeing the face with a patch over the eye, which is a symbol of being tricked, deceived, double-crossed, and that's where the trouble starts. It's almost as though he's been around, but he's naive."

"Yes."

"It's certain that with adults I'd say he's naive. . . . It's not until things start to get out of hand that he realizes, 'Wait a minute, there's something wrong here; this isn't the way it should be.' Just for my own verification, did he at any time relate anything sexual going on?"

"Never."

"I'm going to say I wouldn't be surprised, because it seems there could have been a threat involved. 'If you open your mouth, we kill your family,' as a molester would do to a child, you know?"

"Would he tell you who molested him?"

"I don't know as of yet. He doesn't say. Somebody involved with the church or school."

"I think so," said Jeannie.

"I feel definitely it's an official institution: a church, a school, a youth center. There is definitely a chain of people involved. . . . I keep seeing the wolf, a symbol of evil. Something's definitely very negative, and it's behind the cross. It could be covered up or hiding behind Christianity.

"Okay," George continued, "this little girl tells me from the other side to explain very carefully. . . . There definitely seems to be some sort of sexual abuse. It could have been both by male and female. . . . It was definitely something sexual going on," George now affirmed.

The Clarkes listened quietly. George paused.

"Was Billy inclined to be a loner?"

"He had his moments," Jeannie said, "but he always had friends."

"Was he inclined to look up to somebody?"

"Yes."

"That's what it is. The little girl tells me he feels as if he's part of a crowd, yet he's kind of lonely. He's not part of the crowd."

"He always wanted to fit in," Jeannie admitted.

"He wants to fit in. Exactly. And that's where it happens. So someone—an adult, or someone older than he—befriends him. They sense this. You know, he's naive, he's gullible. He's been around a bit, but he's still a child, and they sense that he's in need of this. This is where the opportunity, the temptation, comes in.

"Again, the perfect opportunity is in a church. Everybody feels he fits in. 'I belong to something. I'm not an outcast.' It's as if somebody is going through a lot of troubles, and suddenly he becomes 'born again' because he feels he belongs. Something happens at school, definitely. Because the little girl, she's telling me what happened.

"Now, don't get the wrong idea," George said. "Your son *is* present in the room. I feel him right there. However, it's almost as if he can't talk about it or doesn't know how to talk about it. He's telling her about it. Now, was he in a Christian school?"

"He had been."

"Oh, okay, because I keep seeing school and church combined. . . . This is not a put-down of anybody's church, but it's as if they confused him in the Christian school. Where, for example, I could sit back and say, 'They are full of baloney,' he'd take it too deeply, too seriously. The little girl who is talking," said George, "they were together in the Christian school. Oh! Because she says the trouble starts in the Christian school—the private school. That's where he takes things too seriously. He felt he could trust her. . . . Somebody definitely put a heavy guilt trip on him. . . .

Somebody in school or somebody who's an adult. A male. There are definitely a male and a female who are the prime suspects in this. I would say, though, that first an older male befriends him, whom he meets at the school or at church."

"Now, when you say older," Jeannie inquired, thinking of Brandon Cooper, "could it be just a year older?"

"Very possible. But it's an older male. He definitely looks up to someone."

"Whom he looked up to a whole lot?" asked Jeannie, apparently beginning to place the person's identity.

"Definitely. He idolized him."

"Ask Billy if the name is Brandon," Jeannie blurted out.

"Don't say a thing," George admonished her gently. *"I've* got to tell you, or I'm going to say you told it to me."

"I'm sorry."

"I'll just leave it and go on. It seems more of an adult, though. Now, could this youngster, Brandon, have been involved with an adult? It seems . . . the befriending comes from there, because Billy feels he wants to fit in. But from there, the next step follows to an adult. Perhaps this Brandon introduced him to someone older, or family or friends. Do you know for a fact that whoever was involved in this was involved in some sort of satanic or evil type of activity?"

"Pretty sure," Jeannie answered.

"Yes, that's what I feel. There's some sort of involvement. I don't know if *satanic* is too strong a word, but I don't know a better word."

"Satanic is the right word," said Jeannie, "if it's who we think it is."

"And it's all covered up very nicely. It's so obviously there, and yet you'd never suspect it. Was he attending club meetings or social gatherings, or something like that?"

"Yes, he did," said Jeannie. "He went on Sunday with Brandon to church."

"Because, again, he's going to some sort of organization, club meeting, social gathering—something like that. Was he in the Baptist church?"

"He had gone to the Baptist church a couple of times," Jeannie recalled.

"Did he go to another?"

"Yes," Sam answered.

"Because he's going to another so-called Christian church, but it's not one that I would associate with your area. He's going to this church, and then from there they go somewhere else. And, he could be with his friend, or a friend of friends."

"He went there one time," Jeannie agreed.

"Now, without telling me: This specific church has another name?"

"Yes," Sam affirmed.

"But it's portrayed as a Christian church."

"Yes."

"Without telling me, is there a good chance I have never heard of this denomination?"

"Yes," Sam repeated.

"Because that's the feeling I'm getting. He gives me the impression I can't say it. I've never heard of this particular denomination."

"At the time," said Sam, "we couldn't find out from him what the name was."

"Did he vow some sort of secrecy? They made it some sort of game; it's like an underground organization."

"When he came back from that, I asked him what they had done," Billy's father remembered. "He said they played games, ate pizza, and drank Pepsi."

"Because he and the little girl now tell me there was some sort of spy fellowship—the kind of thing you must keep quiet about. Again, it's as if kids belong to a club. They keep showing me scenes from *The Little Rascals,* where they belonged to the Woodchucks!" George said, laughing. "They have to keep these vows. . . . Was he into rock and roll?" George asked them.

"Yes," Sam answered.

"But did he get into it heavier? That's what I'm getting at."

"Yes," said Jeannie.

"Because he keeps showing me that he's getting into heavier rock and roll. Things he definitely knows that I would freak out on, he'd find interesting. He wanted to get the shock value of it. Oh my God!" exclaimed George, suddenly turning music critic. "How can you listen to that kind of stuff? Did he have posters up in his room?"

"Yes," Sam and Jeannie chorused.

"That's definitely what I'm seeing: these creepy-looking posters. You certainly wouldn't see them in *my* house! The thing is, he got these types of posters as he got more into it. Was he starting to alienate himself from you? It's as if he was close, and yet it's almost a feeling—a little bit as though he couldn't trust you."

"Apparently not," Sam admitted glumly, "since he didn't talk to us that much."

"He says he felt you couldn't be trusted, or he couldn't trust you. Again, somebody joins a group and has to alienate his family."

"Because he's brainwashed," Jeannie interjected.

"Exactly. That's what I'm getting at. If somebody else finds out, he's going to destroy this. You know, he could put the group in jeopardy. . . . Now, when your son was home, he went to the Christian school for a time. Before he passed on, was he going to a public school?"

"Yes," said Sam.

"Okay. Because he tells me he's in a public school at the time when all this starts to occur. He takes his own life at fourteen."

"Yes," Billy's mother answered softly.

"He says the reason this church is hidden behind Christianity is because of the area you are in."

"We tried to find out where it was," Sam said.

"Yes, exactly, because this is definitely . . . an underground group. Somebody has definitely exposed him to what I would consider satanic-looking things. It could be this promise of power. Was he suddenly into the color red?"

"No," Jeannie said. "His brother loves red."

"Well, it's weird, because he keeps showing me the color red. It has something to do with this situation."

"Could it be blood?" mused Billy's mother.

"That's what I'm wondering."

"Those posters had a lot of red," Sam recalled.

"Yes, it could be connected with that. Do you think it's possible that he could have told you he was going one place and then went somewhere else?"

"Maybe one other time," Sam responded.

"Does the name Becky mean anything at all?"

"Yes," both answered.

"Passed on?"

"No."

"That's his sister," Jeannie offered.

"He kept saying Becky. He must be calling out to her, that he's there." George paused before asking, "Did he choke a little bit, before passing?"

"Yes," said Sam.

"Could he have choked at all, do you think?"

"Yes, because I was trying to keep him from choking," Sam said, recalling the horrible scene.

"There's this choking sensation prior to passing. Did he breathe something in?"

"No, they had tubes down in his chest," Jeannie said, alluding to Billy's brief stay in the hospital.

"Oh, okay," said George, "because I don't know yet how he took his own life. Did he take something? Why does it feel as if I'm going limp inside? Oh, wait a second. Was there blood involved with this attempt?"

"Yes."

"That's why I keep seeing the blood, internally as well as externally. . . . Did he use a weapon on himself?"

"Yes."

"This happened at home."

"Yes."

"He says he did it at home. He said, 'There's bloodshed.' I said, 'Wait a minute. What do you mean? Did you cut yourself?' He said, 'No.' I asked, 'What are you trying to tell me?' 'There's bloodshed.' "

"Yes," Jeannie said in a choked voice.

"At first it was an attempt. I think at that point he wanted to turn back, but it was too late." George then deduced that Billy has shot himself in the head. "Is it possible that he could have seen the people at school? Because that seems to be where the contact is. Contact could have been made at the church one time. Are there other people that go to his school who belong to this so-called church?"

"I would think so," guessed Jeannie.

"I'm trying to say this in a way that doesn't seem too hokey. Satanism is sneaking in. He's trying to bring it into the home, slightly. It's almost as if, if you inch it in, it will take over. He was also getting a little chummier with his sister at that time."

"Yes," Sam acknowledged.

"It's almost as if he were trying subtly to get her involved in it—very subtly, because he became distant with his sister, then all of a sudden started getting friendly with her again. The little girl tells me he became defensive if you questioned him about anything."

"Yes."

". . . Because he was a teenager," added Jeannie.

"Kids can be like this, but the little girl tells me he admits he was inclined to be a little more defensive than usual—especially if you seemed to pry too much. Somebody must have discovered something. You didn't discover anything, as far as you can tell."

"Correct," Sam replied.

"Somebody must have discovered something that added to the threat or the danger, and from there, that's where the trouble started to move in." George then asked about Billy's friend Brandon, "Why does he seem . . . I can't figure him out . . ."

"Shifty," offered Billy's mother.

"Yes, that's exactly the way I feel. There's something that makes me uncomfortable when I dwell on him. This little girl tells me that he could be the one wearing the patch over the eye. You couldn't trust him. Did they pal around frequently?"

"Yes."

"Definitely. There's a strong calling out."

"Yes."

"Could Brandon have been attracted to boys?"

"He could have," answered Jeannie, "but he had a girl-friend."

"His girlfriend belonged to this church also."

"Possibly."

"Does the name Thorpe mean anything at all?"

"Yes!"

"Living."

"Yes."

"Was she a nurse?"

"Yes."

"Was she involved with this church at all?"

"Probably," Jeannie said uncertainly. "I don't know for sure."

"Did you ever meet her?"

"Oh, yes."

"She also is a little on the shifty side. She's like the used-car salesman. She's almost too nice, which would make me suspicious."

"Yes."

"Right," Sam agreed. "There you go!"

"Does she try to come across as a very spiritual, religious person?"

"Yes."

"It all seems to be some sort of a put-on," said George. "I assume she's a Baptist or a Christian."

"Yes."

"Now, does she know this Brandon person?"

"Yes."

"Because she certainly knows this Brandon, the little girl is telling me."

"Yes."

"Her husband is too good to be true; it's the same thing. . . . Don't take this the wrong way: It's almost as if they drip with down-home courtesy."

"You've got it!" Billy's mother exclaimed.

"I see a fishhook," George noted, "a symbol of something fishy. So there's definitely something fishy with the two of them. There's also someone else in the school who would have been involved: an adult male."

"Yes. The teacher."

"Well, I said I won't block anything out. I certainly get the impression that this guy is a real dirt bag."

"Yes."

"That's the only word that comes to my mind. It's the impression the girl gives me. He's a real lowlife, a real dirt bag. Is there a Frank?"

"I take the name Frank," Sam responded.

"Passed on."

"Yes."

"Is he family or just a friend?"

"Friend."

"Billy said to me, 'Tell them Frank is here with me.' "

"All right!" Sam exulted.

"He's like an uncle figure to your son."

"He saw him when he was a baby," Jeannie explained.

"He passed on tragically."

"Yes," said Sam.

"Because he says he went over tragically. He was there before Billy."

"Yes."

"Billy trusts him now . . . because he knows it's somebody that you knew. Frank seems to be a very good-hearted person."

"Yes," Billy's mother asserted.

"So, definitely, you're not surprised to hear that he's there with your son. He would go out of his way to make sure he can help as much as possible. . . . You knew him well," George said.

"He's the only person I ever knew that would do anything for me," Sam said fondly.

"Now he says to me that this is a situation [with Billy] where you never, ever get all the facts. Even if you get the facts, you'll never be able to prove anything. This is like the CIA. There is a neatly covered-up group. He comes right out and says they are definitely in league with the negative or satanic. Definitely no good. Is there a missing person in your town?"

"Yes," Sam affirmed.

"Did that person die? Somebody," George said, "has been sacrificed."

Neither parent appeared shocked. "Oh, they covered it up and said it isn't," said Jeannie.

"There's a murder," George added, "a sacrifice. Was it a female?"

"We don't know. We only know the story."

"It's like a murder, but they [on the other side] refer to it as a sacrifice. This is scary. These people watch every move you make, night or day. You step out of line, and they'll kill you without batting an eye. Somebody is missing. There's been a sacrifice. It could have been a young person."

"We don't know," Billy's mother repeated. "The story is that it was a young girl."

"That's what I'm feeling. It was a female. There's a female presence here who says she's the young female sacrificed. That's why I was getting the feeling of a sacrifice. Your son could have been the next sacrifice."

"Very possible," Jeannie said grimly.

"He could have, out of fear, thought, 'I don't want to deal with it,' and figured, 'They're going to get me, so I've got to kill myself.' But it's almost as if somebody proposed that to him: that he would be the next sacrifice because he was young and innocent and a—"

"He was a virgin," Jeannie cut in, sensing where George was going.

"Exactly! The fact of the matter is that somebody then brought this up to him. Out of fear, he tried to back out of it. There was phenomenal fright and disappointment. That's when he realized they were going to kill his family, and he had to sacrifice himself. It's a sacrifice for reasons of protection."

The dead boy's parents said nothing but nodded their heads.

"Was he home alone?"

"Almost," Jeannie answered.

"Becky did find him."

"Becky was there," she confirmed.

"That's what he says. So he apologizes to his sister. Now, just before he took his own life, was he inclined to be very afraid?"

"Yes," both parents answered together. Shortly before his death Billy moved his bed so that someone looking in the window couldn't see it. He also insisted on keeping the family watchdog with him at night.

"I feel really frightened. I feel genuinely terrified. I'm not exaggerating the word, either, because my stomach is knotting up. It's like the feeling he had before he did it [took his life]. He was genuinely terrified."

"Yes," the boy's mother said.

"Was he not sleeping well? It's almost as if he was up all night thinking they were going to get him," said George. "It was a question of time, this feeling that they were going to get him or get his family."

"Probably."

"It was almost as if he was having a nervous breakdown. Every noise seemed to make him jump. . . . Was he getting calls?"

"Yes," Sam confirmed.

"There's definitely a lot of contact by phone. It's creepy. . . . Was he getting calls from different people?"

"Different people," said Jeannie.

"Did he seem to be upset after he got off the phone?"

"He would never tell us who was on the phone," she said. "He definitely kept it under control."

"And he resented it," Billy's mother recalled, "if you asked him who was on the phone."

"Frank is speaking again. Did he pass tragically in the sense of age as well as circumstance?"

"Yes," said Sam.

"He's been trying to let you know he's taking care of Billy on the other side. He says, 'I'm doing what I can to help him out.' Was there violence in his death?"

"Yes."

"A weapon involved."

"Yes."

"Sounds like guns."

"Yes."

"Let me explain. He says there's murder involved."

"Yes," Jeannie answered, to which Sam added, "He killed somebody."

"Oh, and then he killed himself."

"Yes."

"Oh, no wonder. That's why he's saying there's murder involved. It's funny: He kept claiming, 'It's my fault.' He kept claiming he did the same thing as your son. I said, 'Impossible. It just can't be.' Then he said, 'No, I'm telling you I shot myself.' Was he kind of a mixed-up guy?"

"Yes," said Jeannie.

"At that point, I'm sure he'd have to have been. But he's saying he's gotten his act together over there. This is also his own penance, of his own choice, because he committed murder and then killed himself. He really committed the ultimate wrong. He broke God's law by killing someone and then himself. Did he kill a family member?"

"Yes."

"They've forgiven him because they realize he did it in despair. But he's helping your son, he's earning a penance. Did he shoot a female?"

"Yes," said Sam.

"Because there's a female with him now. Was she his wife?"

"Yes."

"He's not a bad person, though."

"No."

"He didn't mean to do it. This is an accident. There's murder involved, but he didn't mean to do it."

"Right," Jeannie agreed.

George then returned to Billy, asking the Clarkes, "Are you having any problems at home? Anybody bothering you? Because you were intimidated right after his passing. They wanted to know what happened. I think then they realized that you didn't know anything, and they backed off. Did he ever, at any time, express fear of any of these people?"

"No," the boy's father answered. "We discovered the fear in retrospect."

"Was he getting interested in the black arts? Occultism?"

"He may have," Sam admitted, "but not to our knowledge."

"It's as if, suddenly, there's an interest in that. There are books, or something hidden or concealed. Maybe now you might not find them because they're somewhere else. Again, he knew if you found out, you'd disapprove. . . . He apologizes to the two of you," said George, "for what he put you through and because he might have gotten very hostile toward you or made you feel he couldn't trust you."

"Well, not really," said Sam.

"It could have been within himself. Because he kept getting the feeling that there's only so much he could trust you with. He put up a front. He gives me the impression that if I'd been there at the time, I would have sensed something wrong with him. He says that I definitely would have sensed something being unusual. He claims he was very moody."

"Yes," Sam agreed.

Several minutes later George said, "There is one thing he says to me, and the little girl says it, too: 'The less you know, the better.' . . . I think that's why he's not giving all the details. There's something 'funny' about this other person Brandon," George remarked. "I kind of get the creeps every time they bring him up. Was there somebody, an older male at school, who could have befriended him?"

"Yes."

"Because, again, the feeling that it's an older guy who puts his arm around him. . . . It could be someone around my age."

"Yes," said Jeannie, "that fits, that fits."

"Did you meet this person at all?"

"No."

"Then how do you know of him?"

"It's what's written around the picture that I wanted you to look at," she said, alluding to the teacher's yearbook photo.

"Oh, okay. I'll have to get some more information psychically before I do that. But it's as if Billy looked up to this person, you think."

"He might have. We don't know."

"I keep seeing scenes out of a movie I saw years ago about some people traveling in a trailer who run into a satanic cult. Because of what they witnessed, they were murdered. You just don't know whom to trust. Were you getting hang-up calls for a time?"

"Yes," said the mother.

"Because it seems they tried to figure out if you knew anything. And now, I think, they're pretty convinced you don't. I wouldn't even trust some of the law-enforcement officials down there," George warned ominously.

"Yes!" Jeannie exclaimed.

"Because some of them realized when they spoke to you that you really didn't know anything. That's when they started to lay off, because they figured you weren't a threat. Are you planning to move?"

"No," both replied emphatically.

"Eventually you probably will," said George. "Not immediately, but probably in the 1990s. He gives me the impression that you'll probably change residences. You seem to stay in the country, but I feel as if I'm in another area. Is your daughter going away to college?"

"Eventually she will," answered his mother.

"Because it seems that when she goes away to college is when you move. That could be up ahead. I'll just let it go, but that's what he says." Then George relayed messages to Jeannie's mother, Alice, Billy's Uncle Wally, and cousin James, all living, getting each's name correct.

"He's talking more, but he's still holding back something. I can feel it. He's telling me only so much," George continued. "It's almost as if he feels we can't conceive of the danger [these people] could create. Especially since he says, 'I'm up here, and you're down there.'"

"We know, baby!" Jeannie said, her voice breaking.

"Was this church near where you lived?"

"Yes," Sam answered.

"Because he says, 'It's right around the corner.' You'd understand that this is in your town. Is it still there?"

"Billy told me it was near my office, downtown. I don't know where it is. I was curious, but I couldn't locate it."

"But it doesn't look like an actual church," said George. "I'm going to this house, and it's the church. Things are going on inside. It's in a basement. It's underground. I keep going underground. It's not standing there saying 'Church of Jesus Christ.' It's something totally inconspicuous. But he says it's in your community, 'right around the corner.' That's exactly how he describes it. But, again, it's not staring you in the face. Even at your job, you don't know who could be a part of this. Keep a low profile," George cautioned. "Was this other guy, Brandon, into heavy-metal music?"

"Yes," said Jeannie.

"Billy says he picked it up from him."

"Yes."

"Billy looked up to him. He's older, smarter—or so he thought. As our generation would say, 'He's cool. He knows what's happening.' He's seen God, as we used to say, and that's why your son listens to him. Do his parents live in the town?"

"Yes, across town from us."

"The parents weren't as strict as you would be."

"Right."

"A male took him to church."

"Yes."

"Definitely a male with a cruel disposition, and he was older than Billy."

"Same age," corrected Jeannie.

"But I think the father took them," Sam pointed out.

"Oh, okay. Because there's definitely that older male with his wife involved. I wouldn't be surprised if one of these days it's uncovered. You'll never get the full details, and it won't change anything, but one of these days it hits the fan. Suddenly, *Boom!* This comes out in the open. You may be shocked to find out how many people are really a part of this. . . .

"Has anybody noticed animals or pets missing in the area?"

"I don't know."

"Not that we know of," said Sam.

"Are you sure? Because if I looked in the right places, I could find animal remains."

"Yes, yes!" Sam blurted out, suddenly recalling. "They have found animals that have been mutilated in the last few years, even up to a couple of months ago."

"This is all part of their sacrifices," George said. "If I looked around, I could find animal remains, cut up, as if they'd been used for mutilations. . . . Your son claims that around the time he passed on, somebody was missing. Was anybody else missing around that time?"

"There was a little girl who ran away from home," Jeannie offered.

"He just gave me the impression—and I'm not going to ignore it—that someone is missing around the time of a feast day or a ritual."

"Initiation."

"Exactly. I wonder if that's why they give me the feeling they're celebrating satanic mass, or something like it."

"It could be," said Sam. "That's very possible."

"And that's why they were going to get him," George continued. "Now, in his personal belongings, did you ever find anything unusual?"

"The only thing we found unusual was a book that was hollowed out," Sam recalled. "It was about the size for a cassette tape."

"Because he says he did have something rather unusual," George explained.

"That's the only thing we ever found."

"It's funny you should have said 'Seth' earlier," George noted. "I got that name this afternoon [before you came] when I [psychically] heard Jeannie. I heard the name Seth. They kept saying, 'Don't forget the name Seth tonight, too.' Did he pass on, or is he still living? . . . Do you think he could be involved with this? There seems to be some sort of involvement."

"Yes! Yes!" Jeannie insisted.

"Did he disappear around the time of Billy's death?"

"Yes."

"Because Billy gives me the impression that they were going to get Seth."

"Yes."

"Then, all of a sudden, bingo, Billy was selected. Somehow they didn't get Seth."

"Jesus!" his mother exclaimed. "Yes!"

"When you said to me that Seth was still living, Billy immediately said to me, 'He disappeared just before I passed on.' I asked, 'What are you trying to tell me?' I got the impression that he was trying to tell me that Seth was maybe the next sacrifice. And then—"

"He ran away," Jeannie interjected.

"Bingo! When it cleared, Billy was the victim who was chosen."

"Yes."

"There seems to be more pressure among the children, with the older boys having control. There also seems to be—I don't know if I can verify this or not—but I'm not going to block out a thing. I'm just getting such weird, perverted things going on in front of me that, I guess, in this case anything is possible."

"Yes."

"These guys give me the creeps. Did Billy have any contact with them just prior to his passing?"

Both parents replied, "Yes."

"Because he claims he spoke to them, had contact with the two of them prior to his passing. Something must have been exchanged or said, because it seems right after that he [Billy] really goes into a state. He seems to get really uptight and frightened. Were they putting a lot of pressure on your son?"

"Evidently," said Jeannie.

"These people are not joking, they mean business. He might have witnessed something. He might have seen pictures of someone being sacrificed or being cut up. . . . I don't know if he was actually *at* a sacrifice or a ritual, but he definitely saw what they were capable of doing. Also, this girl, they might have had pictures of her being sacrificed. Again, he saw evidence of what had happened. He knew too much."

" 'He knew too much,' " Jeannie repeated sadly.

"Yes. And he knows they knew he knew too much. . . . Why do I keep seeing school buses? Did he take a school bus?"

"Yes."

"Were these clowns on the school bus?"

"Yes."

"Because they had plenty of time to have conversation. I see boys congregating at the back of the bus."

"Yes."

"And, they're giving him the once-over, so to speak. Would you say your son was easily frightened? Was he the type of kid who was easy to scare?"

"No."

"Because I get the impression that if I went up to him and said, 'I'm the bogey man,' he'd laugh in my face. So these people really frightened him. Did anybody do any type of funny drawings?" George then asked.

"Yes," remembered Jeannie.

"These people had ugly-looking, satanic kinds of stuff. I get the feeling—and your friend Frank just comes right out and says, 'These people are satanists.' Is there a bookstore in town?"

"Yes."

"Does it have occult-type of materials in it?"

"Not that I'm aware," Jeannie answered. "The school did."

"Occult-type of things?"

"Yes, in the library."

"Holy Christmas! In a small rural community! I'm

shocked to hear that. There is literature infiltrating the area, he tells me. There are books on satanism or occultism. There might have even been a bookstore that dealt with it. Again, these people are underground. They could also be people you work with. Are you employed also?" he asked Jeannie.

"Yes."

"Same thing. You don't know who it could be. You've just got to act as if nothing is wrong. Either that, or if you speak about it you'll have to get out of there. He comes right out and says that you and your son and daughter definitely would be in danger. Are they aware of this?"

"Somewhat, yes," Jeannie said uncomfortably.

"They don't speak about it, though, right?"

"Correct."

"That's all I want to know, because Billy wants to be convinced that they would not bring it up."

"We'll tell them again. Baby, don't worry," his mother assured him.

"He says they should never, ever discuss any suspicion of satanism. It can go no further than what has happened. He admits that even though he's safe over there, it frightens him a little bit. It seems that the little girl is trying to put him at peace over there. She says that it's all right now. 'You're away from them; they can't get you anymore.' But he sees the fear here. He sees you. He's afraid. . . . That's why it's good that you continue to pray for him, so that he finds peace over there. Is his middle name Edward?"

"Billy Edward," Jeannie replied.

"Oh! Because it's funny. I heard Billy say 'Edward.' I didn't know what he was doing."

"He wants us to know it's really him," she said.

"He claims he tried to signal you before he passed on. He might have left messages that there was danger or who could be involved in his."

"Ask him how," said Jeannie. "I don't understand this."

"In his annual [school yearbook]."

"We didn't see that until after his death."

"Did somebody put something on your property after he passed on? There was an attempted break-in at your home."

"There was at one time that we didn't know about."

"Oh, because it's interesting. He says to me that there was after he passed."

"Yes," Sam replied.

"There was an attempted break-in, to make sure nothing was in the house that he'd left behind, such as messages or pictures. You never found anything. They made sure. Did police investigate at all?"

"Yes," said Sam.

"Your son says you were fed a terrible amount of lies from practically everyone in town."

From Jeannie, a bitter "Yes."

"You can't believe anything you were told. . . . Is he easily riled up?"

"Yes!"

"Because he says, *'Grrrrrr!'* over there. Just talking about it gets him so mad. He recognizes the fact that he was an innocent involved in this, but as he said, he saw what happened after he took his own life. It's suicide, yes, on the record. But in all essence, I don't feel he killed himself. He saw them feeding you all the lies and getting you upset. He knew you were being fed lies, but his hands were tied. There was nothing he could do about it. So now he's glad that God gave him the opportunity to come through and say they were all lies. Do you have a lot of open fields around where you live?"

"Yes," said Sam."

"Has there ever been remains found out in the fields?"

"Yes!" Jeannie shouted. "A baby!"

"There's been a sacrifice outside. That's what I'm getting at. They definitely have gone into these open fields, and chanted and sacrificed."

"Does he know how much we love him?" Jeannie asked, blinking back tears.

"Oh, definitely! Without a question of a doubt. . . . Does the name Kip mean anything at all?"

"Yes," replied Jeannie.

"Passed on?"

"No."

"Does he know him?"

"Yes. That's our dog we got on Christmas Eve."

"Because he calls out about Kip. I'm glad I didn't ignore it. I heard him say Kip, and I thought, *Kip, that sounds like a strange name. I don't think that's right.* But he said, 'No: Kip!' He calls out to Kip and says, 'Hug Kip for me.' "

"Oh, yeah!" exclaimed Jeannie.

"Okay, Billy," George said, laughing, "you win again. I'm glad I didn't ignore that one, as it turns out." He then asked the Clarkes about the dead baby found in the field.

"It's unsolved," Sam said. He handed George a newspaper clipping about the incident. George paused to read it.

"That was the only thing ever printed about it," Jeannie explained.

"This is right in your neighborhood?" George asked, incredulous.

"Yes."

"It's spooky, because I don't know how they sacrifice. They murder, somehow. There is evidence of satanic behavior in your area . . . I think he's starting to fade down, so we'll probably have to end soon. The little girl that was here—I don't know her name—she's going back. Did she have health trouble?"

"Yes," said Jeannie.

"She passed from health troubles."

"Yes."

"That's what she tells me. Did she have something in the blood? Leukemia."

"Yes."

"Okay, now I believe her. I said to her, 'You didn't give me your name, you didn't give me any clues, except what was said before.' She asked that we pray for her. She's taking good care of Billy over there. . . . Also, does the name Richard, or Richie, mean anything? Keep this name in mind especially involved with this monkey business."

"I work with a Richard . . ." Jeannie answered hesitantly.

"I'll leave it to you. Could be. Keep the name in mind, he says, but don't be paranoid."

"Okay."

"Did your son shoot himself in the mouth?"

"No."

"In the face, so to speak?"

"No, in the head."

"Because I feel pressure around the head and face. But, in a way, he missed."

"Yes."

"Because he didn't want to do it. Did he fade into a coma?"

"Yes."

"Because I get that choking sensation, and then he seems to go into a coma and passes on. In Catholicism, Saint Joseph is the patron of a happy death, and I see that, which is a sign that he let go. He was going to pass on. He couldn't survive. He would have been like a vegetable.

"That little girl is going back. Frank, your dad, grandparents, everyone's going back. Your son is also going back. They say, of course, remember to pray for them. Billy sends his love to both of you. He's all right and feels more at ease because he knows that you recognize the severity of this. He puts his finger to his lips, to remind you that silence is golden. You'd better keep silent. Something else may brew out there where you live. There may be another murder or disappearance."

"There has been a murder!" Jeannie blurted out.

"There's monkey business going on down there. He says, at any time if you feel any threat of being pulled into this again, definitely move. . . . He also says, 'Don't go on any guilt trips because this happened.' Sometimes you might have felt this wouldn't have happened if you hadn't moved there. It happened. There's nothing you can do about it. He says he would have tried to make friends if you had moved to someplace else. There's nothing to reproach yourselves about. With that, he's starting to go. . . . Billy goes back."

"Bye, baby!" Jeannie called out.

"Pray for them all." George put down his pen. "Wow, that's scary. I'm just shocked."

The reading, which ran for nearly two hours, also included Billy naming at least thirteen other friends and relatives, all of whose relationships and in most cases, causes of death, George accurately interpreted. But this wasn't what Sam and Jeannie Clarke had come to him for. They wanted to know why Billy put his father's gun to his head. And now they knew.

If it strikes you as inconceivable that a child could be

coerced into taking his own life, consider the infamous Jonestown massacre of 1978. There more than nine hundred members—most of them adults—of the People's Temple ingested strychnine-laced Kool-Aid on the orders of charismatic leader Jim Jones.

In Billy's mind, he had no choice but to kill himself. Who could he have turned to? Who would have believed him? And what would have happened to him if he'd revealed what he knew? At the very least, his involvement in the group's sexual practices, perhaps even pornography, would have been known. From what the Clarkes knew and the unusual number of dead bodies turning up in their area, it's not inconceivable that Billy might have been murdered for breaking the code of silence.

As the Clarkes suspected and as George made clear, the satanic cult in their area had infiltrated the highest levels of the community. Of course, there was the schoolteacher—"the wolf in sheep's clothing" George spoke of in both readings—whose picture Billy had captioned with that legend. And clearly, the behavior and attitude of the local police in "investigating" Billy's suicide was suspect. Whatever the Clarkes' suspicions, they were reinforced when the police ran their private investigator out of town. When George confirmed the involvement of friends (Brandon), the teacher, and several policemen, he was simply adding another piece of evidence to Sam and Jeannie's terrifying puzzle.

That we may fall victim to an organized plot, covered up from the highest level down, is the stuff of classic modern horror stories. In the Clarkes' case, it was all too true, as evidenced by the specificity of detail George relayed to them. When he mentioned that the satanists were "hiding behind the cross," he was unknowingly alluding to a church Billy had attended where it was common knowledge within the community that "something else" was going on. George's description of the attempted break-in to the Clarke home was also accurate. The Clarkes read this as a warning. George was also on the mark when he described the mutilated animals, the dead baby, the murdered girl, and the missing children, and the inordinate number of satanic books available. George's allusion to "another murder" also proved startlingly accurate, although they couldn't confirm it then. The very day the Clarkes left New York to return home, they learned that while they were gone the victim's body was found only five miles from their home, in an area known to be frequented by the satanists. Perhaps the reading's most striking detail was the name of the nurse Billy claimed was also involved: Mrs. Thorpe. What George did not know was that Mrs. Thorpe's nephew was a policeman who tried to convince the Clarkes that their son killed himself over a bad report card or a heavy-metal song.

The Clarkes now had in their hands a wealth of information, but were powerless to do anything with it. Billy's repeated and impassioned warnings that his family exercise extreme caution were not wasted. Back home they received a bogus letter inviting them to a community meeting. They declined and later learned there was no such meeting. The letter was obviously a ploy to get them out of their house for a period. Or, worse, to go someplace. Around the same time, Becky was followed for miles, then her car was run off the road in an area near where two other corpses were discovered. Then the following summer thieves broke into their home but stole only a photograph of Becky that was displayed on a table alongside one of Billy and a picture of Jesus Christ. Why? The Clarkes shudder to think.

Several months after the reading with George, Sam got an anonymous tip that he should compare the date of Billy's death with a calendar of Roman Catholic feast days. When he did, he discovered that the day Billy killed himself was the eve of a feast day devoted to a martyred virgin who was killed as a child. Was this mere coincidence? Likely not, say most experts. As Dr. Stephen Kaplan explains, "Satanism is a desecration and mockery of the Catholic Church, and often satanic rituals are carried out on the eve of certain holy days, purposely, as a perversion of Christianity."

Later several other youths in the area committed suicide. Interestingly, none of their cases received the same intensive media coverage as Billy's. A local newspaper investigating the charges of a cult discovered and printed photographs of sites used for satanic worship. One was a cavern, its walls scrawled with satanic symbols, the numbers 666, inverted crosses, and the words "Satan lives."

Several months later George did a reading for Jeannie's

brother, a minister. As before, Billy came through to talk about "the wolf in sheep's clothing," but stressed the involvement of another friend's parents, too. Dozens of times he repeated his warnings to his family and urged them to leave the area, something the Clarkes are reluctant to do for personal reasons. Following a psychic impression George got one day from Billy, he phoned the Clarkes to remind them to keep an eye on Becky.

In a letter to us the next year, Sam wrote, "Churches, ministers, schools, teachers, courts, judges, neighbors—nowhere to hide. Sometimes it just is too much."

For all the pain and grief the cult caused the Clarke family, they ultimately failed in their one true goal. Billy escaped their clutches to the other side, where he is safe and at peace. They never got his soul.

"I'm Not There"

Even under the best of circumstances, survivors invariably experience a degree of guilt after a death. We may worry that something important went unsaid, or that a conflict continued unresolved. It seems that no matter how good our relationship, when someone close dies few of us really feel in our hearts that we couldn't have done more for him or her.

Fortunately, few of us ever find ourselves bearing the additional burden of being directly or indirectly responsible for another's death. The next readings explore instances where survivors must cope with that. This excerpt is from a reading for a mother, father, son, and daughter:

"Your son passed from something in his head? Because there's pain in the head," George said.

"Yes," the mother acknowledged.

"Something bursts in the head."

"Yes."

"It feels as if something goes crazy with the blood vessels in his head."

"Yes."

"It feels as if it could be or was an aneurysm."

"Yes, that's what it was."

"Your son was young, though."

"Yes."

"He shows me he's in his early twenties," George explained.

"Yes. He was twenty-three," the father answered.

"He says you feel guilty about his passing."

"Yes."

"He doesn't understand why. You feel as though you could have done more."

"Yes."

"Your son says from the other side, 'How could you know? I didn't even know. What more could you know? How could you even know I was sick?' He says you couldn't have known. He says, 'Don't feel guilty.' Be at peace and know that he's okay." Hearing this, the boy's family seemed visibly relieved.

A brain aneurysm is often sudden, uncontrollable, and almost never preventable. But what about when a simple precaution might have spared someone's life? How do parents, and in this instance, grandparents, cope when a child's death results from a momentary lapse in judgment? When there was something that could have been done but was not?

Kristen was ecstatic when she and her husband, Randy, became parents. Their daughter was born on April 28, 1988, with her mother's blond hair and blue eyes. "Michelle really gave me reason to be the best I could be, to strive, to work," Kristen says. "She gave meaning to my life. I really felt whole for the first time. She was too perfect, too special." Oddly, "I always felt a touch of melancholy, even though it was wonderful. All parents worry in the early months, but what I felt was definitely beyond that.

"When I talked to my parents, they would ask me how Michelle was doing, and after giving glowing reports of her latest activities, I would say, 'I don't know, it's too perfect. I feel so happy, the only thing that could ruin my life was if God took her.' This fear would come over me. It went beyond logic. My husband and my parents told me that everything would be fine." At twenty-eight Kristen had no personal experience with death, save for the passings of her grandparents whom she barely knew. "And yet," she said, "I began to fear death more and more. Any mention of it would have me sobbing within sixty seconds." Kristen worried that perhaps she was thinking of her own death.

In February 1989 Kristen was driving in subzero weather on an open stretch of Illinois highway when she lost control of her car. The automobile landed twelve feet up an embankment, against two pine trees and then rolled down and was totaled. Miraculously, she escaped with only bruises. When the car left the road, she remembered feeling "a deep sadness, but yet a calmness." She thought, *So this is when I'm going.* Obviously it wasn't Kristen's time, but in the wake of this accident, her preoccupation with death intensified, only her thoughts turned more and more to baby Michelle.

Monday, June 26, 1989, was a typical day. While Kristen put the finishing touches on her makeup, getting ready for work, Randy took Michelle for an early-morning outing in her baby stroller, the child's favorite activity. When they returned, Kristen got Michelle ready to go stay with Randy's mother, Anne. She knew the baby couldn't be any safer than with her grandmother, or "Noni," as Michelle knew her.

Later that day Anne was driving down a rural road when Michelle began fussing and squirming in her car seat. The grandmother pulled over, took Michelle out of her seat and placed her in her lap, before continuing on her way. Like many people in a similar situation, she thought to herself, *We'll be home in just a few minutes.*

Then the unthinkable happened. Another car ran a stop sign, broadsiding Anne's car. A nurse who lived around the corner heard the collision and ran to the accident scene, where she found Anne unconscious and Michelle pinned against the door, gasping for air. The rescue squad arrived within minutes. An emergency medical technician, coincidentally a family friend, recognized Michelle. He scooped the little girl in his arms and rushed her to the trauma center of a Peoria hospital. About halfway through the twelve-minute ride, Michelle's heart stopped. The EMT restarted it, and at the hospital a full trauma team took over. But her head injuries were severe, and after forty minutes and several more restarts of her heart, Michelle was gone.

"My mother-in-law felt—still feels—terrible about what happened," says Kristen. "Perhaps it was a lack of judgment on her part, but it was an accident. I try to console myself with the fact that this was in the cards. I feel like maybe it was meant to happen, from the signs I'd gotten.

"I really didn't feel like I could go on," she remembers, "without verification that Michelle still existed. So we went to George. It was desperation. It was the last stop for us. But at the same time, it was something positive. It was hope." Speaking of all grieving parents, she remarks, "On one level we're afraid to believe, or we don't know what to believe, because our world has been shattered to the core. Things that happened to us aren't supposed to happen in the natural course of life. We don't expect our children to die. But it could happen to anybody.

"I think everybody's skeptical when they first go to George," Kristen adds. "But I think deep in everybody's heart George's message rings true. It makes sense. You feel it's right. Why should we fail to exist upon death? Seeing him is the ultimate hope, the ultimate gamble."

As soon as Kristen and Randy's reading was under way, George asked, "A male close to you all passed on?"

"No," Kristen answered.

"Well, let's just say yes, because there's a male presence here first. He may be looking for someone else, but he's been the one starting the show off." To Randy, George said, "There's also a male close to you passed on. Are you the husband and wife?"

"Yes," Kristen replied.

"Okay. Your granddad passed on? One of them at least."

"Yes."

"Okay, because there's someone here claiming to be your granddad. A *strong* fatherly presence." To Randy: "Your grandfather passed on as well?"

"Yes."

"One of them. Okay! Because I'm getting a grandfather type. Is there a young female around you? Passed on?"

"Yes," Kristen acknowledged.

"Family?"

"Yes."

"Very young when she passed on?"

"Yes."

"I mean less than ten years old."

"Yes."

"Okay, then I got that right. She keeps saying if I wanted to speak to her I could be this level." George knelt down, sitting on his heels to demonstrate what he meant.

"Yes."

"And you're her parents, yes?"

"Yes."

"She says she passed tragically in the sense of age."

"Yes."

"Is she around four or five years old?"

"No."

"A little older?"

"No."

"Oh! She *is* younger! Okay. Because she's showing me about four or five. Just kind of wondering. She is younger, then."

"Yes."

"I should have known when she said, 'If you kneel down you would be eye level with me.' Did she have any health problems?"

"No."

"Why do I feel pain in the chest? Does that make sense?"

"No." In fact, though, Michelle's chest was crushed in the accident.

"Hmmm. Must mean something. A pain in the chest."

"Perhaps," Kristen answered after a moment of thought.

"All right. I'll just have to leave it with you for the moment. She obviously passes on accidentally. As I explained before, if it's not heart, it's accidental type of passing. Did she lose breath?"

"She was gasping."

"That's probably why I'm feeling pain in the chest. I'm losing breath and getting the pain in the chest again. So that has to mean something. Now, I don't want to add to your grief, but was she very frightened by her passing?"

"I don't know. She was alive when they found her."

"Okay, but she said she was very frightened. It's almost as if I can't talk because I'm so overwrought and nervous."

"Yes."

"Was she 'taken'?"

"What?"

"Again, it's as if I'm talking to a three-year-old . . . *taken.*"

"She was taken to the hospital . . ."

"Yes, but I don't think she means that. . . . Did somebody take her?" George asked, referring to either the family friend who'd accompanied Michelle to the hospital or to her grandmother.

"Yes . . ."

". . . And do harm to her?"

"Accidentally."

"Yes, whichever. She says, like, 'Someone takes me, and

there's harm done,' or something. I don't mean that someone murdered her or anything. The way she's telling it to me, it's as though . . . I said, she's about three years old, and she's trying to explain what happened to her in that language. . . . Any injuries to the head?"

"Yes."

"Did she strike her head?"

"Yes."

"Because I feel like—*Poof!*—I went forward and struck my head," George said, slapping the middle of his forehead.

"Yes."

"There's definitely blood shed, yes."

"Yes."

"You know, it seems that this tragedy damaged the brain or the skull."

"Yes."

"Because I feel that, had she survived she would have been brain injured or something like that."

"Yes."

"So the pressure is right here." George tapped the front of his forehead. "Did she go into a coma?"

"Possibly . . ."

"*Like* a coma. She said to me, 'Like a coma, like a sleep.' I see a vision of Saint Joseph, which means a happy death. So, when the time came that she passed, she passed in peace, but she was in a sleep, more like in a 'state' first. She wasn't what they call brain dead first, was she? Because the thing is, she's in an altered state before she actually makes the transition, and I can't quite figure out what she means."

"It's possible," Kristen answered.

"It's like what we say in Catholicism: She was in limbo. She was here, and she was there, and in between the two states of consciousness, she says to me. What I'd understand as the states of consciousness."

"Yes," Kristen said.

"Vehicle involved?"

"Yes."

"Someone is blaming him or herself for it?"

"Yes."

"She's saying, 'Tell the person to stop blaming him or herself,' or, 'It's not his or her fault.' You know, again, I'm translating in an adult language, but I'm hearing it in little-girl talk. She was obviously in the vehicle, yes?"

"Yes."

"Okay, because she's saying to me she's in the vehicle and there's an accident of some sort. And she *survives* the accident."

"Yes."

"Passes on in the hospital."

"Yes. They worked on her . . ."

"Exactly! That's maybe where she was unconscious. That's why I'm in the limbo state, caught between two dimensions. Someone in the family—"

"Yes."

"Driving—"

"Yes."

"She says she knows that person, for sure. That's why she says somebody takes her and there's harm, but not deliberate. You know it's an accident."

"Yes."

"Is there anyone else in the vehicle with her?"

"Yes."

"Is there another male in the car?"

"No."

"A male was not driving."

"No."

"Okay, she talks about a male." This was probably Michelle's way of communicating something about the medical technician who accompanied her to the hospital. "I'm not sure whom she means by that. Is there a light nearby? Like a red light run?"

"Yes."

"Okay, because that's what I'm seeing . . . a red light flashing or whatever. Did someone run it, or was it like one of those four-way-stop sort of things?"

"No."

"Did somebody go through it? Because that's the thing. I'm seeing somebody running a light, that's what I'm getting at. I don't mean to pull teeth with you or anything, but I keep seeing someone run a red light." Here the light symbolized the stop sign. It was essentially the visual equivalent of a synonym.

"Yes."

"So there is an actual hit—"

"Yes."

"—of cars. Yes. Because she says, 'It's a car accident. There are two cars hit.' Was it more on her side?"

"Hit on her side?"

"The collision. . . . Because, it's like I'm being hit broadside. It's more like, on the driver's side, or something like that."

"Yes."

"And she's thrown *in* the car."

"Yes."

"Is there a grandmother close to her passed on?"

"No."

"Both of your mothers still living, right?"

"Yes."

"Okay. It must be one of *your* grandmothers, because she keeps saying something about a grandmother being there with her that takes care of her."

"Who?"

"I don't know. She just says a grandmother there that takes care of her. Like, who is this woman . . . who has spoken another language? Yes, could've been either side of the family. If there's a grandmother there, it would've been her great-grandmother, technically."

"Yes."

"But she says she's there. Does the name Julie or Julia mean anything at all?"

"Yes," Kristen answered, surprised.

"Passed on."

"Yes."

"It's not your daughter, though."

"No."

"Because your daughter says, 'That's who is with me.' "

"My cousin!" Kristen exclaimed.

"Oh, okay! Because she says, 'Julie.' Was she much older than her?"

"Yes."

"She says it's like her grandma, maybe because she's much older. I said to her, 'Who's taking care of you? If there's somebody there with you that's your grandma, tell me who the name is, so I can tell them.' I said, 'What does she say her name is?' And she said, 'Her name is Julie.' Did she [Julie] pass over young?"

"Yes."

"I mean *years* before your daughter, though, because she [Julie] does say she did pass over young."

"Yes."

"She says she was there to meet your daughter when she came over. So, she'd be like your first cousin."

"Yes."

"Okay, because that's the thing. Now I understand why she says, 'Like a grandmother.' Like I call my older cousins aunt and uncle, because there's a big age difference. They're in their eighties and nineties, and I'm still young . . . for the moment." George asked about Julie, "She also pass on very tragically?"

"Yes."

"That's why she can understand what you're going through, because of the fact she passed on tragically. I just realized I overlooked a very obvious symbol. Before, I kept seeing Bette Davis in front of me in *Jezebel*. The character in the movie, her name was Julie. It just dawned on me, oh, that's why. You didn't look like the *Jezebel* type, so I didn't know what to make of it. But the character's name is Julie in the movie. She says, 'Julie came to me after I came out of that limbo state. She's taking care of me. She's like my "Nana," or grandmother over there.' Well, Julie would be like your own age now, yes. Older even?"

"Yes, older."

"She definitely would be like an older mother, a matronly type."

"Yes."

"Did she pass on as a child, or a very young woman?"

"Julie?"

"Julie, yes."

"A young woman."

"Okay. She's definitely been there for years."

"Yes."

"Were you a child when she passed on?"

"Yes."

"That's probably why she's telling me about passing as a

child. *You* were a child, she was much older. Like, if you were five, she was twenty, that sort of thing."

"Yes."

"Did one of your grandmothers pass over?" George asked Randy.

"Yes."

"Because she does talk about grandmothers and grandfathers to you, all that are there with her. But it seems that Julie is the one who came forward and met her in the tunnel, walked her into the light. . . .

"Your daughter explains that when you pass on, you see nothing but darkness. And she got frightened. Was she inclined to be afraid of the dark? Because she was for this moment, in any case. She keeps telling me, 'I was afraid of the dark.' And then she said, 'It's as if somebody turned a light on,' and she says that's when Julie came up to her and told her who she was. That she [Julie] says, 'Call me Nana, or look upon me like Aunt Julie,' or something. It's that she might have been afraid because she didn't know anyone over there. Julie keeps saying, 'You don't have to worry about her, because I'm taking good care of her until the day when you all come over, and that's a long time from now. Don't think because she doesn't know anyone, she's alone. Other relatives are over here. She's with me. I'm taking good care of her.'

"Does the name Kristy mean anything?" George asked.

"My name is Kristen."

"Oh! Because I heard your daughter sound as if she said *Kristy.* . . . You do pray for her, yes?"

"Yes."

"She certainly thanks you for your prayers and asks that you please continue. Were you and she very good friends?"

"Yes."

"I mean, I know you're mother and daughter, obviously, and I'm sure you loved your daughter. But she says you were like buddies, too, like very good friends. Was she around three?"

"No."

"Younger even."

"Fourteen months."

"So she was just starting to talk."

"Yes."

"That's probably why I'm having trouble communicating. I'm not a parent. You'll have to excuse me. I'm trying to figure it out." George paused, then added, laughing, "And you might think I'd make a good one. I *would not* make a good one, either." Returning to the reading, he added, "Julie is giving me the impression she's well experienced over there. She's been there so long. But did she also pass on in an accident or something?"

"Yes."

"Yes. Because, again, she can sympathize with what you and your husband are going through. She understands because her family went through the same thing when she passed on accidentally. Does the name Janey mean anything to you? Emmy, or something like that."

"No."

"Anne?"

"Yes," Kristen said, acknowledging Randy's mother's and grandmother's names.

"Again, your daughter's trying to say the name, and I can't understand. Passed on?"

"Yes."

"Let's see if I get the right clue. Was she like a grandmother or something to you?" George nodded toward Randy.

"Yes," he answered.

"I assume she's been over there for a while too. She calls her Annie, or Nannie . . ."

"Noni?" Kristen asked.

"I didn't hear. It sounded as though I heard Annie, Janey [this was the name of the woman whose car hit Anne's], or something like that. Did she speak another language, this grandmother? Did she speak Italian?"

"Yes," Randy replied.

"That's probably the one that spoke to me before that said, 'the one who speaks the other language.' Was she called Nannie or something?"

"Noni," Randy clarified. It was a family nickname for both his mother and grandmother.

"Oh, okay. Maybe that's what your daughter was trying to say. It sounded as though she said 'Nannie' or 'Annie.'

. . . I thought I was hearing *Nannie*. But she [Michelle] kept emphasizing she was with her. She did give me the correct language and told me she was your father's mother. But Julie's back again, saying, 'Rest easy now. Be at peace.' Because, she says, 'Your daughter is being taken care of by me. She's not alone over here.' She's taking good care of her. She's all right."

The one question Kristen's reading with George could not answer concerned her feelings about death prior to Michelle's passing. "I don't know whether there were warnings or preparations," she reflects. "I guess I feel that I couldn't change things, but somebody or something was trying to prepare me for her death and a way to deal with it. Looking back, I think it's pretty weird that I was buying books and tapes on death and dying before Michelle was killed."

Is such a thing possible? Ask George whether people might sense in advance, through a vague feeling or foreboding, that physical death might be impending, and he answers, "I would say to treat everything with common sense. You've got to differentiate between normal worry and paranoia, which we all experience to some extent, and a *real* premonition. Without getting carried away, is a premonition possible? Yes. It's possible that Kristen was being prepared subconsciously either by herself or by someone on the other side for her daughter's death."

Looking back on her and her husband's reading with George, Kristen says, "In order to heal, to recover, you have to accept what's happened. There's such an unreality to it all. There are moments when I say, 'My God, I can't believe she's gone.' But you have to accept what happened and that they're okay on the other side. You have to accept that you'll see them again. You have to deal with the intellectual questions, and you have to deal with the irrational, emotional ones. I tell myself I don't blame my mother-in-law. Then I'll turn around and think just the opposite. It's balancing the anger with the hope—the feeling of cosmic injustice, if you want to call it that. You always have to fight against the emotions of emptiness and bitterness.

"We miss the people who have died," she continues. "But we want to know what to expect. What is there for us when we die? When we get our comfort from our loved ones, we know what awaits us. If you can go into it with no fear, you can live your life more freely. We can be happier. We can take more risks because we know it's okay. We know what we're doing is not in vain. We know it's okay for us to live. We don't have to be afraid, and that's invaluable. I mean, who gets the opportunity firsthand to know it's going to be okay to die? That's what George gave me."

Two of modern medicine's most controversial bioethical dilemmas are determining when life ends and when, or if, it is ethically correct to terminate artificial life support. Despite widespread debate on the part of physicians, theologians, lawmakers, and the public, these questions defy easy answers. Across the nation there is a growing movement to give family members more say in these difficult decisions. However, as one bereavement expert we spoke with pointed out, when a loved one assumes responsibility for discontinuing life support, he or she must later come to terms with the guilt and doubt that often follow. Even when one knows what is best, it's hard not to look back days or years later without wondering if the decision made was indeed the right one.

What does the other side have to say about the issue of when life support can or should be terminated? The next two readings offer some idea of how those who've passed view physical death.

Paul was working with his brother Jim at a construction site when Jim was struck on the head by a large falling rock. Though it was an accident, Paul couldn't stop feeling he might have prevented it. Exacerbating his feelings of guilt over Jim's passing was his decision to terminate life support when doctors declared his brother brain dead.

"A male close to you passed," George said to the young man.

"Yes," he acknowledged.

"He does pass over young."

"Yes."

"He's related to you by blood."

"Yes."

"Is it your brother?"

"Yes."

"The passing is beyond his control."

"Yes."

"Okay. Then I'm glad I didn't try to clarify. I don't know what it means, but you probably understand. I keep seeing a scene from the movie *Dangerous Liaisons*. He says it's out of control. Your brother claims his passing is beyond his control. He's at peace now. Could he have gone over in excitement? Because he claims he went over in a little anxiety. But he says he's at peace now. His passing is accidental."

"Yes."

"Okay. Because he doesn't pass from health problems."

"No."

"You do pray for him? But you could more frequently."

"Yes."

"Well, he looked at you when you said that. Not that he's a saint, as he puts it. But he knows it could help. It definitely helps. This again could be symbolic—just say yes or no: Is there a vehicle involved in his passing?"

"No."

"Okay. Then it's a symbol of an accident. That's what I'm trying to figure out, because he shows me a vehicle accident and it could mean one or the other or both. In this case it means an accidental passing," George explained, attempting to discern accurately the meaning of the symbol that flashed before him.

"Yes, it was an accident," the young man confirmed.

"Your folks still living? He talks to me about your parents, but . . . Wait a second: Your mom is still living."

"Yes."

"Your dad's passed over."

"Yes."

"Okay. Because your father must be with him. There's another male around. Two males around. Somebody claims to be losing his son. He's kind of at the wrong place at the wrong time."

"Yes."

"That's what he says. Is he a little on the wild side?"

"Yes."

"You know, he says I'd definitely raise two eyebrows to him," George said. "Did he kind of hang out with the wrong crowd?"

"No," the man answered, baffled.

"Was he around them when this occurred?" George asked, somewhat confused.

"No."

"I don't know what he means by that, but he claims, he's 'around the wrong crowd.' Well, let me leave it go. Did he suffer injury?"

"Yes."

"Anything to his head?"

"Yes."

"Because I feel as if somebody just hit me over the head. There's a strike to the head. A blow to the head. He falls."

"Yes."

"He falls from height."

"No."

"He just falls from being hit. Because he falls. I hit. I fall. He's hit. I don't know how he means that. A gunshot could be a hit. Don't say anything, but he says he's hit." George didn't immediately comprehend Jim's spirit communicating that something fell *on* him, a point he would clarify a few minutes later. "Did this occur out in public?"

"Yes."

"Okay. 'Nothing could prevent this.' Does that make sense?" George asked.

"I hope so," Paul answered.

"Because he says nothing could prevent this. 'It's beyond my control or your control,' he says. Somebody feels guilty about his passing. Seems as though they felt they could have prevented it or helped it or something like this. And he keeps saying, 'No, you're putting yourself on a terrible guilt trip for no reason.' It's beyond control. Was somebody with him when he passed on?"

"Yes."

"Were you with him?"

"Yes."

"Because he claims you're with him when this tragedy occurs," George explained.

"Yes."

"Was he kind of—I mean this nicely—was he kind of a wiseguy?"

"Yes."

"That's why he says he was 'with the wrong crowd': He's

kidding *you!* I don't want you to take it the wrong way. When he said that, he seemed to have a smile on his face. He's breaking your chops, more or less. That would be him. You know, he's inclined to joke."

The young man nodded.

"He also apologizes for the way he passed on. Does that make sense? He apologizes basically, I think, because you obviously witnessed it or were there, and you have to live with it. You saw what happened," he said, as Paul began crying. "He claims he didn't suffer prior to his passing," George added, indicating it wasn't clear why the spirit was stressing this point. "I'll just let it go. He claims he didn't suffer. Did something fall on him?"

"Yes," his brother confirmed.

"He started saying 'falling' again. And I'm saying, 'What are you talking about, falling? I already covered it.' And he says, 'No. Something falls *on* me.' If you had seen, you couldn't have prevented it. It was beyond your control, he says. There was nothing you could have done about it. He says, 'I can tell you until I'm blue in the face.' He says he knows you won't listen, but he's going to try anyway. You and he were out of the home together."

"Yes."

"I don't know what he means. You understand. You were working or something."

"Yes."

"This happens on the job."

"Yes."

"Okay. Obviously you were on the same job together. Something falls on him. Strikes his head."

"Yes."

"He dies instantly," George said.

"No," the man answered.

"It certainly knocked him unconscious, though, because I don't feel I'm conscious of any pain or suffering. He could have been in a coma or something like that because he says, in a sense, it kills him instantly. He injures his neck also."

"Yes."

"It feels as though he broke his neck or part of it. There's injury to the neck. Were you doing physical work?"

"Yes."

"I'm not saying this is what it is, but I feel that it's on a construction site."

"Yes. That's what it is."

"Okay. Because I don't know if that's just my clue for physical work or [something much more specific]. In this case it's both. But he says it's like a construction site. Something falls on him. He's struck in his back also."

"No."

"It must have sent pressure down the back. I imagine if it hit his head, he must have felt it down his spine. There's pressure down the back. There's talk of age. Is he younger than you?"

"Yes."

"He keeps saying he's the younger brother. You blame yourself for this?"

"Yes."

"He keeps saying, 'Will you stop blaming yourself for it!' God has given him the opportunity to be discerned so he could put your conscience at rest, because you keep blaming yourself for it. You feel you should have known. You could find a million excuses as to why you could have prevented this. He says, 'To be honest, there was no way to have controlled the situation.' That's why he says he's in the wrong place at the wrong time. Did a beam or something fall on him?"

"No."

"Something heavy enough like it?"

"No."

"He says it's heavy. Can I take it that it was?"

"No." Here Paul understandably failed to take into account a basic law of physics: The effect of gravity on a falling object increases the force of its impact.

"I don't know. He gives me the impression it's pretty heavy. Was it a tool?"

"No."

"I'm just going to come out and ask you. What was it?"

"A rock."

"Oh. Because he's telling me that it's heavy, and you're saying to me no, and he's saying, 'Yes it is.' Probably if it fell from a height, maybe it was the impact. He said it was solid, and if it could hit me, I'd feel it. You're saying no. He's saying yes. That's what made me think it could have been a tool or something."

In the above exchange, George experienced a situation that occurs during some readings in which he insists that the communication from the spirit is correct, although the subject disagrees. In this instance, George psychically felt that "something heavy" struck and killed the young man, although the subject answered incorrectly or misunderstood George's meaning.

"Your dad passed before your brother," George continued.

"Yes."

"Because he claims your father crossed him over. Was he in a coma for a period of time?"

"Yes."

"Was he on a life-support system?"

"Yes."

"You had to pull the plug, so to speak."

"Yes."

"Because he keeps saying you did the right thing. I feel as if somebody just pulled the plug out of the socket," George explained. "You were there?"

"Yes," Paul acknowledged.

"He says he knows you were there even though he was unconscious, so to speak. . . . Your father greeted him in the next stage, but he knows that you helped cross him over also. He knows you were there. Because he never came out of it, true?"

"Right."

Paul, who'd regained his composure, began crying again.

"Were you in charge on the job?" George asked.

"Yes."

"That's why you feel responsible, because you had authority over him. He keeps saying that you were his boss. He does have a good sense of humor."

"Yes."

"Because he keeps joking, 'That's why I'm definitely with the wrong crowd.' He's kidding you that you were his boss, and he says that's why you feel responsible."

Paul sat quietly and listened attentively, but did not respond.

"Definitely continue to pray for him," George said. "It's the best thing to do for him at this time, and just know he's all right and at peace. He certainly loves you as his brother. He does not hold any type of hatred or disappointment against you whatsoever. He says, 'You feel very disappointed in yourself. You almost want to see a therapist about it.' You put yourself on a terrible guilt trip and that's just snowballing. He says you're always punishing yourself."

Paul nodded his acknowledgment.

"Your father passes on pretty young," George said.

"Yes."

"Your mom is still living."

"Yes."

"Is she open to this? Because he does ask for her. 'Tell Mom you've heard from me. I'm okay.' He's there with his father. He keeps saying he's all right. Does this happen in another state, not New York?"

"Right."

"Does this happen in the summer?"

"Yes."

"I feel as if I'm in warmer weather. I feel as if I'm in the summertime—"

"Right."

"Does the name Gene mean anything?"

"No."

"I'll leave it with you. Also the name Jack mean anything at all?"

"Yes."

"Passed on?"

"Yes."

"He says Jack is there with him. Also there is a Bob?"

"Yes."

"Passed on."

"Yes."

"More than one?"

"Yes."

"Because there are two—like Bob, Sr., and Bob, Jr."

"Yes."

"It's got to be your dad and brother, right?"

"No."

"No?" George asked in surprise.

"My father is Bob," the young man explained.

"Okay. Your father is Bob. Is there another Bob? Wait. No, there *are* two who've passed on."

"Yes."

"Father and son. Oh, your *grandfather* and your dad. Okay. My mistake. They were right. Because they said, 'Father and son,' and I just jumped. I said it was your brother, and your father and you said no. They said, 'Yes, father and son, but you got the wrong ones' . . . Does the name Danny mean anything? Friends of yours? Daniel or David?"

"No."

"All right, I'll let it go. Sounds as if I heard the name Kevin, too. Kevin or Kenneth."

"No."

"Nobody passed on, though. They're flying in too quickly, and obviously they're not making any sense. Did you as a family have to decide to pull the plug?"

"Yes."

"Because he keeps saying you did the right thing. He never would have come out of it. He would have been like a vegetable. He was kind of trapped. He says you set him free. Somebody was holding his hand," George said.

"Yes," Paul confirmed.

"It's just as if the monitor stopped. He says he knows you were all around. He just couldn't communicate physically. He knows you were there. Your mother was there, too."

"Yes."

"He claims that he knows the family was there, and he says your father was waiting on the sidelines for him. . . . He did have a very lively personality, right?"

"Yes," Paul answered through tears.

"Because over there he's back to his old self. He says, 'Go home and have a good night's sleep.' You know, take it easy. He says, 'Stop punishing yourself.' You don't take orders very well."

"I don't." The young man smiled slightly.

"Because he's kidding you. He says, 'Now for once I'm in charge. I'm telling you: go home and take it easy.' You and he seemed to have had a very good relationship even if you didn't say it. He says, 'There's no place for anger over here. You can't hold it. I have no reason to. It's not your fault.'

I think I'm hearing . . . Does the name Randy mean anything?"

"I don't know."

"Also a Jim."

"Yes."

"Passed on."

"Yes."

"Is that your brother?"

"Yes."

"Okay. I don't want to sound hokey, but he tricked me," George said. "Because I kept saying, 'Give me your name.' I felt he was going to. First he told me to think on the name Randy. I don't know why. I just said okay. He said, 'Get out the name Randy,' and I did. Then I heard him say 'Jim.' Sometimes they do that. There must be a way they have to distract part of my brain to get me to listen. They must have distracted my conscious brain so the subconscious could receive the name. He does ask that you definitely continue to pray for him and your dad and the others that have gone over. . . . Do you have any more siblings?"

"Yes."

"Because he does call out to them. A total of four or five."

"There're four," Paul said.

"Counting your brother, there are five?" George attempted to clarify.

"Four." Again in a few minutes Jim's spirit would confirm George's first response. As you'll see later in this reading, there *are* five children.

"Okay. That's what he's telling me, then. . . . He was on life support for a period of time?"

"Yes."

"Because he says he certainly wasn't there for a week. He was there for a period of time. . . . He says he did everything in his power since he's passed on to try to reach out to you, especially in some way or another to let you know that it's not your fault. Because I'm feeling relief from him. It finally happened. I don't want to sound conceited, but he says he had to find somebody legitimate to get the message to you to let you know he's all right. He says it's been a very hard task to find somebody. He says to me, 'Take it as a compliment.' He's going to step aside now. I keep seeing an apple core, and that was the 'core of distress' here and in the next stage with him, too. Because he saw the anxiety you were going through. So definitely continue to pray for him. He jokes with you again. He says, 'Don't make me hold my breath.' He's not mad at you. He still loves you. You haven't failed in any way. Just be at peace. 'Tell your mother and family you have heard from me.' Is there another sister?"

"Yes."

"Did your mom lose a child?"

"Yes."

"That's why he keeps telling me there are five children. You would have had another brother," George said.

"Yes!" Paul confirmed.

"That's why he keeps telling me there're five. He's telling me he has another brother and a sister. I argued in my mind, because you told me there're four children, counting you. He said, from the other side, 'That's impossible.' He kept saying no and that he knew what he was talking about, that there's another brother. That's why I felt you had another brother. He says to ask you about the miscarriage. He says his brother was there to cross him over also. The two of them are together with your dad."

"Yes."

"Maybe that's why I'm seeing senior and junior, again. They all say to pray for them. Tell your sister you've heard from him also. He sends his love, and your other brother calls out to you, the other brothers, and your mother. He's kind of someone who always feels he's right."

"Yes."

"I mean, not that he was difficult, but he was convinced he was right. Like when he said I was wrong. He told me you were giving me the wrong information. He said to me, 'I know what I'm talking about.' . . . Do you have children of your own?"

"Yes."

"Did you name one after him?" George asked.

"Yes," Paul acknowledged.

"Because he keeps putting white roses in front of me and he says you named a child after him. So he's been born again, not in the religious sense. He says he's around your son Jim as a guardian angel."

George paused as he listened to the spirit's message and then repeated aloud what he psychically heard.

"Okay. He says, 'I've waited long enough. Pray for me. For once and for all, put yourself at peace. No guilt or anxiety.' Just be at peace and know that he's okay. He's going to close now. Your father says, 'This is Dad signing off.' 'This is Jim signing off.' Your brother goes back. They're going back. 'Remember to pray for us,' he says."

After the reading, Paul was pensive. He stood alone with his thoughts for several minutes. His eyes were misty. Then he spoke briefly. "I feel as if a tremendous weight is off me," he said. "Maybe this is the beginning of trying to deal with what happened. Maybe tonight I'll be able to sleep."

Suzie and Dennis Martinek are bereaved parents whose daughter Molly died of a stroke and a suspected brain aneurysm in 1987 at age fourteen. Born with a congenital defect, the girl suffered with cardiac and related problems her entire life. As a result she had brain abscesses and by age ten had twice undergone near-fatal brain surgery. Molly had known all along that she was seriously ill and could conceivably die at any time.

"I told her, 'Naturally I'm going to die before you, because that's the way things are,'" recalls Suzie, like her husband a teacher from the San Diego area. "'Parents die before their children.' But I said, 'If you should happen to die before I do, or before your dad, or if we go before you, we've got to make contact.' She said okay, that she would definitely try.

"We were at the Mayo Clinic. Molly was scheduled for surgery July 22, 1987, at about six-thirty in the morning. At about one o'clock in the morning, she'd gotten ready to go to sleep, then she started talking to me kind of funny. I said, 'Molly, don't do that, you're scaring me!' I could see that one side of her face was drawn up, and I realized that something had gone terribly wrong. I feel it was a stroke.

"The doctors said they felt that she'd be fine. Molly went into intensive care for a couple of days. She was supposed to have the surgery to reconstruct her heart the next morning, but she never did. She experienced intense, incredible head pain, which was probably leakage starting from the aneurysms. They did all sorts of tests and found she had had quite a few clots for a long time. She was paralyzed on one side, but when she awoke Friday afternoon, she said she felt a little bit better. Then, boom! The whole inside of her head blew out from the aneurysm.

"That was Friday. They put her on a respirator, hoping some pure oxygen would take pressure off the brain, but the brain swelled and then compressed down on the brain stem. They took an EEG [electroencephalogram] on Saturday, and it showed very little brain-wave activity. At that point it seemed possible that we could have kept Molly on life support and brought her back to San Diego, but we knew that's not what she would want. She wouldn't want to be a semi-vegetable if she came out of it. It just wouldn't be Molly.

"We decided to see what was going to happen. If Molly wasn't going to survive, we wanted to be sure that whatever organs could be donated would be. The doctors later discovered that Molly had blood clots throughout her body, which damaged every single organ except one kidney. It was clear that sooner or later Molly would require more aggressive life-support, but to what end? Every time they stuck her with a needle, I asked, 'Why one more needle? Why one more blood test? Why one more anything?'

"After a second EEG on Sunday showed absolutely no brain activity, we realized, She's dead, and there's nothing we can do about it. The doctors said there was no chance. And you could see it in her eyes. If you've ever seen anybody who's at that stage, the eyes aren't 'there' anymore."

Suzie paused. "On Sunday we decided to shut off the respirator. We figured that if she stopped breathing, that would be it. It would mean that her brain stem was damaged beyond recovery and there was no way she could survive except on life support. To us, that would be not saving her life but prolonging the inevitable, her death. If she did breathe on her own, though, we would have to decide how to proceed. As the doctors told us, in that case, she might continue in that state for years. I knew that wasn't what Molly would want.

"We were spared facing those choices, though. When the doctors turned off her respirator, Molly stopped breathing. She was gone. I look back on those hours. There were just three days between the coma and her death. We had to have been guided, somehow, because it was almost a release.

"What we went through the whole time she was alive is what the experts call anticipatory grief," Suzie explains. "You're constantly in a grief state because you always have hope. Afterward, though, I had second thoughts. 'Did we shut off too soon? Should we have kept her on life support?' I never, ever thought I could have done it. I always said, 'Oh, no, I would never do that, even if it took years, just having her body kept alive.' But when it actually came down to it, I knew that was what she would have wanted.

"Of course, you get back home, and all of a sudden stories leap out at you from the newspapers: 'Person Brought Back From Coma After Seven Years Brain-Dead.' Intellectually you know this is inaccurate reporting. You know there had to be some activity during those seven years. But it still haunts you a little bit. You think, *Gosh, if they did it . . .* Though we knew in our heart of hearts that she was gone."

As George began the reading, he asked the attractive, well-dressed couple, "A female close to you pass over? Because there's one older and one younger. Let me go with it. There's talk about a daughter. Did you lose a daughter?"

"Yes," Dennis acknowledged.

"Oh, okay. That's the young female, obviously, that came up between the two of you. There's talk about a grandfather. I'm trying to figure out if she means yours or your wife's. Did your dad pass on?"

"Yes," Dennis answered.

"Okay, because she keeps saying, 'Grandpa is with me.' I didn't know which one she meant. So I'd better listen carefully. Did he pass on before her?"

"Yes."

"Because she claims he was there to meet her when she came over. I take it she passes as a youngster."

"Yes."

"Okay. Because she tells me to go lower than sixteen. She's less than thirteen?"

"No."

"Oh, okay, because she keeps showing me thirteen and sixteen. She's right between there, then. Was she actually in her sixteenth year?"

"No. She was in her fourteenth year," Suzie clarified.

"I'm curious as to why she shows me sixteen and tells me to go down. So she's fourteen. Her passing was obviously tragic," George continued.

"Yes."

"She knew she was going to pass on."

"She knew she might. Yes."

"She had lung trouble."

"Yes."

"You both took care of her, obviously. She thanks you for being good to her prior to her passing. You took good care of her. This illness affects her blood."

"Yes."

"She keeps telling me that I'd find it in the blood. She's touching my arm and telling me it's in the blood flow. She went through a hell of a time," George said.

"Yes," Dennis confirmed.

"I mean, not that she's complaining. . . . But she's telling me, 'You wouldn't want to go through it.' I'm sure I wouldn't. Did she have a lot of blood tests? She's being injected, or there are transfusions."

"Yes."

"It seems that she had it from day one. She claims that. In a sense, it could be heredity. There may not be evidence of it, but it seems somebody else [in the family] had it. It seems that it was there before. It affects blood cells."

"That's not what she died from, but she was born with it," Suzie explained.

"Oh, okay. She keeps telling me there's trouble in the blood. I'm glad you explained that to me. That's what she's trying to tell me, and I'm just overlooking it. But she does state that it affects the blood cells. The way they look or something," George said.

"That's right," Dennis acknowledged.

"She says that—not that she had this illness—but she says it's like having AIDS. You have one virus that can cause other problems, and that's probably what she's driving at. She had this, and it caused trouble breathing and trouble walking. Did it also affect her breathing?"

"Yes."

"Was she operated on?"

"She was getting ready for an operation."

"I feel that she suffered a great deal, but she's not complaining. It's as if she was starting to learn to live with it. Her attitude was 'What am I going to do? This is the only choice I have.' . . .

"No matter what, you never gave up hope and faith," George continued, "and this certainly rattles your cage, so to speak. She's not trying to make herself sound like a Pollyanna, but she sounds as though she always tried to look at the bright side of things. Because she says to me, that even though your struggles didn't have a happy ending, look at it this way: that this is still a happy ending, because she's alive and living someplace else. She claims that she lives with your father over there. . . . Did she know him at all [on earth]?"

"Yes."

"Maybe not as well as she knew your parents," George said to Dennis. "But she says she knew him, in any case. Your father feels he could have been closer to you," George remarked to Suzie. "Is that true?"

"Yes," she acknowledged.

"He's embarrassed to have to say that's a fact, and now he has the opportunity to make up for that. God's giving him the opportunity by taking care of your daughter in the next stage. He feels he could have been closer. It's funny; it's not that he's a bad man. He just feels he could have been a better husband and father. There's talk about your mom. She's still here."

"Yes."

"Because he started to talk about her. And I asked him if she's there or here, and he said, 'She's there.' You have other children."

"Yes."

"She says you have another child."

"A grandchild."

"But you, yourselves, have another child," George insisted.

"Yes," Suzie acknowledged, referring to Molly's step-siblings.

"You do. Because she's saying there's one other child. So that would be the grandchild, then."

"Yes," Dennis answered.

"Now, this daughter is *your* daughter."

"Yes."

"Okay. Since she's passed on, there's been a birth of a niece or nephew."

"Yes."

"That's probably why she's bringing it up. She's aware that it has come to pass. Did this illness affect her brain at all?"

"Yes."

"I feel a lot of pressure up here," George said, placing his hands on his head and indicating where he had sympathetic pain. "Would it make her not be able to speak well, because I feel as if I can't get the words out. But she's fine now. She says she's one-hundred-percent normal as we would understand it. Did it affect her eyesight at all?"

"Yes."

"I feel that she's fine now. She can see clearly. She's fine all around. She's a very spiritual individual; not that she's religious. What she went through, I'd say she carried the cross very well. . . . You've been dreaming about her."

"Yes, I have," Dennis replied.

"Because she says she comes to you in dreams, when you're in a receptive state, so to speak. It's to let you know that she's all right. . . . It seems as though she's trying to do things, because she says she works with young people over there, especially those who cross over from illnesses. It's almost as if had she stayed here, she'd have become a nurse or a doctor. She seems to be very involved with helping, social-type work, as we'd understand it here. She's always 'on call,' as she says. She's very adaptable to her situation. When she got over there she was not surprised that she had passed on. Her attitude was 'I've passed on. Okay.' Her grandfather greeted her. She asked him, 'What do I do?' She liked the fact that you don't have to go through a lot of struggle there the way you do here. . . . It's funny: even though she had trouble speaking, she was still a talker."

"Yes."

"She's obviously a talker. But she says that sometimes she had to struggle to get the words out, and now everything goes very smoothly, and she's fine. She calls out to the other children and, again, she sends them white roses, kind of a spiritual blessing. Is there another wedding or birth coming up?"

"Yes."

"Because she does speak about another birth. . . . I won't stake my life on it, but it may be another boy," George said.

"Oh!" Suzie exclaimed happily.

"She keeps talking about another grandson. I'm usually inaccurate about that," George confessed. The couple laughed. "Things can change. Souls can alter, but it feels like the birth of a boy. Again, I may be off on it because at one point she showed me a son and a daughter. She might be trying to tell me there's a nephew and a niece. I'm getting mixed up, so I'll leave it with you. But she is aware of a next birth. Does she go into a coma?"

"Yes."

"I see a vision of Saint Joseph, which means a happy death. She lets go in her sleep, more or less. When she passed on was she on life support or something?"

"Yes."

"Because I keep seeing her hooked up to something like that. . . . She says at one point you were afraid, wondering how long she was going to linger. She says, 'Thank heavens you were spared having to make that decision.' It's another thing she seems to say to me, that obviously she was not going to come out of it. Technically, she was brain dead. She says to me that the body stayed alive. . . . It seemed she was always trying to do good things for you. She thanks you for being so good to her, so this [passing once the respirator was turned off] was her last opportunity to do something good for you.

"She didn't want to have to see you going through making that decision, so she snapped, she left the body. She said when she was in a coma, she basically knew she wasn't coming back. I mean, she was in bad enough health to begin with, so she certainly did not want to come back brain dead.

"Did you take her to Disneyland?" The Martineks nodded. "Because she thanks you for taking her there. One thing about her: she's a very appreciative youngster. I mean, she accepted everything as a grace, more or less. She has tremendous faith. I see an anchor with her, which is a sign of faith. She has tremendous hope, plus she's a very giving individual.

So even for the short time that she was here on earth, she left a tremendous impression with you and the people she came in contact with. Does the name Kathy mean anything at all?"

"I have an Aunt Kate," Suzie acknowledged.

"Did she pass on?" George queried.

"Oh, years ago."

"Oh, okay. Because she says Katherine. She was trying to break it down like Katy, Kitty. Katherine is there with her also. Does the name Molly mean anything at all?" George asked.

"That was her name!" Suzie exclaimed.

"That was her!" Dennis added.

"I keep hearing somebody singing 'Sweet Molly Malone.' I heard the song, and I said to her, 'Are you trying to tell me something, or am I daydreaming?' "

"I used to sing that song," Dennis explained.

"Really? Because I heard her singing it, and I thought to myself, *What is there to lose if I'm not correct? Maybe she likes the song or something.* So it's a double message: not only my clue for the name but also something that you can singularly remember her with. Did you make her 'famous'?"

That question brought a smile from her mother. "We established a family award at her school," she said.

"Because she says she's like a celebrity. Not that she's a movie star, but she says you made her famous, established. She's known."

"Yes, that's true."

"Did she have kind of dark hair? She's definitely a brunette."

"Yes."

"Okay. Not as fair as you are. I see her . . . and she looks younger than her age."

"Probably did," Dennis answered.

"By a couple of years. Not by that much. I see a female with dark hair, moderate length, and it seems that she has your eyes. She seems to be between the two of you. Did she believe there was something after death?"

"Yes."

"So you know, again, everything falls neatly into place for

her. She knew there was something after death. She went into the light. . . . She also says John is with her."

"Yes. Two of them."

"Is one of them a friend of yours?"

"Mine," Dennis answered.

"She calls him Uncle John or Johnny. I guess he passed on young. He's not that old, and he's a friend of yours, but I don't know if she knew him or not. The thing is, he's there with her also. . . . Does the name Harry mean anything?"

"Oh yes."

"Passed on?"

"No."

"Anyone close to her?"

"No."

"She knew him. Well, the thing is, she just called out to Harry. But did somebody close to Harry pass on?"

"Yes."

"Not that you minded doing it, but she apologizes for your spending money on her treatment. There was just so much that had to be put into this."

"Everything we did for her was a joy," Suzie said without hesitation.

"Well, she knows that. She feels so bad. She just doesn't want you to think your efforts were in vain. Because she says, okay, maybe she's not alive here, but still she had to be here long enough that, in those fourteen years, she made a good impression."

After discussing the fact that Molly knew her father said the rosary for her, George turned to him and said, "Your first name is Dennis, right?"

"Right."

"Okay. Because I just heard the name. You're a professional?"

"Yes."

"She says to me, there's definitely movement within your profession. I think this is symbolic: The name Gloria mean anything to you?"

"Oh yes! Oh yes!" Suzie exclaimed.

"Did it have something to do with your daughter?" George asked, somewhat startled by her response.

"Yes," Dennis acknowledged. The Martineks explained after the reading the name's special significance: When Molly was young, she and Dennis sometimes played a game where she assumed the identity of Gloria, and he pretended to be a character named Johnny. Suzie confided to George and me, "I had decided before seeing George that three specific things would be evidence that the messages were coming from Molly. One of them was 'Gloria.'"

In the reading, George said, "She wrote it [the name] over your head. I asked her what it's about. Is that her nickname? She just said you'd take it. It's not a name. That's why I said it must be something symbolic."

The couple laughed as George continued. "The thing is, this means something specific to you, because she wrote 'Gloria' over your head. It's something specific enough that you will know you're hearing from her today."

"Yes!"

"That's definitely her I'm making contact with. She told me to say it and say it's a symbol and let it go."

"It sounds like her," Dennis confirmed.

"You know, she explains everything to me carefully, and she's been doing it since I started. She said, 'They'll know what Gloria means.' Apparently you do, because when I saw you react, I heard her say, 'I told you that they'd know.'"

"Yes."

"Were you two at her grave recently or something?"

"She's not buried."

"You have the ashes?"

"Yes, they are with us all the time," the woman answered.

"Okay. Apparently you've been to her grave, in a sense, because she says you're very near her. Tonight you'll be at her grave site. Apparently that's what she means. She says, 'I'm not there.' . . . She seems to beam with radiation over there, which is a sign that she's very much in God's light. She's a very charitable, loving individual, and her light reflects it. When you feel good, you glow, and that's the feeling I'm getting. I keep thinking as she comes near me, I feel as if I'm glowing. This is certainly a very loving individual."

"Yes."

George mentioned some family health problems that Dennis confirmed, then continued. "You know, as much as she knows the two of you miss her tremendously, yet you have to accept the fact that she's alive someplace else."

"Yes."

"She says when your day comes, which isn't in the immediate future, you certainly know who will be there waiting for you. In any case, there's hope of something to look forward to. She definitely is a model of hope. She never gave up."

"True."

"She got frustrated when she had trouble speaking. I can see why, especially if her brain was affected. Did she have a blood vessel break up here?" George queried, at the same time touching his head.

"Yes," Suzie answered.

"It feels as though, because of this trouble with the blood, there's pressure. It builds up. It might have gone up to the head, to the brain and the—"

"Okay."

Later, George said, "Your daughter, she's inclined to be very artistic."

"Yes."

"She seems to be artistic with colors and writing."

"Writing. Yes."

"She said it's still her hobby over there. It's as if she writes in colors, she tells me."

"Yeah?" Dennis responded.

"Oh wow!" Suzie said, smiling.

"She keeps insisting that if she writes a poem, she'll write the feelings in words, but the emotions are in a color. For example, love is pink; passion is red; sorrow is black, as we would portray colors here. And she keeps telling me to emphasize certain things, because you would know what she's talking about and I wouldn't."

"Yes."

"She writes Gloria over your head, but it's in colors. . . . She's very fond of Christmas," George said.

"Yes."

"She says she's closest during the holiday season. Do you take the name Tom, passed over?"

"Alive," Suzie corrected.

"Close to your daughter."

"Tom's my brother."

"He's going through a lot of changes: family, job. He has trouble getting his act together."

"I think so."

"Try to be close to him. You're close with your parents."

"Yes."

"Say hi to them for her."

"Yes."

"Are you getting a new vehicle?"

"We just did."

"Congratulations. You left her room intact."

"Yes."

"She visits. . . . Your daughter is very family oriented. She doesn't come across like the typical teenager. She's very considerate of other people's feelings. . . . She's like the unsinkable Molly Brown."

That remark brought laughter from her mother.

"Do you take the name Anna?" George asked.

"That's my mother," Dennis acknowledged.

"Did your parents speak another language?"

"Yes. A little bit."

"Is there a Joseph passed over?"

"That's my father," Dennis answered.

"Your mother is Catholic."

"Yes."

"She's very devout."

"She's Christian now, more than strictly Catholic. But she is very devout."

"She prays for your daughter."

"Yes."

"I think they're going to close. Joseph is going back. He says Molly may live with him over there, but he says she keeps him in line!"

"Oh yeah."

"He says even though she's younger than he is, she's more advanced in a lot of ways spiritually. So he learns from her—as people learned from her on earth. She doesn't bully anyone over there. They learn by example. They're going back. Dad's going back. Everyone's going back. Your daughter went back. Did you call her Moll?"

"Yes we did."

"I keep hearing that Molly Malone song and seeing the symbol of Molly Brown and the book *Moll Flanders,* which would be a symbol of the name Moll. And she says she's going back. She says, too, that she sends her love to both of you. She says she knows that you love her, and the feeling is mutual. She says to look at it as if she went away to join the Peace Corps. That's basically the work she does on the other side. She writes 'Gloria' over your head in colors. It's the third time now she's done it, and that's the symbol that's linked to her. And with that, she signs off."

Reflecting on her daughter's passage, Suzie muses, "I cry every day. It's funny, time doesn't really make it better. I can cry until I get a headache and my nose gets stuffed up, and it doesn't change anything."

Dennis agrees, saying, "I don't think time has healed anything. It's the same as it was at first."

"We left her room exactly as it was," Suzie says. "Everything hangs in her closet as it was. Some people find that odd. It's fine with me. It's nice to go in there.

"I was always hoping to hear from her. I would have gone to a psychic if I had known a reliable one. But I didn't. The few I'd ever been to in my life were jokes. It's not that I didn't or don't believe in the hereafter, it's just that I'm a very skeptical person. And if I don't see it, I don't usually believe it. And, of course, you want to believe something so wonderful as that. I did believe that this information came from Molly; I'm positive of that. Who else could it have come from?" To which Dennis adds, "There was no other way George could have gotten it except through Molly."

"I think the comfort," she observes, "comes from knowing or having an idea of what the relationships are over there, on the other side. I think going to George is a great comfort, but I wouldn't expect some miracle to come from it, because it's not going to. We're here, and our child isn't, and that's hard to live with."

George had alluded to Molly writing "in colors," not knowing that she wrote poetry. Some time after their reading, the Martineks sent us a book they'd published of their daughter's poetry. Clearly Molly was just as George had described her: happy, positive, appreciative.

Rainy Day

Stepping out into the bitter cold,
I put up my umbrella and start walking.
I hear the grit
Beneath my feet and the pitter patter
Of raindrops on my umbrella.
I see nothing but green all around me
And the mist of my warm breath in the air.
The smell of the rain refreshes me.
I taste the crisp fresh air as I kneel down to
Smell the sweet scent of the wildflowers.
I seek shelter underneath a huge redwood tree
And the smell of smoke reminds me of
Our warm fireplace, where I long to be.
                                    —Molly Martinek, 1986

6

To Know the Real Story

George was asked by a hospice care worker to visit a hospitalized person with AIDS. The patient, Peter, was forty and in the final stages of a long battle with the disease. He had seen George on television and read about him. Peter wanted to learn as much as he could about life after death and had many questions for George.

"I have to admit that I probably didn't cover my reaction very well when I walked into his hospital room," George recalls. "Peter was behind a screen, and when I first looked at him, I was taken a little aback. I'd never seen anyone looking so ill. Then, I have to admit, I became very angry that a person could suffer so. He knew his time was coming; you didn't have to be a genius to figure that out. It was obvious that he was a very giving, loving, charitable soul. You could tell he was a very good person."

After being introduced, George and Peter talked casually. George was reluctant to bring up immediately the subject of death. However, Peter took the lead, and the conversation quickly moved in that direction.

"George, please tell me what can I expect when I pass on," he asked. "Will I be free from this suffering? I'll admit to you that I'm a little afraid of the unknown. I believe in the hereafter, but I'm still not sure. Will somebody be there for me?"

"Someone is passed on in your family, and I assure you that certainly he or she will be there for you," George answered without hesitation.

"You know," Peter said, "a few times here in the hospital, I woke up in the middle of the night, and I swear I saw my late father sitting in one of the chairs here in my room. And it's funny, because I was closer to my mother than I was to him."

"Well, you can't go on those grounds, because it can be whom you least expect that will come to greet you. So maybe it's your father, knowing you could pass on at any time, and he's waiting there on the other side for you," George explained.

"What can I expect?"

"There might be that moment of darkness," said George, "and then you'll go toward the light. Don't be afraid. Don't be paranoid. You're not going to hell. Go toward the light, because that's God. Your loved ones who've passed on will be there waiting."

Peter listened raptly as George continued. "Your father can come right for you in this hospital room and say, 'I've come to cross you over.' Don't be afraid. Go with him."

"But part of me says I'm not ready to go yet," Peter protested sorrowfully.

"Well, do you think you have a choice?" George asked softly.

"No . . . It's pretty obvious I don't."

"Remember," George gently pointed out, "that once you pass on, the suffering is over. Everyone who has passed from AIDS has come through from the other side to tell me the pain and suffering have been immediately relieved."

In 1981 George stated on my radio program, *The Joel Martin Show,* that the world would experience an epidemic which he described as "a new strain of virus."

"It will be of epidemic proportions," he said then. "It will create a panic. You'll walk down the street and not know who is infected with it. It's going to be like a plague, and it will hit a select group. Kids. But large numbers of people will be affected with a dread disease as well, and people will compare it to the plague of centuries ago." Although George never said the word, was he predicting AIDS? Sometime later on television, he said it would somehow be "related to a mutated smallpox virus."

In the mid-1980s, before the full impact of the AIDS crisis was understood, I asked George for *We Don't Die,* "Why don't [those on the other side] give us advice on how to find the cure for AIDS?"

"They say that in the case of AIDS, the disease has been around for centuries, maybe since the beginning of time," George said then. "It's not anything new. They do say that it's a very intricate and complicated disease, and yet its cure is right under our noses; it's very simple. I've been told that the answer has something to do with protein. But, again, even if they try to communicate an answer to me, I'm not necessarily going to understand what they're saying."

In late 1988, George received a letter from a reader, who had read *We Don't Die*. In the book George said that those on the other side seemed to suggest that an AIDS cure or vaccine "has something to do with protein." Shortly thereafter, the young man joined a National Institutes of Health clinical trial in which volunteers were inoculated with an HIV protein-based vaccine formula.

Today George says, "I'm surprised that a cure for AIDS hasn't been found. With scientists always boasting to me how superior science is to what I do, I always wonder why they can't evaluate this relatively weak virus and find a cure. But instead, some of them turn around and say, 'If you're so psychic, how come *you* can't tell *us?*' For some reason, that's not where my gift lies.

"Unfortunately, until a cure or a vaccine is discovered, there's going to be a lot more suffering. I can only say to those who are HIV positive or who have AIDS, your life *is* going to go on. You are not going to die. You're not going to be sent to hell. You're not going to suffer in the afterlife."

According to the federal Centers for Disease Control, between June 1981 and November 1990, 157,525 AIDS cases have been reported. Of those, 98,530 have died—more than the number of Americans who perished in the Korean and Vietnam wars combined. In 1990 the World Health Organization reported that AIDS "will be more widespread in the next century than previously thought." WHO estimates that six million to eight million people worldwide have been infected with the human immunodeficiency virus, or HIV, which causes AIDS. The WHO forecast that fifteen to twenty million people will be infected by the turn of the century is considered a *minimum* estimate.

Public-health officials predict that by the end of 1992, there will be 365,000 AIDS cases in this country and that 263,000 Americans will have died from AIDS. The United States is unusual in that the largest percentage of persons with AIDS have been white homosexual men. Elsewhere in the world, the disease is spread mainly through heterosexual contact, or, in the case of the Romanian orphans, blood transfusion.

Experts agree that millions who previously considered themselves "safe"—i.e., non-drug-using, nonpromiscuous heterosexuals—may in fact be in grave danger. An estimated one million Americans are infected today, yet most of them don't know it. Because the first symptoms of AIDS may not appear for up to ten years after infection, the number of potential victims is staggering. The Reagan administration's stubborn refusal to address the AIDS crisis has caused us to fall behind in the only effective weapon against the HIV virus: education. In those "lost" years, a noisy parade of self-righteous religious Fundamentalists, conservatives, and social reactionaries have nearly succeeded in drowning out the voices of reason and compassion.

In the meantime, not only have intravenous drug users and homosexuals been stricken, but also hemophiliacs and others who've received blood transfusions. Also entire families have become infected, as the virus is passed between husband and wife, from mother to child. In 1990 the *Journal of Gerontology* reported that an estimated ten thousand people over sixty will have contracted the virus by 1992. Despite routine blood screening for the virus since mid-1985, there is still a 1 in 28,000 chance of contracting AIDS through a transfusion. Because HIV tests screen not for the virus itself but for antibodies to the virus, through mid-1990 there have been six cases of persons infected through "tested" blood. How is that possible? Apparently the blood donors were infected with the HIV virus but so recently that their blood contained no antibodies. No one is safe.

Recently a New York congressman referred to AIDS babies as "innocent victims" of the disease. To that we would reply that *every* victim is innocent. To believe otherwise requires us to see some people as "guilty" or "deserving." Such thinking is ethically repugnant. George has learned through readings that AIDS is *not* God's "punishment" for its victims any more than lung cancer is His punishment for the "sin" of smoking.

Not surprisingly, as the AIDS crisis worsened, many people with AIDS and loved ones of those who had died from it came to George for readings.

"We're not supposed to die when we're young," a young man with AIDS told him. "I mean, when your grandmother passes on, okay. You expect to die when you're old. But when you're young? No. People, friends are dying from AIDS in their twenties, thirties, forties. It's not normal. It's not supposed to happen that young. We're not ready to die."

AIDS is unique in that those who contract it almost always know someone else who has it or has died from it. A reading with George takes on a special significance in a situation such as Charlie's. He is a person with AIDS who has seen the crisis evolve from a rare medical mystery to a full-blown epidemic. For people like him, a reading provides powerful support to help him deal with his illness. The fact that Charlie and the friends he speaks of are homosexual does not diminish the poignancy of his struggle.

"Out of about fifteen to eighteen friends," he says, "I'm the last that is living. All the others died in their mid-thirties. Nothing was known about AIDS in the early 1980s. We were such a close-knit group, we helped one another. I was able to glean a tremendous amount of information about AIDS as a result. So when I found out I was HIV positive, I knew what to expect. I'd seen it from both sides of the sickbed, so to speak. At one time I was the care giver, and now I'm the person in bed.

"I'm not saying I'm made of stone or don't have feelings, but I have a tremendously strong belief in my own personal spirituality. The way I see it, this is a temporary condition. I just have to get through it the best I can. This life is a temporary passing to something I consider much more permanent and glorious. I've been told that through George by my friends who've passed away. They've told me beautiful things. They've told me not to worry.

"These are people who've had a very low sense of spirituality, because every religion turned us away," Charlie says sadly. "As homosexual men, we were told that we were not part of 'their' religion. We were told we were condemned to hell. We grew up hearing this, and at the end of our lives AIDS actually became a gift to us because we got back our spirituality, which will serve us forever."

Among the questions people with AIDS often ask George: What will it be like to pass on? Where will I go? Drug users and homosexuals ask if they're going to be punished or condemned. Similarly, loved ones of those who have passed on from AIDS virtually always want to know, Where are they? Is the suffering they endured here over? Are they free of pain and at peace on the other side?

Today diagnosis is often made earlier and medical advances treat the potentially fatal symptoms and complications more aggressively, allowing patients to live longer than thought possible even a few years ago. However, until there is finally a cure, AIDS is a protracted death sentence. As with every passing, behind the mounting AIDS statistics are personal stories of pain and courage. There are long-term survivors fighting back, helping others, and leading active lives. There are tens of thousands who have been diagnosed as HIV positive but are otherwise healthy for now. There are also, sadly, those who live in excruciating pain and fear. Some have chosen suicide over agonizing, lingering death. What happens to them in the afterlife?

Sometimes those closest to the person with AIDS, such as parents, have the greatest difficulty understanding the disease. Frequently, in George's experience, it is not until someone has passed on from AIDS that misunderstandings and conflicts are settled and apologies made, between the dimensions.

"He's saying he feels he could have been closer at the end," George told the father of a young man who'd died from AIDS.

"Yes," the man answered.

"Your son thanks you for your prayers."

"Yes."

"And he apologizes for the emotional distance that was

between the two of you in this physical plane. He's sorry the two of you weren't closer when he was here."

Several years had elapsed since George's first reading for the family of a man killed by AIDS. In that time he had also conducted many readings, occasionally in the hospital, for AIDS patients preparing to make the transition to the other side. Through it all, George remained nonjudgmental. However, like any compassionate person, he cannot help but react angrily to the controversy raging around the AIDS debate, causing needless pain for people whose burden is already near-intolerable.

"The AIDS victims who have come through from the other side in readings," George says, "have told me the first thing they notice when they pass on is that they are immediately relieved of all their suffering. A lot of them are working on the other side with people who have passed on from AIDS so that they can help them to cross over, especially if they are in fear." For one young man, George had a specific message from the spirit of a friend who'd died from AIDS: "Your friend says, 'Tell him I love him and miss him, and not to be lonely. I'm still with him. I know he's working with AIDS people on earth.'"

"Yes," the subject acknowledged.

"And he says, 'I'm doing the same thing on the other side.'"

George notes, "One thing those who pass on from AIDS don't have to deal with on the other side is the prejudice they may have experienced here. There won't be any hatred or fear of them in the next dimension because they had AIDS here on earth. There are no religious fanatics or self-righteous people to tell you you will go to hell. Personally, I've never believed that. If God is all-loving and merciful, as I believe He is, then there's no place in hell for you if you're a good human being.

"Some people would say that a person is sinful because he is a homosexual, a drug user, or sexually promiscuous. I'm not going to condemn anyone on those terms any more than I would for the color of their eyes. We have modern-day scribes and pharisees who tell us what and how we should think, and in doing that they deprive us of using the greatest gifts God gave us: our brains and our hearts.

"Besides, the unfortunate fact is that if the projections prove true, in the coming years the bulk of AIDS cases will be people whom society considers 'mainstream': high-school and college students, married couples, the elderly, and children.

"One reason why many AIDS patients panic as death approaches is that we've all been so conditioned. Someone asked me, 'Should I go back to church? Should I confess and save my soul at the last minute?' Unfortunately, instead of helping them with love and mercy, as Mother Teresa does, the churches often would rather keep them in fear and despair, to force—even bully them—into doing what the churches want them to do. What conceit! What arrogance! Instead of patting themselves on the back because they've saved a person's soul before he passed from AIDS, they should instead show mercy and love before that person dies.

"I think these people want to be reassured that even if they are not overly religious, they don't have to be. A lot of gay people are not religious because they've been told in so many words by people like New York City's Cardinal John O'Connor that religion has no use for them. I just think they want to be assured that God is still there and that God still loves them as they are.

"Parents want to know, 'After my son suffered with AIDS, is he in hell now because he was gay?' To me, if that came through, it would not be from God. If you read the Bible carefully," George points out, "it's obvious that Jesus found the company of society's so-called outcasts preferable to the self-righteous. It's my feeling that the 'outcasts' who are good people are going to go to heaven faster than the self-righteous. We know that Jesus Christ embraced the lepers. If He were here on earth today, does anyone truly believe He would turn away people with AIDS? Do you think He would make a judgment on them at all? Christ knew the so-called outcasts were also God's children. He also knew that they would probably be more open to His teachings and beliefs.

"Mother Teresa was one of the very first in the Catholic Church to step forward and say that people with AIDS are

Christ's children too, and that we have to take care of them. She started one of the first AIDS hospices. She didn't make judgments. I read a controversial comment from one priest who has a ministry for AIDS patients. He said, 'The Church doesn't always speak for Christ.' That's sad to hear. Someone who came to me recounted a story about having attended a funeral for a friend who passed from AIDS. During the service a priest made it a point to say that the deceased had been a good person, 'even though he thumbed his nose at Christ and turned his back on society' through his homosexuality. I was appalled to hear that, and can only imagine how much pain it caused that person's family.

"What happens on the other side," says George, "is that those who've passed from AIDS see God as He really is—total love, mercy, and compassion—and then they realize that they've been duped, in a sense, all those years by the messages of guilt and abandonment some churches tried pushing on them. That's when they realize that they are truly at peace and one with God, because they know that God would never reject them under *any* circumstance. Frankly, neither should we."

Frequently the spirit of a person who has passed on from AIDS will tell loved ones here that, much to his relief, he had not been condemned to hell and that in addition to the end of suffering in the physical body, he is not being punished on the other side. "When I got here," one spirit said to George, "no one judged me. I was brought into the light by other relatives who'd passed on before me. No one condemned me for having AIDS, and I have the same chance now as anyone else to grow spiritually.

"I've met other friends who passed on from AIDS," he added. "They came up to greet me and to offer help. I'm adjusting to life here. I'm free of pain and am at peace."

George says, "The families and friends of those with AIDS come to see me, and you can see they are filled with love. They want to support those close to them who have AIDS, whether they're in the here or the hereafter. But there are others who seem so fearful, who hate everybody and everything. A lot of survivors tell me they feel devastated by the loss of someone they love to AIDS. I would say there is a continuing and growing need here for AIDS bereavement groups and support groups specifically for those with AIDS and their loved ones.

"I did a reading for an individual who has AIDS and obviously only a short time to live," George recalls. "He admitted to me that he's afraid to die. He said he didn't know if he was ready. He wanted to see his sister get married in about a year. I said to him, 'You *will* be able to see her get married. But you just won't be in the physical body. You'll be there in the spiritual body.'

" 'But they won't see me,' he said.

"I answered, 'No, they won't see you, but with the love they feel for you, they're going to know you're there.' "

Of course AIDS is not the only disease that takes a harrowing toll on its victims, but one cannot deny the magnitude of physical suffering it brings. Again, as the readings show, it is the physical body that is afflicted, the only part of us that truly does die. Any subject whose loved one passed from AIDS is encouraged to hear that the misery ended with life on this side. Spirits who've passed from AIDS seem particularly keen to reassure their friends and family that on the other side they've returned to "themselves."

"Do you take the name David?" George asked.

"Yes," the subject, a young man, acknowledged.

"He's passed on."

"Yes."

"You've lost a male friend? Because he's standing behind you right now."

"Yes."

"He passed away recently."

"Yes."

"He says you knew him well."

"Yes."

"His was a tragic passing."

"Yes."

"He tells me he knew he was going to pass on."

"Yes."

"He calls out to his parents. 'Tell them you've heard from me.' "

"Okay."

"He was like a loner?"

"Yes, even though he was around a lot of people."

"The illness affected his blood," George said.

"Yes."

"He tells me he had a rough time before passing."

"Yes."

"Did he have AIDS? Because that's what he's telling me. I see blood cells affected."

"Yes."

"He's sure glad it's over with! There's a feeling of relief that his suffering is over."

"I believe that."

"He says that when he had the illness he was always tired."

"Yes."

"Now on the other side, he says he's back to his old self again," George said.

Often gay men who've passed from AIDS attempt to heal rifts with fathers who either disapproved of or didn't understand their sexual orientation. As the next reading demonstrates, happily, these fathers (and mothers, sometimes) and sons usually are able to reconcile.

Mike is a stereotypical tough, veteran Irish cop. Tall and handsome, with snow-white hair against a ruddy complexion and an intense gaze, he worked his way up from patrolman to high-ranking official in the New York City Police Department. The cops-and-criminals world he lived in contrasted sharply with the more genteel environment his son Michael, Jr., knew as a designer.

Mike, Sr., and his wife, Peggy, had never met George before their reading with him at a public appearance George made before several hundred people.

"Did somebody lose a son?" George asked. "Somebody claims to be the son passed on."

"Yes," Mike answered.

"He was a young boy by today's standards. A young adult."

"Yes, a young adult."

"He's over twenty-one."

"Yes."

"Did you not get all the answers about his passing?"

"I could say yes."

"He shows me Sherlock Holmes, symbol of mystery. You didn't get all the answers about his passing. There are unanswered things."

"Yes."

"I mean, there's nothing you can do about it."

"That's correct."

"Apparently your son wants to verify that if you have a suspicion or if you feel empty, that you are correct in your feeling," George explained. Mike closed his eyes and nodded. "Did your mother pass on?"

"No."

"Your mother-in-law?"

"My mother-in-law, yes."

"Because he says, 'Mother's with me.' So it had to be his grandmother. It has to be your mother-in-law, then."

"Yes. They were very close, even though she died years ago."

"Okay, that's the thing. She comes in. He says he's there with his grandmother. When you said no to your mother, he said 'mother-in-law' to you, to let you know she's present."

George paused briefly to write down rapidly some of the words and phrases he psychically heard, then continued: "Was there any bloodshed involved in your son's passing? Bloodshed *internally?*"

"Yes."

"It's not bloodshed in the violent sense," George clarified.

"No."

"Your son had an illness."

"Yes, he did."

"It feels creepy. . . . It affected the blood cells."

"Yes, it did."

"That's what he tells me. A form of cancer."

"Yes, it was."

"A rare form."

"Yes," Mike answered.

"It's almost as though he didn't know he had it."

"That's correct."

"It's funny. It's there, but it's—"

"He may not have known until the end."

"Until it actually started taking some toll on him physically. Did it attack the bones at all?"

"Not that I'm aware."

"Was he very weak from this illness?"

"Yes, he was extremely weak."

"I feel as if I'm having trouble with the legs; I feel as if I can't get around."

"He did have trouble. That's right," Mike confirmed.

"In the legs?"

"Yes, in the legs and getting around. He used a cart."

"It must have attacked the muscle and the bone somehow."

"Yes."

"It's like a form of leukemia, almost."

"Well, we might say that."

"A form . . ."

"Yes."

"That's why I had to say a form, because I couldn't come out medically and say what it is. I'd understand it as a form of leukemia," George explained. In fact, by this point the spirit had told George explicitly that he died of AIDS. Why George withheld that information will be made clear later.

"Yes," Mike replied.

"In any case, he does tell me to let you and your wife know that he is fine and at peace. It's almost as though he was misdiagnosed or mistreated, but not in the physical sense. [It's] as if somebody didn't know what it was, or he thought it was this and treated it for this, or nothing could be done when he realized—"

"That may have happened in the last year and the year before [he passed]," Mike replied.

"It's almost as if there's a form of . . . I don't want to say malpractice. I want to say mistreatment. Somebody's trying to help, but he doesn't understand completely what it is."

"Yes."

George paused again to write frantically the messages he received psychically from the spirit.

"He's a very bright young guy," he continued.

"Very bright," Mike acknowledged.

"Very creative also."

"Extremely creative."

"Did he have something to do with music?"

"No."

"Or an art, in that sense?"

"An art."

"Okay. Because there are musical symbols around him, which could also symbolize creativity or an art. Did your son earn his livelihood through this creativity?"

"Yes, he did."

"Because he says to me that he—"

"He was—"

"No, no, don't tell me!" George insisted, then laughed. "I sound like the Wizard of Oz: 'Don't tell me, don't tell me.' . . . Did he have anything to do with theater?"

"No." Strictly speaking, the correct answer was yes.

"Okay. Then it's a symbol of creativity," George said.

"But he was a type of showman," Mike put in.

"Oh, all right. Because I see a stage in front of you. A theater. And he says his work was theatrical."

"He designed shows," Mike said.

Here George remained characteristically firm about the creative symbols he psychically sensed. However, the communications from the other side in this case could not pinpoint exactly which of the creative arts the spirit was involved in. Other times the messages are more precise. It is one of the enigmas of the psychic-mediumistic process that specificity of detail can vary from one reading to another.

"There was a little bit of a lack of communication between you and him," George continued.

"I would say at times," Mike confirmed.

"Because he apologizes for that."

Mike did not answer but slowly nodded his head.

"I mean, every parent, I'm sure, has a lack of communication with his child, to some degree, but this would stand out."

"Yes."

"And he knows you understand."

"And I do."

"Okay. That's why he wants to let you know that he understands. He knows that you do."

"Yes."

"He could irritate the situation."

"I agree."

"He admits that. He definitely could. A very moody guy."

"On occasion."

"He just apologizes. Let it go. Definitely, between the two parents, I would say you had the greater lack of communication with him."

"That's correct."

"And that's why he's glad you stepped forward, and this is why he singularizes you more so, because the greater lack of communication was between you and him. And now it can be resolved. . . . It's almost as if there was a time when he wasn't talking to you, or he was very cool toward you."

"That's correct."

"And he says to just let it go. He seems to have made good money."

"He did."

"He was definitely established in his work."

"He was."

"Because he certainly knew his business."

"Yes."

"He was very creative, very artistic, and yet he was involved in other things," George said.

"He was," Mike acknowledged.

"You know, maybe that's why I'm getting the confusion about the variation of creativity. Because he seems to have his hand in a number of things."

"He did. He traveled extensively."

"Okay. That's what he meant by theatrical: putting on a show." George laughed, then quipped, "See how poorly my brain functions? . . . Is there a Pete, or Peter?"

"Yes."

"An uncle?"

"Yes, his favorite uncle."

"Do you take the name John?"

"Yes."

"Father?"

"Yes, my wife's father."

"John . . . he had regrets."

"Yes."

"Drinking, and the way he treated people."

"He didn't treat his family well," Mike acknowledged.

"Do you have a daughter?"

"No."

"Did you lose a daughter? Because your son asks about a daughter."

"Well, we had a daughter, yes. She died. She was—"

"Like a miscarriage. A stillborn," George clarified.

"Well, she died before she was born."

"Okay. . . . He asks me to ask you about the daughter. So he's probably trying to tell me to tell you that the sister that passed on is also there with him. Because he says [something] about being very close with his sister. So apparently it's in the next stage of life, not this one. Just remember to pray for him," George concluded. "He's going back."

Interestingly, George never used the word *AIDS* at any time in the reading. However, afterward, George told Mike, Sr., and Peggy privately that their son's spirit asked him not to make public the fact that he had passed on from AIDS. He explained that his parents, especially his father, had difficulty accepting his life-style and illness. "He's had a hard time dealing with my passing," Mike, Jr.'s, spirit said during the reading. George honored the request, and instead said he died from "a form of cancer . . . a rare form . . . [that] affected the blood cells."

"When George spoke to us privately," Mike recalls, "he told us he knew our son had passed from AIDS and how he'd asked George not to say it aloud. Mike was not even forty when he passed on. George was one-hundred-percent accurate. We went back to him for a private reading more than a year later. I felt Mike come into the room; the same feeling I had when George did the reading for us in public. We have the feeling we're still connected to him and that he's there to talk to. The feeling that Mike was there during the reading was so strong that I knew something was happening. I never had such a feeling go through me. You don't expect to see this gift from God in this day and age. Maybe years ago, yes. But not in our own time."

Joe and Mary are in their sixties: the kind of people George is fond of describing as "down to earth," honest and unpretentious. Even after decades of marriage, the pair act like young lovers, so considerate of each other and so clearly in tune that one often completes the other's thoughts.

"After we saw what George did on TV," Joe says, "we thought we should get in touch, through him, with our son, to find out how he was doing." Mary adds, "I wanted to hear that my son was happy, because I knew he wasn't happy in life. Even before he got AIDS, he had a rough life. But when he got AIDS, it got too difficult. He was suffering."

"I knew Tony had AIDS three years before my wife did," Joe admits. "I had taken him to a doctor who diagnosed him as HIV positive. I kept it from Mary until the last six months."

Mary remembers vividly the day Joe told her. "The bottom fell right out of me. I did realize Tony was looking terrible; he was losing weight. How did I take it? I don't know . . ."

"You took it hard," Joe says to her, gently reaching for her hand. "You didn't realize it, but—"

"I didn't believe it."

"It was hard to accept," her husband agrees. "We talked about it with him. As a matter of fact, there was one time when our son sat with Mary, and they discussed his dying. Tony knew I could handle it better; I think he was worried if she could handle his dying. We'd always known Tony was gay. We accepted that. It was hard because of our religion and upbringing, but we did. We couldn't say to our son, 'Leave us, get out, we don't want to know you.' We stayed with him all the way. This is the way it had to be, and we accepted it.

"How does one accept knowing you are going to die?" Joe asks rhetorically. "To me, it would be devastating to say, 'I know I'm going to die.' How do you handle it? My son was strong. To me, he had guts. It's so hard to put into words."

"Once he said that sometimes he was angry with me," Mary remembers. "But I knew why. He was angry with me only because . . ." Her voice trails off.

"Because if she would get mad at him," Joe interjects, "it would make it easier when he died. Then you could tell yourself he was 'bad,' and you were glad he died. But he didn't mean it. He was only doing this to antagonize her to make it easier for her."

"I knew that's what he was doing," Mary says.

"There's one wish that Tony had: to die at home and not go into the hospital," Joe says. "We took care of him to the bitter end."

"He died in his sleep one morning, in his bed. We knew it was coming. We didn't know when."

"Since Tony passed away," says his father, "we've both been in therapy. What he—and we—went through was a terrible experience. We needed to hear that he was okay, that he's happy, that there's a heaven. That's a comfort, to know he's at peace."

In their reading with George, a portion of which is extracted here, Joe and Mary did hear from their son.

"A male close to you passed?" George asked.

"Yes," Joe answered.

"You lost a son."

"Yes."

"He says he knew he was going to pass on."

"Yes."

"He was closer to his mom than to you, his dad," George said.

"Yes," Joe admitted.

"He says he had health problems. It was bad. He tells me he suffered greatly."

"Yes."

"I psychically see horns locking in front of me. It's my symbol that he and you locked horns."

"Yes."

"Your son says he wouldn't wish the disease on his worst enemy. He went through a very difficult time."

"Yes."

"When physical death came, he was ready to let go." Then George asked, "Do you take the name Joe?"

"Yes."

"Your son says there was trouble in his blood."

"Yes."

"The illness spread."

"Yes."

"It's AIDS," George said. Joe confirmed he was correct. "Your son was outgoing, exuberant. Now he's back to his old self on the other side. He gives a sociable, warm, loving vibration."

"Yes," Mary said, "he was like that."

"Was he distant from you for a while?"

"Yes," Joe acknowledged.

"Well, you definitely miss each other."

"Yes, we do."

"He says he knows you loved each other."

"Yes."

"On the other side, he helps others now who've passed on in bitterness," George explained. "Do you take the name Kenneth, or Kenny?"

"Yes. He's a family friend who passed away."

"Ken or Kenny says he knows your son. They're together now on the other side. Do you take the name Jack?" George asked.

"Yes, that's our other son," said Joe.

"Because your son calls out to him. 'Tell Jack you've heard from me,' he says. Your son . . . passed not too long ago."

"That's right. About a year and a half ago."

"Jack is receiving good news?"

"Yes."

"Do you take the name Mike?"

"Yes," Mary answered, "that was my dad."

"He says you called him Poppa, or Pop," George clarified.

"Yes, that's right."

"He says to always continue to pray for your son who's passed on."

"Okay. I do."

"Do you take the name Catherine?"

"Yes, she just passed on," Mary explained.

"Well, she says she's with your son now. They didn't seem to know each other here, but they do in the next stage of life. Your son commends you for some community or social work you're both involved in. Although he says now you're retired."

"Yes. We both do volunteer work for an AIDS hospice."

"Do you take the name Johnny?"

"Yes."

"He's passed on."

"Yes."

"He calls to his wife who's still on the earth."

"Okay."

"He's a nice man. He gives off a nice vibration."

"Yes."

"He knows your son on the other side."

"Yes."

"Do you have a daughter?"

"No."

"A daughter-in-law?"

"Yes."

"Your son speaks of a birth."

"Yes, there's one coming up soon."

"Do you take the name Ralph?"

"Yes. There are two. One is a friend of our son. The other is an uncle who passed away many years ago," Joe explained.

"Your son is very independent on the other side," George said.

"Yes, that's him. He was always like that."

"Who's Bobby?"

"Our son's nephew."

"Because your son is around Bobby like a guardian angel."

"Oh, great!" Mary exclaimed happily.

"Your son says to stop smoking. Do you smoke?" George asked Mary. "He says you're long overdue to stop."

"Yes, I know," she replied softly.

"Do you take the name Mary?"

"Yes, that's me."

"Did your son pass on at home?"

"Yes."

"He thanks you for that."

"Yes."

"Do you take the name Patrick?"

"Yes."

"He's passed on."

"Yes, it's an uncle."

"Well, your son says he's okay and is at peace now. He wants you to know that," George said.

"Oh, good. Thank you."

"He extends the white roses to his brother, to congratulate him on the upcoming birth."

"Okay."

"This is their first child."

"Yes."

"Well, I'm usually wrong about the sex, but I'm feeling it will be a boy," George offered, to which Joe and Mary both laughed. "Your son says to pray for him."

"We do."

"Was someone devout with Saint Bernadette? I see her around you."

"We had a young niece named Bernadette who passed on," Joe answered.

"They're fading now," said George.

After the reading, Joe and Mary reflected on the experience.

"I feel Tony is alive and well in the next stage of life, as George calls it," Joe said. "All the names of family members he mentioned; this blew my mind. George said my mother is taking care of Tony and to not worry about him. That was just fabulous. It made us feel like a million dollars.

"Just hearing they've reached a place where they're at rest and at peace and doing the things they've really wanted to do—what else could there be? They're happy. They miss us, and they're okay, and not to worry. That makes you feel good."

"To know he's not suffering anymore the way he did here with AIDS . . . ," Mary added.

"We'll be reunited someday," Joe said confidently.

"I hope so," Mary added, smiling.

"We'll be together again. Just as he's with all our family now."

"In the meantime," said Mary, "I pray for him every day."

In a reading for a man who'd made a long, lonely journey from the Deep South, George discerned the spirit of his son, a victim of AIDS-related pneumonia. It became clear during the reading that father and son were close.

"Your son says he felt he'd rather pass on than continue to endure the suffering he went through from AIDS," George told the man. "Your son kept things to himself."

"Yes," the subject acknowledged.

"He led a double life, so to speak."

"Yes."

"He was a very private person."

"Yes."

"He wants you to know that contrary to great religious myths, he wasn't sent to hell. He wasn't a bad person."

The father nodded approvingly.

"He calls to his sister and brother. He says he was especially close to a sister."

"Yes, he was."

"But he says there is marital discord—a lack of harmony on the home front between you and his mother."

"Yes."

"He wants you and his mom to patch up some marital differences. He's trying to play peacemaker from the other side."

"Okay."

"Your son says he hopes for harmony on the home front. 'Please try once more, Dad,' he says. And he adds that he knows you're not disappointed in him."

One of the problems George often has is understanding what a spirit means when it describes its relationship to a subject. As we noted in chapter one, on the other side George has learned that we communicate with and know one another purely through emotion. The next reading is one of many in which the attachment the spirit feels for the subject is expressed in terms of the heart.

To a young male, George said, "Someone comes in from the other side and claims he's like a spouse to you. He says there was an emotional relationship, like a marriage."

"Yes," the subject replied in a distinct Texas drawl.

"He says he's still close to you; you feel him around."

"Yes."

"Your spouse comes through and tells you to go on with your life."

"Okay."

"He tells me you worry too much."

"Sure."

"He says to go on with your life."

"Okay."

" 'Know that I'm near you,' your spouse says." George repeated the words he heard psychically.

"Yes."

"Your life is happy, but a bit lonely."

"Yes."

"Well, know that you're certainly not alone."

"Okay."

"Your spouse sends his love to you. He, your dad, your brother, they all go back. Your spouse hands you white roses, symbolically. He thanks you for being good to him prior to his passing. And he sends his love, again, and asks you to pray for him," George concluded.

No matter how long one has to "prepare" for death, we each leave with our own expectations and fears about what awaits us on the other side. In the next two readings, you'll find spirits who passed with different ideas but "came through" with the same conclusion: We don't die.

"A male friend passed," George said.

"Yes," answered a young man in his twenties.

"He passes from a disease."

"Yes."

"He says it's AIDS."

"Yes."

"He passes in a coma."

"Yes," the subject acknowledged.

"He says when he was here he questioned life after death. He was skeptical. But he admits he was curious."

"Yes," said the young man.

"He tells me that his attitude when he was here about life after death was 'We'll find out when it happens.' "

"Yes."

"He says now he is alive in the next stage; it's just not in the physical sense as we understand it. Your friend who passed from AIDS is very adaptable in the next stage. He had AIDS-related pneumonia. Because I'm getting a heaviness in the lungs. It's sympathetic pain."

"Yes, he went through that."

"He was a good person," George said. "There was love and closeness between the two of you."

"Yes."

"On the other side, he helps others with AIDS cross over. He's got to be on the move."

"Yes, that's him."

"He always liked to be involved."

"Yes."

"Do you take the name Matt, or Matthew?"

"Yes. I'm Matt."

"He says he had to come through first and then go back quickly because he's got lots of work to do on the other side."

"Yes, that sounds like him."

"He says he's your guardian angel in business. He's going to do his best to help you with your career here. I see Felix the Cat, the symbol of good news or surprise. It goes back to your career. Your friend says your life is coming back together again. I'm seeing pieces of a puzzle going back together. Your life has to go on. One chapter closes and another opens," George explained.

"Yes, I understand," Matt replied.

"Know that he's okay and that he's at peace. And whether you believe it or not, there is life after death! He survived the transition we call death, he tells me. He calls out to the old crowd. 'Tell them you've heard from me,' he says."

"Yes, he would do that."

"And he calls to a female friend to whom he was close."

"Yes."

"He's very much to the point. He's abrupt. He says to me, 'I'm finished. Don't force me to hold on.' And he goes back."

"Yes. That's the way he was."

In another reading for a young man, George psychically discerned that his lover, Donald, had passed on from AIDS. Donald's spirit told his lover, "Don't worry, you don't have

AIDS." The subject confirmed that he'd tested negative for the disease, then added wistfully, "But I still wish I could die and be with him."

"No, don't do that!" George warned him. "Your friend says absolutely no. Don't come to him that way. It's the back door to the other side." Then George relayed this cryptic message: " 'I'm fulfilling the promise we made before I passed.' "

After the reading, the subject explained to George, "Before my boyfriend Donald died, we made a pact. Donald told me to go to you, George. He said he would come through to let me know he was still with me."

While many survivors make peace across the dimensions, this reading tells the story of a father who could not come to terms with his son's homosexuality and AIDS, or himself, until he followed him over to the other side.

"I'd known Gene was gay since I was eighteen," his sister Kim told us after the reading. "It was a shock, and it was something I had to deal with, but I loved him anyway. Gene and I were very close. The love was there no matter who he was or what he was.

"I kind of pried it out of him that he had AIDS, just like I'd pried it out of him that he was gay. I remember, we were watching a TV movie about a young man who tells his parents that he's gay and has AIDS. Gene didn't want me to watch it. Now, he'd been back and forth to the doctor recently, because he didn't feel well. Then he finally told me he got a test result back that day and said, 'I've got AIDS.'

"I answered, 'Don't joke, Gene; that's not funny.' He said, 'Kim, I'm not joking.'

"From then on, there was no keeping me away from him. I didn't want him watching that movie by himself, so we watched it together. We cried. I remember Rock Hudson being in the headlines at the time because he had AIDS.

"My parents knew Gene was gay, so it wasn't a double hit for them. My mother took it very well; she was with my brother until the end. My dad, on the other hand, didn't take it very well at all. He was afraid of AIDS and his son, on top of it. And then having the hard relationship they had throughout their lives anyway. They weren't very close. So when Dad learned that Gene had AIDS, he kind of backed away from him. They talked, but they didn't want to.

"Dad didn't want to go see Gene because if, God forbid, Gene were to hand Dad a glass to drink out of, or if Gene even just wanted to drive Dad's car, Dad couldn't handle it. Gene didn't need it either, so the best thing was for him to stay away.

"Gene knew I was talking to Dad," Kim went on, "and he wanted him to come visit. I told Gene what Dad said about him having AIDS, and Gene said, 'That rotten so-and-so,' in so many words. The irony was that my dad was very good-looking and much younger-looking than he was. He looked thirty, not fifty. He'd split with his second wife. He had an obsession with women. With the number of sexual partners my father had, he was in just as much a risk group to contract AIDS as Gene was!

"Gene told me that he didn't want Dad around. 'Three years down the road,' he said, 'Dad will get AIDS, and he'll blame it on me. You just go tell him I don't want to see him either.' But in the end, during Gene's last six to eight weeks in the hospital, he called Dad himself. And Dad did come up to see Gene. Dad stayed in a motel, though, because he knew Gene had stayed at my place. Before he went with me to see Gene, he asked, 'What am I going to do if Gene tries to hug me?' I said, 'You can be sure he will.' Gene was an affectionate person. A person with AIDS wants a hug, he deserves a hug.

"When Dad walked in, Gene hadn't seen him in so long, he immediately jumped up and hugged him. Well, from that point on, my father sort of came to the conclusion that he really loved Gene.

"Of course, when Dad went home," she added dryly, "he *bleached himself* before he got into the bathtub. He wouldn't put his toothbrush next to anyone else's, because my stepsisters and stepmother thought my father might have caught AIDS from his son! They were really that uninformed.

"Gene wanted to write a book about AIDS to help other people. He wanted people to know that AIDS could hit anyone. He wanted to clear the ignorance. He went public where he lived, in Virginia, trying to make people aware of AIDS. He helped, affected, and touched a lot of people there before he went. And because he went public, he had tons of friends.

"Gene was twenty-five when he passed away," Kim said. "Dad didn't want to go to the funeral. I guess he was very torn up about it. We laid Gene to rest in Virginia. Dad went to the memorial and to the mountain where we sprinkled Gene's ashes. Dad was very quiet and emotional, but he kept his feelings inside.

"Less than two years later, my father killed himself. He'd lost his upper-management job after twenty-nine years and was forced into retirement. He had all kinds of financial problems. And, like I said, he was obsessed with women. Like George observed in the reading, my Dad was like a little boy who never grew up.

"When George was talking to me during the reading, I sensed my brother's and my dad's personalities. My father used the expression *SOB* all the time. In the reading, George said my father told him he could be a real SOB. He used to always say that and always referred to Gene as a sissy, just as George said.

"Also, like George said, Dad just lost it. Something snapped. He shot his girlfriend Diane four times. The police think she was running away. Then Dad embraced her. It looked like he'd kissed her. And then he shot himself in the head with another gun.

"After Dad's suicide," Kim said, "I cleared out his apartment. I found a photo album with pictures of the AIDS quilt in Washington, D.C.! Dad had taken pictures of the piece of the quilt that was of Gene. In the picture, my father was kneeling down by the quilt, his head in his hands. I guess his girlfriend took the picture. You could see the man was tormented. It was as if he were thinking, 'Did I lose a son? Did I lose something I loved, and I didn't know it?'

"Gene tried to deal as best he could with the fact that he was going to die. I know he wasn't afraid. When he got real sick, he went through denial. Then there was another two-week period of denial toward the very end. He thought he was cured. By then he was suffering with dementia, so he wasn't in his right mind. At the end he sort of hallucinated. He had a false sense of well-being. He said that my late grandmother was there with him; he would quote Scripture we knew he didn't know. That's how we knew our grand-mother *was* there with him.

"He had told me, when he was well, that if there was a way for him to come back, he would." And he did.

"Don't say anything, but I see a double-barrel shotgun in front of you," George told Kim during a group discernment. "I take it to mean that you've been hit 'double barreled.' "

"Yes," she answered.

"Emotionally. I don't mean literally."

"Yes."

"I see Saint Anthony over your head, dressed in black, which is distinctly a sign of a recent death or tragedy."

"Yes."

"The lightning bolt over your head; whatever it is, it must be quite shocking."

"Yes."

"This is like a shocking type of tragedy."

"Yes."

"There's talk of your mom. Your mom's still living?"

"Yes."

"Okay. Because I hear somebody calling to your mother. You've been doing a lot of praying recently, because I keep seeing that symbol around you."

"Yes."

"You must be going through a lot of distress, because I distinctly see Saint Philomena over your head, which would be a sign of extreme distress in a female due to this tragedy. It seems as though one followed the other; one concluded, then another one began."

"Yes."

"Your dad passed on?"

"Yes."

"Because someone here claims to be your father."

"Yes."

"I don't know why, and don't say anything, but can you confirm why he says he needs your prayers desperately?"

"Yes."

"Okay. As long as you understand: He says he needs your prayers *desperately*! And I'm not saying he was an overly religious man, or anything like that. This is somebody who just definitely knows, since he's gone over there, that he needs your prayers. But you obviously have been praying for him, and he's very thankful. He broke the law?" George asked.

"Yes."

"I'll leave it with you, as long as you know what it means. He says he broke the law spiritually. Now, I don't want you to get the wrong impression that he's suffering in hell or anything like that. That's not what I'm heading to. He just knows that what he did was the wrong thing to do. But he knows that God is giving him the chance to make up for it. That's why he needs your prayers so desperately. . . . There must be a suicide involved," George continued, "because I keep seeing the Sacred Heart of Jesus over your head, which is clearly the sign of a suicide. Your father's parents passed on, too."

"Yes."

"Did you lose a son or a brother?"

"Yes. My brother."

"Your father keeps saying, 'There's a son,' and I don't know if he means his son or yours. Your father just 'lost it'?"

"Yes."

"I mean on the earth. He just totally loses it. I'm not saying he's a mental case, but I feel as if I'm having a mental breakdown. I don't mean this literally, but it's as if he goes in and out of his mind. This is why everybody else's relatives in the room just kind of stood aside [on the other side] to let him come in first, because he needs it. He desperately needs to come through. I hope I'm right." Suddenly George asked Kim, "Are you a Christian?"

"I was raised that way."

"Because he asks you to pray to the Sacred Heart of Jesus for him. Again, I'm not saying he's overly religious. I'm not trying to push religion. It's a spiritual thing. Your father took his own life?"

"Yes."

"Your brother passed before him."

"Yes."

"He says your brother tried to help him over there, but he's got to do ninety-eight percent of the work himself. He was very distraught over your brother's passing."

"I think so . . ."

"Maybe he didn't show it, but he goes to pieces. I would say he and your brother were not that close, because there's a lack of communication on the earth. Your father wouldn't let himself be close to your brother—not the other way around. Your brother passes on, and there's a combination of angry and guilty feelings. He kind of abandoned your brother, and yet he didn't want to. There's this terrible conflict of feelings. Your father feels he could have been closer to you also. Is that true? Because he apologizes to you for a lack of communication. He's capable of being a real SOB."

"Yes."

"That's the best way I can describe it. He tells me he knows he's not allowed to use the words [on the other side], but he apologizes to you also. He says he could have been a better husband. You know, he feels he could have been closer to his children. Was he inclined to show favoritism?"

"Yes."

"He apologizes for that. He really did a number on himself on earth: his passing, taking his own life. He's doing a number on himself, and he's having a time healing himself over there—just as much as he had a time here on earth. He's having the biggest problem dealing with himself. That's the biggest struggle. Your brother just took him as he was and has basically forgiven him for a lack of communication."

Kim quietly nodded her acknowledgment.

"Your brother and father were not speaking? If they were, they were very reserved. But still your father lost his son. It still shakes him up. . . . It's funny: It seems as though they were closer, maybe when he was a child. It seems years ago they were closer, and then the whole relationship was just shot to pieces, more or less. Your brother passed from health trouble?"

"Yes."

"He knew he was going to go."

"Yes."

"It's as if he subconsciously prepared himself that it was just a matter of time. . . . He took care of himself?"

"Yes."

"He definitely blesses you for being so good to him prior to his passing. You and he seemed to have a nice rapport. There was definitely a close relationship, and he doesn't want you to think that he's dead. He says he's very much alive. Definitely continue to pray for him. He's a very gentle soul."

"Yes."

"Was he fond of nature?"

"Yes."

"He's artistic. He's a very cultured person, very good with nature. A very gentle, caring human being. It's funny: your father couldn't deal with that."

"No, he couldn't."

"There's a conflict because of this. Your father's more down-to-earth; kind of macho, in a way."

"In a way . . ."

"It's almost as though he wanted his son to be the all-star football player, and he turned out the opposite. That just blew his mind; he couldn't deal with that."

"Yes."

"It's almost that he looked upon your brother a little bit like a sissy, because he wasn't a macho man."

"Yes."

"Your father have a very, very bad temper?"

"Yes."

"His temper did him in, he says."

"Yes."

"Because he says he has a very violent temper. Did he drink?"

"No."

"Okay. Then it's just my symbol of a bad temper. Did your brother live with you?"

"He was nearby."

"Was he *very* nearby? Because he thanks you for being so good to him prior to his passing. He's very fond of animals."

"Yes."

"There are animals around him over there. I feel as if I'm seeing someone in the woods," George said. "I don't mean this as a put-down to him, because your father says he was kind of 'sissyish.' I keep seeing scenes out of the classic *Snow White,* where she's out in the woods among all the animals. He doesn't like human beings as much as he likes animals."

Kim chuckled. "Can you blame him?" George joked. "He says there are lots of animals over there that he takes care of.

He's adjusted, but he's still being rehabilitated. You know, he had a rough time here on earth both emotionally and physically."

"Yes."

"He's still 'on holiday,' as they put it over there, where they're letting him relax and adjust according to what he needs. Your father says, for the time being, he's in the colder levels. He put himself there, though. Again, he says he 'broke the law very badly.' I don't know how he means everything, so let me just go with it. I don't want to sound like a Fundamentalist. I'm not telling you he's condemned to hell or anything. What I'm saying is that hell is not a hot spot over there; it's a cold spot. He's in those colder levels until he deals with himself—which he knows. But he has the opportunity to do it at his own pace. That's why he asks that you pray to Jesus for him frequently. He's saying to pray to rescue him and bring him deeper into the light. Your father shot himself."

"Yes."

"I'm [psychically] hearing gunshots go off in the room. . . . Your brother has come to your father's assistance over there a number of times, but he says, again, that your father has to find his own way. Did your father have an argument with someone prior to his passing?"

"Yes."

"A family member or a friend?"

"A friend."

"Somebody he knows pretty well. Was there a business failing?"

"Yes."

"Because there's a business argument or business failing, plus everything was piling up on your father. I feel as if there's an anvil on my shoulders. I'm weighed down with stress."

"Yes."

"It seems . . . there's a big argument and a falling-out of friendship. There's definitely a big gap in communication."

"Yes."

"Your father committed murder?" George asked, surprised at what he was hearing.

"Yes," the woman answered.

"Because he claims he shoots the other person."

"Yes."

"Did he shoot the other person, then kill himself?"

"Yes."

"Okay. Were they romantically involved?"

"Yes."

"He's saying they're 'partners,' and I took it like business partners. Now I know what he means: romantic partners. Your father abandoned your mother?"

"Yes, a little."

"Yeah, he feels he did, emotionally. Was this basically like his girlfriend?"

"Yes."

"Because he says he shoots her. . . . Then he took his own life. That's why he says he breaks the law so severely. It's double. He takes somebody else's life as well as his own. Boy, he had some temper! When he got going, duck!"

"Yes."

"It's funny: It's like they loved each other, but too power-fully, because it's abnormal love. It's too overwhelming. His girlfriend is there also, and she states that their love is too possessive. 'It's just the wrong way to love.' She tried coming to his assistance, but again, the biggest problem in his life was himself. It's funny: all in all, it's not like he's a bad person. He just didn't know how to handle himself. He's sensitive, but he doesn't know how to express it."

George continued writing, then returned to the spirit of Gene.

"Your brother passes from an illness in the blood."

"Yes."

"He says that he passed on from AIDS."

"Yes."

"Because I'm feeling as if I have pneumonia. He says that he's trying to help both of them over there. Your brother is a very caring individual—very compassionate and caring in the next life. Your dad is overcoming himself. So they ask that you pray for him daily and even light a candle in church and consecrate him to the Sacred Heart of Jesus. You and he might have had a lack of communication, but he's still your dad. It's as if he's a boy trapped in a man's body. That's what I feel like: I'm dealing with a big teenager. It's his way or no way. He was inclined to react too quickly with a bad temper, and he didn't think about the consequences of what he was doing. I feel that he shoots the girlfriend and then realizes what he's done. 'Now what am I going to do? There's no way out except to kill myself.' So he shoots himself. Your brother was not the happiest person in the world."

"Right."

"It seems he likes it better there. You know, he's really not for this world. That's why I say he's happier there. I'm seeing the artist Vincent Van Gogh. . . . He did make the most of this plane, but he still likes it better in the next stage. He's much happier there. He just wants to let you know that he's at peace. . . . He doesn't mind being alone. He has his own 'little mansion' over there."

That description brought a smile to his sister's face.

"You know, he can be on his own. Not that he's not giving. He's willing to give and to serve on his own course, the course that's best for him. Definitely pray for him also. Continue to keep your father in mind first and his girlfriend as well. With your father, mostly, because he's really put himself in a bad state. He says God is extending him the grace to come through, so he can kind of clear his conscience. He's trying to understand himself. . . . Do you take the name Lee, passed on?" George then asked.

"Living," she corrected.

"I heard your brother say 'Lee.' Are they friends?"

"Yes."

"He's calling out to him. I don't know. Maybe he wants to let him know he's all right. Tell Lee you've heard from him. I'll just let it go. Does the name David mean anything?"

"Yes."

"Passed on?"

"No."

"Your brother knows him also."

"Yes."

"Again, maybe another friend he knows. He calls out. Were they involved at the time he passed?"

"I don't know."

"There seems to have been some romantic involvement at one time, because he says, 'Tell David you have heard from me' and ask him to pray for him. . . . Do you take the name Rick, or Ricky?"

"Yes."

"Living also?"

"Yes."

"Again, it's somebody he knows. Your dad knows him, too."

"Yes."

"Why does your father apologize to Rick? Make sense?"

"Yes."

"I'll leave it with you. Your brother calls to Rick, but not as profoundly. Then all of a sudden your father steps forward and says, 'Tell Rick that I apologize.' He cheated him? I don't know how he means that. . . . I would say that within the family, he was closer to you."

"Yes."

"Because, definitely, it's as though you and he never parted. Out of both parents, he was closer to your mother. He says, 'Tell Mom that you've heard from me.' . . . Pray that [your father] finds peace and forgives himself; that he overcomes his own ego, his own struggle. That's the greatest of all sins: your own ego."

George paused momentarily, then continued.

"Your brother goes in his sleep."

"Yes," Kim replied.

"It seems as though he just falls asleep and lets go, because he says he has a very peaceful passing. He wakes up in the next stage. The friend, David, they seem to have been good friends. He was with him until the end. He emotionally supported him. Whether he was there or not, he knows he was there. That's why he expresses the thanks and says to pray for him. Do you take the name Jack?"

"Yes."

"Passed on?"

"No."

"Again, somebody your brother knows."

"Yes."

"Your dad knows him also. Again, your father apologizes to him. There must be a reason; again, the feeling that I've been cheated. 'Tell Jack you've heard from me.' He calls out to him also. . . . Who's Danny?"

"He's my son," Kim said.

"Passed on?"

"No."

"Oh, I heard your brother call to Danny," George explained. "Were they that close?"

"Yes."

"Your brother looked upon him as a son, almost. So he says that as soon as he's finished adjusting, he's going to ask if he can be like a guardian angel [to Danny]. . . . Did you know your father's girlfriend?" George asked.

"A little bit."

"She calls out for prayers also."

"Okay."

"I think with that they're going to step aside, because your brother says other people are trying to get through now. Definitely pray for him continually, as he instructed. He calls again to your mother. Your brother just says he's okay. Do you take the name Don?"

"No."

"Ron?"

"Yes."

"Ron—a friend? Your brother would know him."

"Yes."

"It just seems that he's calling out. He says his friends were very supportive in the last years. Your father says they have to go back now. The first thing they have to adjust to [on the other side] is obedience. He didn't do that here either. They're going back. Pray for them, especially your dad. Again, your brother sends his love."

The year before Gene died, he wrote a poem, which was read at his memorial service. Here is a portion of it:

This world, another world, or up there somewhere,
I still exist, and with love and happiness live.
Take time to know the real story.
Take time to know your soul, and you will find you
And God are as one, and always have been.
I carried my mother's love, my father's name, and my
Family's honor.
God bless you, 'til we speak again.

Questions Answered

"We never get used to death, we are never ready for it," said a minister at a funeral service. "But in life there are no safe places." Those who come to George often know that all too well.

Any loved one's death is painful to handle. But when that passing is shrouded in mystery, or when survivors doubt the "official story" of what happened, grief lingers, and they are left emotionally paralyzed, unable to move forward with their lives. As the following reading attests, often the only person who knows the whole truth is the victim.

One week to the day past his twentieth birthday, Greg was returning home from visiting his grandparents. He called his parents before he left to say he was on the way. His father, Ron, looked at the clock; it was 8:30 P.M. "The weekend that Greg was killed was excruciating for me," he recalls. "That entire weekend I just kept praying, God, please bring him home to me. I had some sort of premonition that something was going to happen to him."

A short time after Greg left his grandparents' house, a couple of hours' drive away, they heard sirens wailing by. Greg's grandfather remarked to his wife, concerned, "I hope that's not Greg." Then dismissing the thought as ridiculous, he and his wife left to meet friends. On their way, they came to a cordoned-off intersection surrounded by emergency vehicles. Police detoured traffic around the accident scene. Unbeknownst to the elderly couple the car they saw consumed in flames contained their grandson. Though they continued to their meeting, Greg's grandfather could not shake what he later described as a "funny feeling."

On their way back home that night, Greg's grandparents noticed the accident scene still cordoned off. Back in his house, Greg's grandfather called his son and daughter-in-law to ask if Greg was home yet. It was 10:15.

"No, Dad. It could take him a couple of hours," Greg's mother answered, unconcerned. Still, Greg's grandfather sensed something was wrong and returned to the wrecked car. After he identified himself, a police officer confirmed that the demolished car was registered to Greg's mother and that the body of the driver, a young male, was still trapped in the wreckage, burned beyond recognition. It was Greg. When the gas tank ruptured in a collision, the car had burst into flames.

"Grief isn't even a strong enough word to describe what we felt," says Greg's father. "It was complete emotional incapacitation; agony, with lumps in our throats and tightness in our chests; the most severe of human experiences. It's what only a parent who has lost a child can comprehend."

Even though Greg's accident appeared to be simply that, Ron was troubled by questions and strongly suspected that foul play may have been involved. He simply could not believe that Greg, an unusually mature and sensible young man, drove carelessly or in any way caused the accident. In Ron's mind there *had* to be more to it. It's indicative of our deceased loved ones' concern for us that one of the first pieces of information Greg relayed to his father through George concerned the true cause of his death.

"A male close to you passed over," George said to Ron during a group discernment. "There are two generations? Seems as though one's older. One's younger. There's a young male around you. A young male close to you passed over."

"Yes," Ron answered.

"He says, 'Put it to rest.' Do you understand what he means?"

"I think so."

"I'll just leave it with you. . . . I keep seeing Sherlock Holmes in front of you. You may be trying to make a mystery out of it, and it's not. It's as though you're reading into it."

"Correct. We're looking for the answer," Ron admitted.

"He keeps trying to tell me to block it out, to be at peace about it. He says he didn't suffer prior to his passing."

"Okay. Thank you."

"Is he a very direct type of guy?" George asked. "He doesn't want me to question him. He says to just say what I'm hearing. 'Tell them I didn't suffer before I passed on.' He doesn't have patience with me."

"That's him," Ron agreed.

"He seems very anxious, and he knows what he's talking about. Now, this could be symbolic, so just say yes or no: Is his passing an accident?"

"Yes."

"He does not pass from a health problem."

"No."

"He says his passing is an accident. He emphatically states that."

"Right."

"He's also trying to get me away from health trouble. Okay, okay. I won't argue with this guy! He also apologizes for the way he passed on. Does that make sense?"

"Okay, son."

"Okay, so long as you understand."

"Yes."

"You do pray for him. I wouldn't say you're overly religious, and neither is he, but he's thankful because he knows it's of value. And he keeps saying to continue praying for him," George said.

"Okay."

"He doesn't waste time, true? He has no time to waste."

"Right."

"Probably that's why they let him in first. They figured it was easier and safer," George explained with a smile. "Again, this could be symbolic, so just say yes or no. A vehicle involved in his passing?"

"Correct."

"Okay. Because that could also symbolize an accident. That's why I have to be careful how I interpret [psychic symbols]. Did he go to sleep? It looks as though he falls asleep. Did he fall asleep at the wheel?"

"That's what we want to know," Ron said.

"It looks as though I'm falling asleep. He goes off the road, yes? It seems he loses control of the vehicle, and I feel as if I'm going off the road. I'm losing control of the car."

"Oh, okay."

"He falls asleep. And I think you find it hard to believe, because I'm dealing with a very levelheaded guy."

"Correct."

"That's why he says you're not at peace about it, because this could not have happened to 'our son.' He's not a dope. . . . As he puts it philosophically, 'Even the best of swimmers drown.' "

"Okay. That has meaning, too."

"He's not far from home."

"Right."

"That's why it looked so strange. He's almost around the corner. Just about."

"Yes."

"Your son was at the height of his life."

"Yes."

"I mean, he could have still gone further. But he's got his act together."

"Yes."

"I feel I'm going places. I'm achieving."

"Correct."

"He was a little mad at first when he went over [to the other side]. It's like, 'Here I am at the height of my life, and now I'm dead.' But he says it doesn't matter. He realizes his life is just going on. He was resentful at first. And your grandfather kind of calmed him down, because he was inclined to be a little high-spirited," George explained. "He told him, 'Why do you feel cut short? You're not cheated. You're still alive. What are you complaining about?' "

"Okay."

"And so he's fine now. Was he married?"

"No," Ron replied.

"Seeing someone at the time?" George asked, confused.

"Yes."

"Was he close to marrying?"

"Yes."

"Because he keeps talking about the fact that he's married. Emotionally he probably was; literally he wasn't."

"Correct."

"Because he calls out to his fiancée. Tell her you've heard from him and that he's okay."

"Okay."

"He also seemed to be successful with his job. I'm sure he had his ups and downs, but he basically is like the perfect son."

"Yes, that's correct."

"Somebody to be proud of."

"Conscientious."

"Yes."

"His faults are so trivial, you know. They're lovable faults."

"Yes."

"Financially he seems to have been doing well."

"Yes."

"He's making you proud of him."

"Yes."

"Because he says in the next stage of life he's still an achiever. He's still somebody who goes places. And that's the thing: You might have been suspicious that maybe there was foul play or something. He says he falls asleep. Again, he makes that statement, 'Even the best swimmers can drown.' "

"Okay, I've got you, son."

"He keeps saying that he falls asleep, and that's it. He seems so emphatic about it, as if he knows that you're wondering if there's more to his death than meets the eye. And this is his way of putting you at peace. He keeps stating, 'Put it at peace. Put it at peace.' Unless he looks younger, was he in his twenties?"

"No, just twenty," Ron answered.

"I feel as though I'm dealing with someone who's more grown-up."

"Absolutely. That's correct."

"He very athletic?"

"Absolutely."

"Because I feel—I can't say I see him clearly—but I feel somebody in front of me that's obviously more athletic looking than I definitely am."

"Correct. Absolutely."

"You have other children."

"Yes."

"Is he your oldest?"

"Correct."

"I'm trying to figure out why he's singularizing himself as the son. Now I know why: He's the eldest. Your first child. That's why he says it hits home so much more. You've lost your eldest son."

"Yes."

"Does the name Greg mean anything?" asked George.

"That's his name!" Ron exclaimed.

"Oh, that's who you're hearing from. Did someone call him Greggy?"

"Yes."

"Which he doesn't like," George added.

"I guess not."

"It's as if somebody might have years ago, because I heard him say, 'Don't call me Greggy.' "

"Okay."

"Did he work in sales?"

"Yes."

"Because it seems as though he can acquire cash. He knows how to get blood from a stone, as they say. He's very good with handling finances."

"Excellent. Yes."

"Was he on a sports team?"

"He was."

"Was he a swimmer or something?"

"He swam," Ron verified. This also explained Greg's earlier statement, "Even the best of swimmers drown."

"Not professionally, but he was probably good at it. . . . I'm not trying to sound corny, but was he 'Daddy's boy'?"

"Yes," said Ron in a voice choked with emotion.

"Not that he's accusing you of favoritism," George added.

"He knows how much he meant to me."

"That's what I'm getting at. He kind of knows, 'I'm Daddy's boy.' "

"Oh, yes."

"Under the circumstances, such as this, he doesn't think there's anything corny about saying that."

"No, no, it's not corny."

"He knows that you both love him, and the feeling is

mutual, because he's a very loving, giving individual,'' George said to Ron and his wife.

"You've got it."

"He says to definitely tell all the family you've heard from him and he's okay. And certainly if this young man were alive, he'd get his point across. He comes on like gangbusters behind me. He definitely is going to let me know he's here in the room."

"Yes."

"That's why, as I said, I'm not surprised he's coming in first," George said.

"Very assertive," Ron confirmed.

"He probably 'salesmanned' his way up to the front of the line [over there]," George joked.

"He would," returned Ron, smiling. "Some things never change."

"He's a sharp talker, very shrewd. He says he's very busy in the next stage. As much as he wants you to hear from him, he wants to settle the score. His attitude is, like, 'I'm on a coffee break. I've got to hurry up, because I've got things to do over here.' He's always got ten things going at once. Was he going to school at the time [of his death]?"

"Correct."

"He says he's going to school, again, over there. He says, 'I'm going to school here, and I have a job here. These are things I do.' He's a very giving person."

"Oh, yes."

"And the thing is, that's what he does over there. He helps. He's very good with people his own age. He helps young people over there. And he says, 'You name the job, [I'm] involved in it.' He definitely has ants in his pants."

"This is true."

"As he did here. . . . He did have a lot of jealousy around him. Maybe from a job or such. Not that anybody would have done harm to him, but it's just that you know how people are. It was there," George said.

"It could be," Ron answered.

"Because there's no jealousy there [on the other side]. Everybody is happy for what you can achieve, and there's an equal balance in God's world, more or less. It's not like here, where people resent you getting ahead," George explained.

"Yes."

"He says when he got over there, he was living with some-one whom you called 'Pop' before. He says now he's on his own. He's very independent."

"That's funny," Ron interjected.

"It's like he went to visit him [Pop] on vacation and stayed with him to learn the 'new country,' and now, 'Okay, I'm on my own.'"

"Okay."

"He's crazy about cars?"

"Yes."

"He says he does miss cars over there a little bit. He hasn't gotten over that yet. But he's learning to. There are certain things you can create realities for. But there are more impor-tant things to do. Do you still have contact with his fiancée?"

"Yes."

"He keeps calling to her. I get the feeling of him calling out to her, 'Tell her you've heard from me,' and that he sends his love."

"Okay."

"The name Max or Mike mean anything at all?" George asked.

"Dog," Ron said.

"Passed on?"

"No."

"I heard him call out to Max. Is that your family pet?"

"No. I know whose pet it is."

"Was he close with the animal?"

"Yes."

"He just said, 'How's Max?' Now, you're sure this pet's not passed over."

"Not as far as we know."

"Then I'll take it that he must be calling out to it."

"Okay."

"He holds the white roses to himself, as a symbol of peace. . . . That he's okay. You've been dreaming about him," George observed.

"Yes."

"He says he keeps coming in dreams. He's trying to let you know he's all right. . . . You're always going to miss him, and you're always going to experience this tragedy. But just know that your grief is temporary; that someday you will be together with him again."

"Okay," Ron said softly.

"It's not in the near future, though, as he says." George laughed. "He definitely has a dry sense of humor."

"Yes, exactly."

"When he said to tell you it's not in the near future, he said it kind of sarcastically, but kidding."

"That's for me. That's for me," Ron replied excitedly. Later in the reading Ron interjected, "He knows I have some other questions."

"But basically, again," said George, "he's all right and says just be at peace. And *don't* read into his death. He says it's what he claims. Believe me, he gives the impression that he was as shocked as you were. Did he hit the windshield or something? Did he strike his head?"

"Probably. Maybe."

"I feel a hit to the head. It seems to have been a clean strike [from] whatever injury he sustained."

"Correct."

"Because it kills him immediately," George said.

"Yes," Ron responded, no doubt relieved to hear Greg was unconscious while he was burning.

"He loves to talk, yes?"

"Yes."

"Because he says, 'I've got to go now, because there are people behind me starting to get impatient.' "

Both Ron and his wife smiled.

" 'I'll share it with you. I'll tell it to you.' His attitude is now that he's achieved over there. He's so glad God has given him the chance to share it with you, what he's achieved in the next stage."

"All right."

"To quote you before. 'Some things never change.' And he says that's right in his case—it's never changed. . . . Now, this could be symbolic: Are you saying the rosary for him?"

Ron's wife, mostly silent throughout the reading, said, "Yes, I do."

"Oh, okay. Because he's holding white rosary beads out between the two of you, and that's a sign that you're saying it for him. And if you're not Catholic, that's my sign of constant prayer. So I had to be careful how I interpreted it," George explained.

"I have to admit he came through like a bolt of lightning. Sharp. Precise. Clear. It's as if I were having a conversation with him in the room, and he was telling me all about himself," George concluded.

Today Ron recalls, "In the reading, George said he saw Sherlock Holmes in front of me, and my son said I'm trying to read things into his accident. I had been agonizing almost to the point of becoming seriously ill, because I *had* to find the cause of the accident. It was just inconceivable to me that he would be careless at the wheel. People were telling me to put it aside. 'Ron, you're destroying yourself.' I'd answer, 'That's my option.'

"I have not prayed the rosary in perhaps fifteen or twenty years," Ron says. "The Monday that we went to George, I was walking around the house, and I said to my son, 'Greg, if you get a chance, try letting us know whether to keep up the rosary.'

"Now, when George said that my son is holding out the white rosary beads between us, I instantly knew that my wife was also praying the rosary. And then my son said in the reading that it wouldn't hurt if I did it more often. And I have.

"I feel at times like we're almost healed. We will always have this missing, yes. But we know where Greg is. We know that he is at peace and okay. I know that whenever I want to talk to my son, whenever I want to express my love for him, all I have to do is say the rosary. It's like a father wants to give his child a gift. I can do this every day, and I pray that God gives him whatever spiritual benefit God knows he needs most, and that He elevates him as close as possible to Him. That is my prayer."

To Ron and his wife, Greg brought happy news and relieved them of nagging doubts. Sadly, this is not the case for everyone George reads. As the following three readings demonstrate, spirits sometimes impart information that is troubling or shocking. These excerpts also show some of the frustrating limitations to communications between this dimension and the next.

•　　•　　•

"You've lost a daughter," George said to two women, one middle-aged, one younger.

"It was my daughter-in-law who passed," the older woman answered.

"She comes through like a daughter. You were very close."

"Yes."

"She passed tragically."

"Yes."

"It's not accidental. Someone is to blame."

"Yes."

"There is suspicion that she was murdered."

"Yes."

"She says she doesn't blame anyone. She was murdered at home."

"Yes she was."

"Someone broke in, she tells me, but it doesn't look like a forced entry."

"That's right."

"It happened in daylight, during the day."

"Yes, it happened in the morning," the woman explained.

"Was there a business failing?" George asked.

"Yes."

"It's as if whoever did this was out to get her husband, your son."

"Yes."

"There were threatening phone calls."

"Yes."

"The person responsible is the man connected with your son's business failing."

"Yes."

"There were signs of a struggle."

"Yes."

"There's a weapon involved."

"Yes."

"I psychically hear gunshots. A gun is involved."

"Yes."

"Your daughter-in-law was trapped, restricted. She couldn't get away."

"Yes."

"She was alone at the time."

"Yes."

"There were no witnesses."

"That's correct."

"She says, from the other side, 'It's the man with the business failing.' He came for your son, but she was in the wrong place at the wrong time."

"Yes."

"Are you on bad terms with your son?"

"No."

"Because it feels as if he's at a distance. It feels as if he's away," George said, obviously confused.

"Yes, he's in prison," the woman answered.

"He's being blamed for her death."

"Yes."

"She sends her love to him. You have contact with him."

"Yes."

"She says her husband is not guilty."

"We agree."

"Your son had no alibi."

"That's correct, but there was no evidence against him."

"The problem for your son is that there was no sign of forced entry."

"Yes."

"Your daughter-in-law says, again, 'Your son is innocent.' "

"Yes, that's what we thought."

"She calls to her children."

"Yes."

"She's asking you to pray for her—and your son."

"Okay."

"I'm seeing the name Gloria, which is my symbol of good news ahead. Do you take the name Matt or Matthew? She's calling to him."

"Yes, her brother, Matt."

"They were close, she says."

"Yes."

"She says everyone knows your son is innocent—except the system."

"Exactly, my son is serving a long prison sentence."

"Your daughter-in-law is emphatic that your son is innocent. She's frustrated on the other side because there's only so much she can do."

Although George and other psychics are frequently called upon by law-enforcement officials to help solve crimes, the word of a psychic holds no legal weight in court. In a case such as this, one can't help but wonder why the murdered woman couldn't bring forth some information that would lead police to her killer and free her husband: a key piece of evidence, perhaps. George often stresses that those on the other side do not always have all the answers. But why not? It seems that there are limitations to what they know, and it should be remembered, probably countless restrictions on how effectively what they do know can be communicated through George. Countless times even George has wished it could be otherwise.

To say that George never knows what to expect is an understatement. Rita, a woman in her early forties, came to him seeking answers to some critical questions. She grew up on Long Island, New York, where her best friend was a boy named Tom. Because she'd been abandoned by her own father as a toddler, she came to view Tom's father, Joe, as her own. Rita's and Tom's mothers were also best friends. When anyone asks Rita how long she and Tom have been friends, she replies, "Since the stroller." When Tom's son, Carl, was born, Rita was honored to be named his godmother.

After Tom's parents retired to a small Florida town ten years ago, and Tom moved west, the family lost touch with Rita. Through friends in the old neighborhood she heard of Tom's problems: a series of failed businesses, his wife's accidental death. Most shocking were allegations of Tom's involvement in a criminal enterprise. However, nothing could top Rita's shock and depression when she learned that Tom's parents had been brutally slain in their home—and that Tom was the prime suspect.

After months of severe depression, Rita took up a friend's suggestion that she visit George. As she later revealed, she went hoping to hear that the police were wrong. Although she was able to find out some answers, others eluded George, in part because Rita couldn't confirm certain information.

"We'll start with this," George said to Rita. "Male close to you pass on? This situation have anything to do with the death of a male?"

"Yes," she said quietly.

"Because since you walked in the room, while we were talking, I definitely feel a male presence . . . who is not family. He says he's not family but he *is* family." George looked puzzled. "And he states that he's right behind you, and it's like he was listening to our conversation. Now, this is someone you knew well—a close friend. He pass recently?"

"Yes."

"Because he hasn't been there long. Funny guy? He's got a nice sense of humor. A cynic? He's like Missouri, the Show-Me State; he's got this kind of an attitude. He's openminded, though."

After a few moments of silence, George shrugged and said to the woman, "Maybe I'd better not interpret this: He thanks you for being good to him prior to his passing. Does that make sense? Maybe just being a good friend or whatever; I didn't want to say you took care of him. I don't know how he means it, so I'll let it go. . . . He pass on in the last year?" George asked.

"Yes."

"Yeah, because I said 'the last year,' and as soon as I did, he said, 'No, no, no, *this* year, this year.' He knew he was going to pass on?"

"No."

"Funny, he says in the back of his mind he knew he was going to pass on. I'll leave it with you. His passing was sudden?"

"Yes."

George snapped his fingers. "Like that? He's one moment to the next. He's here"—*snap!*—"he's there." He kept scratching on his tablet. "Did you pray for him?"

"Yes."

"Because he does thank you for it. He's not holding his breath, though—that's a wisecrack from him. . . . Just say yes or no to this: Was his passing accidental? Or did it have the suddenness of an accident?"

"Sudden, yes," Rita answered, shifting uncomfortably in her seat.

"Was he having trouble with his chest?"

"Yes."

"Anything bother his heart? Even like the way he passed on? Affected the heart, or anything like this? Must mean something, because there's a pulling at the heart. . . . He not believe in life after death? Well, let's just say his attitude was 'I'll find out when it happens.'"

"Yes."

"He's saying that he's alive, there *is* life after death, it's been proven to him. Did you work together? Maybe not in a normal job, but in another line? Because there's work contact. Maybe not nine-to-five contact, but that's there. . . . Did he have trouble with his head?"

"Yes."

"Internally? Something burst in the head?"

"No."

"Was it something in his head that contributed to his passing?"

"Yes."

"That must be what he means," said George, touching the back of his head, "because he tells me, 'Stay where you are.' Was there something pressing within the head? Did he have a health problem in the head, like a tumor? It's like a pressure in the head . . ."

"Yes," the woman replied, "he did have a health problem with his head prior to his demise."

"All right, the thing is, he might be giving me that just so I know the reason he passed on was from up here." Again George indicated the back of his skull. "That's all I have to know. Did he have trouble with his eyesight?"

"Yes."

"The pressure from up here could cause problems in other places. He lived with this?"

"Yes."

"Because that's the thing. I don't know if he knew it was there or not. I don't know. He lived with it, he tells me. But definitely the pressure up there seems to be making itself known." George looked up with a start. "Something snaps?" he asked. "I mean, I'm going nuts, it's a feeling of"—he snapped his fingers again—"popping again. As soon as I realize what it is, I'll understand what he's trying to tell me. Did this affect his senses at all? Because he's telling me that on the other side he's back to his old self; he's fine. There must be a reason why he says that. Was he young when he passed?"

"No."

"How old?"

"Mid-seventies."

George seemed very surprised. "Was he very young at heart?"

"Yes."

"Oh, okay. If I didn't know better, I'd think this guy was about forty. He seems very young at heart. . . . Was he married? His wife passed over? Before him?"

"No." Obviously Rita misinterpreted George's question, because he replied, "Well, he claims his wife is there with him. The two of them are together. They lived near you?"

"Yes and no," Rita said.

"They were neighbors."

"Yes. At one time."

"Okay, because he claims, 'We're neighbors.' He does have a peaceful passing—"

"No," she said emphatically.

"No," George insisted, "he says he does. He says, 'It wasn't as bad as it looked; it was a peaceful passing.' Once he had let go, he let go. He shows that he passed peacefully. Did anything hit his head? Because I just felt as if I got hit in the head!"

"Yes."

"All right, he might have had a problem up here internally. But now I feel, like, a hit to the head, because he keeps touching the top of the head. Was he hit by someone?"

"Yes."

"It feels as if someone's hitting me on the head. Was he kind of at the wrong place at the wrong time?"

"Yes," Rita answered ruefully, "you'd have to say that."

"He knows the person that hit him."

"I don't know . . ."

"Was he 'technically' murdered?"

"Yes."

"Because he says that technically he's murdered; we would call it that. But he's very forgiving, like, 'They didn't mean to do this, it just happened.' Was he held or trapped or something?"

"Not that I know of."

George sighed. Piecing together the clues of this reading was going to be particularly difficult. Rita knew few details of this vicious crime, only what she'd read or seen in the local media and the few facts she could pry from police. So she could not corroborate much of the information George was receiving from the deceased's spirit.

"It feels as though he was restricted," George went on. "He was killed by a blow to the head; that's what he says. He was killed by a striking, a hit to the head. This happened in his home."

"Yes."

"They arrest anybody yet?"

"Yes."

"And it *is* somebody he knows."

"Yes."

"Okay, because he keeps claiming he knows who's done this to him, in the sense that it's not a stranger on the street. Was the person who struck him family?" George asked, incredulous.

"Yes."

"Okay, yes, because he says he or she is family, and that's why I'm a little taken aback. Is this person family by blood?"

"Yes."

"Could there have been more than one person?"

"That's a possibility," she conceded.

"You know, one might have done the act, but somebody else knew or was around or something; it seems to be more than one person. Yeah, he was murdered by his own blood. He's shocked because he was murdered by his own blood. Does that make sense?"

"Yes."

"Do you believe he was murdered by somebody in his own family?"

"Yes."

"Now, the circumstances of the hit: Was it basically an act of violence or in anger?"

"I don't know."

"Technically he was murdered, but he tells me it was 'like an accident.' "

"I can understand that."

"Let's say he's not as hard on the person as maybe the law would be," George said. "He says he's forgiven. He seems nice, pretty easygoing."

"Yes."

"Because he says that over there there's no place for anger and revenge, and he says—" Suddenly George stopped moving his pen. "Wait a minute. There seems to be a male around him, a male at the time. A male do the hitting?"

"Yes."

"It's definitely a male who commits the act of violence." Referring to the murder victim, George reiterated, "He's a very easygoing man. Again, he forgives. He says there's no place for hatred over there. 'You can't fit in over here if you have those types of feelings. On the earth you can fit in, you can survive; here you can't. If you don't have the purity or the oneness of God, there's no place for you here.' He seems very adaptive spiritually, a very spiritual person. . . . Did somebody try to rob him? Is something missing from the home? Did somebody try to make it look like something it wasn't?"

"Yes."

"Did you live near him?"

"Yes," Rita answered, thinking of their days on Long Island.

"But not at the time that he passed over. As a matter of fact, did you hear about this on the media?

"No."

"You were contacted?"

"In a roundabout way, yes."

"All right. It's just, like, you heard about it from outside sources. A younger person strike him?"

"Yes."

"And it *is* his family by blood. He keeps bringing that up. He is the type that would be shocked by that fact, I think.

I guess that's why he keeps bringing it up. Like, 'I can't believe he did this.' He's shocked that his own flesh and blood would do this. *Hmm,* curious . . . Did his son do the killing?"

"I don't know," Rita replied, although at the time of the reading police were holding Tom based on circumstantial evidence and had not yet charged him.

"Are you pretty convinced his son is the one?"

"I don't really know, but the police say—"

"I want your opinion only because he's telling me his son killed him. He's saying his son is guilty of his murder! Were they not getting along? It seems like some falling-out . . . there's definitely some argument, some altercation. . . . Money involved?"

"Yes."

"I guess you don't have to be psychic to know that in any case," George quipped, "but there seems to be some sort of money trouble involved. The son felt cheated or something?"

"I don't know." Rita did know, however, that Tom had been involved in some failed get-rich-quick schemes in the past and was struggling to stay solvent.

"Has the son been arrested recently?"

"Yes."

"It seems they had no leads or clues at first?"

"Yes."

"Did the son try to cover it up?"

"Yes."

"Yeah, again, I'm seeing someone covering up tracks." George was clearly frustrated. "It's like pulling teeth. . . . When he first went over there, I have to admit, he gives me the impression that he was so shocked this happened to him, he didn't know what to do with himself. But then somebody helped him to get over it. Now, the blow to the head was very severe, and that's probably why I felt as though the heart was pulled back when he was hit; everything else went wrong, too. Did you know the son?"

"Yes."

"Was he like a pal to you, too?"

"Yes," she said.

"He says you know the son; that's probably why you

know *him*. Now I know the connection. Are you kind of shocked yourself?"

"Yes," she said, shaking her head from side to side.

"Yes, because he says, 'Shock.' Maybe you kind of question your values, or the value of your friendship, things like this. You're shocked by the whole situation. . . . Did you kind of know the son was guilty?"

"I don't *know* it, but that's what I feel." She'd spoken to Tom once on the phone following his arrest, praying that he would say something to the effect of 'Rita, I didn't do it!' Instead, his callous tone and remarks such as 'They're going to have a tough time pinning this on me' dashed her hopes. After hanging up with him, she was crushed and for weeks after questioned how she could ever trust anyone again.

"The feeling," George said gravely, "is correct. Otherwise they would say, but it seems that the son is definitely guilty. There was a falling-out? It's definitely something with money, a business, some sort of falling-out. Is there a Howard involved?"

"Not that I know of," Rita replied. As it turned out, Howard was her deceased father, but, as often happens, she was so caught up in the reading that she didn't focus.

"I'll just let it go. . . . Did [the son] have an [substance] abuse problem?"

"Not that I know of." That may have been true, Rita admitted afterward. She'd heard the rumors and feared the worst.

"It just seems as though he's not in the right frame of mind. Was he a little mentally off or something? He seems out of harmony with himself . . ." Once again the name Howard came up. "There's a Howard passed on," George insisted.

"Yes."

"That's your family, yes? I can tell he's family. He's saying, 'Don't cut me off, don't cut me off.' But I'm having a hard enough time with this." Apparently Rita's father was horning in on the reading, and as far as George was concerned, at a most inopportune time. While George cannot control which spirits come through, he can choose to ignore those who distract him.

"Was there a weapon used to strike? Not in a traditional

sense, I just realized. . . . Did this son murder more than one person? Because the mother steps in and says, 'He's guilty of another murder.' " George seemed startled. "Did he murder his mother, too?"

"Yes."

"Whoa! 'Cause she was very quiet, and then all of a sudden she stepped in and said, 'He's guilty of my murder, too.' Now, the son himself is young, yes? In his thirties or forties?"

"Yes."

"Were the parents both killed on the same day?"

"Yes."

"Were the parents kind of retired?"

"Yes."

"They moved to a retirement house in Florida."

"Uh-huh."

"The son live with them? Or, let's say, he had access to the home."

"Yes."

"Because it's as if he's there, but he's not. Both of them say their son was guilty of murder. It's as though they're not comfortable having to say that from the other side, but it seems to be fact. Did both parents suffer injuries to the head?"

"Yes."

"Killed almost the same way?"

"Yes."

"Because that's what the mother says, too, same thing, a blow to the head again . . . I seem a little shocked," George said, "as if it's hard to think this person would be capable of this."

"Yes," she acknowledged.

"You know, he seems like your average everyday nice guy."

"Yes."

Again George focused on the murder weapon. "He used a tool?"

"A tool, no."

"But it's not a gun or a knife. That's the thing; they say to me it's not a weapon in the traditional sense." George was correct, for although the police did not discover a bloodied pipe at the scene of the crime, forensic pathologists who examined the bodies concluded that a pipe or similar object was used to crush their skulls. "Both parents were murdered at home?"

"Yes."

"Was anybody in the house with them at the time?"

"Not that I know of."

"Any pets in the house?"

"No."

"Because I feel that there was someone else there. I could be wrong. . . . It seemed as though they were a very nice family, yes?"

"Yes."

George paused, anticipating additional information from the other side, but both spirits seemed reticent to say anything further. "It's funny," he told Rita, "the mother keeps saying to me, 'What are you waiting for? What do you expect to hear?' And I said, 'What do you mean?' And she said, 'Well, what can we do about this?' " Rita appeared as frustrated as George, clearly expecting some sort of message or guidance from them. "It just seems as though, as Norman Bates says in *Psycho,* 'We all go a little mad sometimes.' Basically, they look at it that way: He just lost it for the moment and acted accordingly. Was he under a lot of stress?"

"Yes," Rita acknowledged.

"There's a lot of pressure around him, so he might have reacted, just for the moment, under stress. His parents, did he think they were very demanding, or inclined to come across that way, expecting too much of him?"

"Yes and no."

"Because it could be his interpretation: this feeling of demand or being dominated, things like this. . . . I don't mean to laugh, but the mother keeps asking, 'Are you expecting more?' "

"Yes," the subject answered. She later told George and me that she wanted the deceased man and woman to tell her whether or not to adopt their three grandsons who would be left orphans should Tom be imprisoned. But neither spirit came forth with advice, for loved ones who've passed to the other side never formally direct; they offer information for the living to act upon of their own free will. Rita, too, boiling inside with rage at Tom, hoped for the murder victims to voice her own feelings of bitterness—which, of course, they did not.

George continued: "Is there a Katherine passed over?"

"Yes."

"Anything to do with them?"

"Yes."

"Okay, because I just want to make sure it's not any more of your relatives popping in. She's passed over, yes? Is she the mom?" George didn't have to wait for Rita's confirmation. "Okay, yeah, because the parents just started talking again, and she said, 'I'm the mother you're talking to.' Was she very creative? Musically inclined?"

"No."

"All right, then, let me take it symbolically: I'm hearing musical notes, so it could just be a sign that they're in harmony over there. The mother, she comes to you sort of like an aunt figure, maybe because you were a friend of her son's. She looks upon you as if she were your aunt."

"Yeah," Rita said.

"She know your parents?"

"Yes."

"Wait a minute, now: Your mom is still living, your father passed on. They knew your father? Vaguely, from the way you're answering, I take it?"

"Yes."

"Your father is Howard."

"Yes."

George laughed. "I keep getting Howard. They keep telling me, 'Howard, the father.' That's *your* father, Howard. They're on the same plane over there. They know he's over there, they've met over there, that sort of thing. They related to him at all?"

"No."

"Just friends—as your mother was friends with them. Is your mother also a Katherine?"

"Yes."

"That's why I keep hearing it twice. Because Katherine, the lady that's passed on, keeps calling to your mother. Did they know your mother better than your father?"

"Yes."

"Name Jean mean anything?"

"No," Rita answered hesitantly.

"Jean or Joan?"

"No."

"Well, they ask that you pray for them. Both parents seem to be very close to this particular son, and they say forgiveness was the first lesson they had to learn. But it's as though they didn't have to learn it; they were already ready to forgive, because, okay, they passed on, they 'died,' in our world, but they're alive in the next one. Does the name Mike or Michael mean anything?"

"No."

"Anybody involved with them at all? Somebody passed on?"

"Not that I know of."

"Are you not speaking to their son?"

"Correct."

"You want to, though."

"Yes."

"They kind of ask you to speak to him. It's your decision, but they make the request all the same. They just ask that when you speak to him, if you think you can handle this, 'Tell him he's forgiven.' You might have to wait till after he's convicted. But they do say to tell him 'We forgive him.' He is pretty remorseful, though, yes? Is that the right word?"

Rita held out her hands; judging from her conversation with Tom, she truly didn't know.

"Name Henry doesn't mean anything, does it? Or Steven?" These and other names that George mentioned may have been relatives of the deceased that Rita would not have known. Or were they the names of persons connected with the murder? Unfortunately, at the time of this reading, there was no way for her to know. "No," she said.

The subject's pained expression prompted George to ask, "Is there still something you're waiting to hear?"

"Yeah."

"I know it, because I can feel it, and it's driving me crazy. . . . I don't know if they don't want to talk about it, or they're not ready, I don't know what it is. You have to do what you want, but they're not discouraging you. It's almost as if you want to bring him a message from them? I'm sure you would, but that's what they keep saying, 'Tell him that we forgive him.' "

A lengthy pause followed, then George looked up.

"You want to know 'It's all right?' " he asked Rita.

"No, that's not it."

"I don't know what they mean, then, because the mother keeps saying 'It's all right.' What's all right?" This continued for several minutes, George sighing in frustration, partially because of the deceased spirits' reticence, but also because of Rita's lack of knowledge of the crime and of the family. He was sure that some of the names she failed to recognize were other departed relatives surrounding the couple on the other side.

"Why do you want 'the answer'?" George asked in exasperation.

"It would depend on what I eventually end up doing," she said haltingly. Trying to adopt the young boys, that is.

" 'Cause that's what Katherine says: 'Why do you want the answer?' Why are you people being difficult?" Both George and his subject laughed. "Would you have to make a change?"

"What do you mean 'make a change'?"

"I don't know. She says, 'about the change.' Job? Residence? Anything like this?"

"No."

"Then I don't know what she means," George admitted. "This situation kind of shatter your life personally?"

"Close, yeah."

"I see broken glass, something being shattered. Yeah, because it can alter your life?"

"Strong."

"Strong what?" George asked.

"It's a strong experience," Rita admitted.

"Can't read 'em," George said. "They're just so blank, it's like grasping at straws. It seems that they won't speak about it. I guess I just have to accept the fact that maybe they don't want to speak about whatever it is."

Finally, after well over an hour, with Rita's question still unanswered, all the spirits appeared to go back, her late father Howard accompanying the other two souls. "It's funny," George said, "it seems as if they're over it and they've forgiven, but part of them doesn't really want to talk about it, or maybe not at this time. But again, in regard to whatever 'this' is, it's your personal decision to make. It's all right that you make your own decision, they said. So I guess that's what she meant before when she said it was all right. And with that they sign off and ask you to pray for them."

George and Rita sat silently for a few seconds, both obviously drained. In this instance the relationships were so unusually complex—Rita was a friend, not family—and so many pieces of information were missing that George could not interpret the clues with his usual accuracy. Furthermore, although George has helped law-enforcement agencies solve crimes, with excellent success, this reading was a first for him. As he said afterward, "I don't think I've ever had a situation with parents who'd been murdered by their own child." He had to overcome his own shock that such a brutal murder could be committed by a son, and so it took him awhile to voice what he'd been hearing.

"I kind of argued with them," he told Rita and me. " 'You're kidding, this can't be true.' The mother said, 'Well, he killed my husband; why couldn't he have killed me?' I said, 'All right, I'll relay it,' " believing Rita would deny it.

The reading's shortcomings point out the subject's crucial role. Rita's recent emotional distance from the son and family and her lack of knowledge regarding the actual crime certainly prevented George from pursuing several names she could not identify. Did any of the names Rita couldn't confirm belong to an accomplice? We'll probably never know.

Paula was thirty-five, attractive and youthful-looking, with dark hair and large eyes. She and George had never met nor spoken to each other prior to her reading in April 1989. There was no way George could know that Paula suspected her mother may have been a victim of Richard Angelo, the "Angel of Death."

A male nurse at Long Island's Good Samaritan Hospital, Angelo was accused in 1987 of killing four patients and assaulting three others by injecting them with a muscle-paralyzing drug. The sensational case was front-page news

in the New York area for many months and also reported
nationally. The heavyset, bearded, twenty-seven-year-old
nurse was also suspected in many more deaths at that hospital. For the six months that Angelo worked the graveyard
shift, "dozens of his patients either died or needed to be
revived by an emergency team," the *New York Post* reported. There was also a significant increase in the number
of patients suffering cardiac or pulmonary arrest while he
was on duty. "Graveyard shift," indeed.

It would be nearly two years before police and prosecutors
completed their investigation. Eventually thirty-three bodies
were exhumed in the search for evidence against Angelo.
However, traces of the drugs could not be found in all the
remains, either because of the time elapsed or because the
muscle-paralyzing drugs had dissipated. Two of the drugs
that Angelo is thought to have illegally administered—Anec-
tine and potassium chloride—are considered "untraceable."

Angelo gave police a videotaped confession admitting
that he injected patients with the muscle-paralyzing drug
Pavulon, then attempted to revive them "so that I could be
a hero in the eyes of the hospital staff." A police detective
who testified at the Angel of Death's eight-week trial in 1989
was quoted as saying he "showed Angelo a list of sixty-eight
names of patients on the special-care unit who had gone into
respiratory arrest during the time Angelo worked there, and
Angelo started to cry. He said, 'There are so many here.' He
didn't think he did that many, but he just didn't know."

The detective testified that Angelo confessed to having
injected seven to ten patients. But in his videotaped confession when Angelo was asked if he knew exactly how many
patients he had injected, he admitted, "No."

In this reading Paula's mother came through with information that seems to substantiate her daughter's suspicions.
George also received information that, in retrospect, pointed
to a second meaning: Paula's imminent death.

"Someone claims to be the mother passed on," he said.
"She passed tragically."

"It depends," Paula replied.

"Your mother passes young by today's standards. She
passes in her sixties. She was not supposed to pass on."

"We don't think so."

"She says she was not supposed to pass on. I'm going to go by what she says. She's a victim."

"We think so."

"She says she's a victim. Let's see what she means. I'm writing murder backwards: REDRUM. She was murdered, but she was not murdered—not in the legitimate sense. She claims she was murdered, but not traditionally. Her dad passed over."

"Yes."

"Because her father's with her. Her mother, too."

"Yes."

"Both her parents come through with her. And I hear another language. Did she speak something that sounds like Italian? Because that's what it sounds like to me."

"Yes."

"Your mother was hospitalized."

"Yes."

George wrote the word *poison* on his pad. "She claims she was there for some kind of health treatment. Is there some sort of malpractice situation? Just say yes or no."

"Yes."

"She was involved in malpractice while in the hospital, she says."

"Yes," Paula replied, even though the family had not brought a lawsuit against the hospital.

"Is there a Maria passed on?"

"Yes."

"Your mother knows her."

"Yes."

"Is she like an aunt or grandmother?"

"Grandmother."

"She's coming through to help her. Did you know your grandmother Maria at all?"

"Yes."

"She's a very religious woman."

"Yes."

"[Your mother] says, 'Maria came through to help me.' They met in the next stage of life and they crossed her over. Your mother injected?"

"This is what we think."

"Your mother says she was poisoned."

"Did she really?"

"She claims she was poisoned. She was injected. See, the thing is, it wasn't supposed to happen like this. It's a malpractice. Not that her doctor did it. But it's as if . . . it was being done for a reason and it backfired. Is there a Millie passed on?"

"Yes."

"Your mother says, 'Millie is here with me also.' "

"Yes."

"Your mother was in the hospital for treatment—heart attack, whatever."

"Yes." ·

"She was in there for some sort of specific treatment, and she claims she was poisoned through injection. She says that there was a weapon in her death, and I was going to ask you if it was a traditional one. And she said to me, 'No.' She says she was poisoned. Was her body exhumed?"

"Yes."

"Does it show that she was poisoned? I don't know. Can they tell that? It seems that her body was exhumed, she says. And you can tell she was injected or something, or she was poisoned. There might have been a trace of an overabundance of some sort of drug in the system, in any case. Because that's what she means when she says she wasn't supposed to pass on. When she went over, her father said, 'What are you doing here? You're not supposed to be here yet.' And so she was at the mercy of somebody else. . . . Did she have anything to do with that guy they arrested?" George asked.

Paula nodded.

"Now I know why I keep seeing that. I took it as a symbol. It's the actual thing. That nurse that was arrested for . . . Now I know why I keep seeing the Angel of Death! He's called the Angel of Death! I thought it was a sign that somebody was going to die. Because she says she was at the mercy of the Angel of Death. And I'm, like, 'Huh?' Now I put it together, because the media labeled him that. She said she was under somebody's care, and she says it was not a doctor. She says it was a male. I just realized it's a male nurse. . . . She had contact with him, yes?"

"Yes."

"She says she was at the mercy of the Angel of Death. . . . Your mother seems to be kind of a nice lady, and she feels sorry for him. Because, she says, 'He didn't mean to do it, but it backfired.' Like what's been discussed in the media—he wanted to do something courageous."

"She says that was how she died?" Paula asked.

"She claims she was at the mercy of the Angel of Death," George repeated.

"She didn't die of natural causes?"

"No. She seems to give me the impression that someone put whatever drug in those people's systems and used it to disrupt the heart. It's almost as if she died of a heart attack. That's why I asked before, 'Is she in for heart treatment?' It feels as if something goes into my system to create a heart attack or make me feel as though I'm having one. And she tells me that the person also killed a number of people. And when I heard that, I saw the face and started to realize . . . It's just as though I'm seeing a news flash. . . . Your mother is at peace, though. She doesn't hold any hostility. She knows what happened. That's the thing. Did she have a heart attack? Is that why she went into the hospital?"

"She had a tumor—"

"But did she pass on from a heart attack?"

"—but they said she died of a heart attack."

"She claims she passed on from a heart attack encouraged from this poison, or this drug, that was put into her."

"Cardiopulmonary arrest," Paula confirmed.

"And she says Philomena was there to meet her when she came over."

"Philomena was my great-grandmother."

"Your dad passed on."

"Yes."

"Before her."

"Yes."

"Because he was also there to meet her when she came over."

Paula's mother was never officially named as one of Angelo's victims. However, in the course of the reading, George quickly discerned that the woman was murdered by a poisonous injection while hospitalized. When George psychically saw the Angel of Death—Nurse Angelo's nickname—at first he thought it was "a sign that somebody was going to die," since usually the symbol is a portent. Paula explained that she always suspected something was amiss when her mother died unexpectedly. Learning that Angelo had been one of her mother's nurses only confirmed those suspicions, although, again, Angelo was never charged with Paula's mother's death.

Nearly two years after he was arrested, Angelo, whom the prosecutor called "a monster in nurse's whites," was convicted of the murder of two patients and of manslaughter and criminally negligent homicide in the death of two others. He was also found guilty of assault of one other patient. He was sentenced to fifty years to life in prison.

Sadly, Paula did not get to see the man she believed to be her mother's killer brought to justice, at least not in this dimension. On Thanksgiving Day 1989 she died of a sudden heart attack. This raises another possible interpretation of the Angel of Death George saw during her reading seven months earlier. Had it been only a reference to Angelo and her mother's passing? Or had George also received a sign that Paula, too, would soon pass?

The genuineness of a communication is sometimes easier to establish when the spirit knows something the subject does not. Examples like the following effectively rule out telepathy, or mind reading, on George's part. These readings are of interest because they span two years, and in both George insists his information is correct, despite the subject's initial vehement denial.

"Your uncle passed?" George asked.

"Yes," the woman acknowledged.

"Your uncle feels he could have been closer to the family and he apologizes for that."

"What?" the woman exclaimed.

George, nonplussed by the subject's response, continued. "Your uncle says he's very ashamed of himself, that he could have been closer to the family and he apologizes for that."

"What?" the woman asked again, appearing offended.

"Your uncle . . . gives me the feeling that he's ashamed of himself."

"That is totally inaccurate!"

George was surprised. How could he be so off target? Had he somehow misheard or misinterpreted the spirit's communication to him? It took him several moments to recover from the subject's vigorous denials.

"I don't know what my uncle had to apologize for. He was a great guy," she maintained. "He was a pillar of our community, a churchgoer—*every* Sunday. He was a fabulous person."

George, having regained his composure, listened carefully again to the messages he heard and sensed psychically. He did not retreat from his earlier statements; rather, he steadfastly held to them.

"I don't understand. He keeps telling me he is so ashamed. He says he's sorry he did this to the family." George was insistent.

"Did what?" the woman asked skeptically.

"I don't know," George admitted, "he won't say. He just says he disgraced the family."

"I don't know what he's trying to say," the woman answered, her voice rising.

George, equally perplexed, spent the next few minutes listening more closely to the spirit's message. "He also said he cheated the family." This George interpreted as logically as he could. "Does he mean financially?"

"No," she answered without hesitation. Then she added, "Are you sure you're speaking with my uncle? Maybe you've got someone else coming through."

"Yes, I'm sure. He's your uncle," George answered with certainty.

"But there's no reason he should apologize or feel ashamed. He didn't cheat us. He was a great guy. He and my family had a very good relationship."

Beyond this obvious impasse, the rest of the reading continued. George was otherwise accurate as to names and details about various circumstances in the woman's life. As she left, the woman told George she would play for her husband the audio tape she had made of the reading. "He's going to wonder, too, why you said these things about my mother's brother," she admonished.

Much to George's surprise, two years later, the same

woman returned to him for a second reading. Each year, George sees several thousand people. While he might vaguely recognize a subject, he simply cannot recall details of the tens of thousands of readings he's performed over the past decade. George remembers thinking the woman looked familiar, but he couldn't place her. After polite greetings, the reading began.

"Your uncle apologizes. Is there any reason why he'd apologize?" George asked.

"You're goddamned right he should apologize! That son of a bitch! I'd like to go to the cemetery, dig him up, and rip him to pieces!" the woman exclaimed angrily.

George was startled. Obviously he'd hit a nerve, but he continued, listening carefully and then repeating what he'd psychically heard. "Your uncle is confessing that he molested his nephew," he said with understandable reluctance.

"Yes!"

"He says he was sexually molesting your brother."

"Yes!"

The remainder of the reading largely dealt with apologies from the uncle's spirit, who, after confessing, apologized repeatedly and profusely.

"It's as important for him to come through to confess as it is for you and your brother to hear it," George explained. "It's ten times more important that they accept God's grace to come through and confess to clear their conscience on the other side. He says the sin was not only the sexual act of molestation, as bad as that was, but also the emotional effects of it. The abuse, the humiliation, the degraded feeling. The other side gives me the impression that the physical does not survive but the emotional does. That's why an emotional hurt is ten times worse than a physical hurt. The physical can be destroyed. The emotional cannot.

"Your uncle said that when he went to the other side he had to face and judge himself. That's what they call the judgment after you die. He had to follow his life and had to watch his life and see the humiliation and horror he caused his nephew. Plus, he sees from the other side what he's going through. So he put himself into a hell-like state more or less of his own free will because of what he did."

"Who punishes my uncle on the other side?" the woman asked.

"Himself," George answered without hesitation.

"How?"

"Because those who commit such acts are continually haunted by the demon of ugliness that they've created. He keeps apologizing to your brother and to you for abusing and molesting him."

The woman told George that she'd had a reading with him two years before and failed to acknowledge the messages. "I don't understand," he said. "If you didn't know then that your uncle was abusing or molesting your brother, how did you find out between then and now?"

She explained that when she returned home from the first reading, she played the tape recording of it for her husband. He was also at a loss to comprehend the enigmatic apology from her late uncle.

Several weeks later, still puzzled about the message, she replayed the tape for some other family members. As her middle-aged brother listened to George's message, he froze, then burst into tears. Having regained his composure, he finally told her that from the time he was a small child until he was thirteen, their uncle had sexually molested him. Like many sexual-abuse victims, he'd been too afraid and ashamed to tell anyone.

This shocking disclosure not only clarified his sister's reading with George, it explained a lifetime of serious emotional problems. For years, he'd seemed frightened, withdrawn, even unbalanced. Despite years of therapy, he made little progress. Now the pieces fell together.

"Why did my uncle wait until now to confess? Why didn't he say what he was apologizing for two years ago when I first came to you?" the woman asked George.

"He didn't confess until you knew for a fact this was true," George explained. "When your uncle was sure that you knew the wrong that he'd done, then he confessed. When you first came to me, you didn't know what he had done wrong, and you might have been even more upset to learn then what he was apologizing for. As it turned out, you discovered the secret—what your uncle did—from your brother."

"My uncle committed a terrible sin," the woman said sternly.

"Sin is not only the physical act but also the emotional abuse, because emotions survive as negative energy," George answered. "Murder, for example, is a sin, of course, but the anger or hatred accompanying that evil act of taking someone's life survives bodily death. The Nazis have a special place in what we would call hell. Their own negativity created devils and evil spirits. Touching your brother where he shouldn't have was sinful. So was humiliating him."

"Why did my uncle come through at all?" the woman asked George. Like some people, she was upset by the role her uncle was playing in the family, even in death.

"Well, because of the ugliness that your uncle perpetrated on your brother, he is not on a higher level on the other side. He's on a dark level. But this is a help to him also. When his spirit was in the room, the feeling of his energy was kind of cloudy. The vibration was not as bright as, say, somebody who's been a very good person, where you feel uplifted or elevated. He seemed very dim. I've had that happen in other readings when child abusers and sex offenders or molesters have come through to confess and apologize."

"What does he want from us?" the anguished sister asked. "Hasn't he done enough harm?"

"He basically wants to hear from you that you forgive him. He's admitted he was wrong. He's apologized profusely. He knows he was sick, and he was the one with the problems, not your brother. He never did anything to deserve the abuse your uncle forced on him. He is the innocent victim. Just as he is trying to overcome what happened to him so he can go on with his life here, your uncle is trying to work out his mistakes on the other side so he can progress spiritually there. His coming through can be a help to both of them. It's up to you, of course, whether to forgive him. The other side says forgiveness is greater. But it's still your decision. Your uncle is saying it's very important that he accept God's grace to come through and confess to clear his conscience over there."

Reflecting on the numerous readings that included confessions like this one, George says, "As much as people think

I've had a bad childhood—being misunderstood, put on tranquilizers, ridiculed by others kids, and so on—since I've started doing readings I've found out there are people who have it ten times worse than I've had it. My experiences, as bad as they may have seemed, were like nursery school compared to what some of the people who've come to me have gone through.

"I recall a reading for a young woman in which her father's spirit came through to confess that he had sexually abused her for years when she was young. Her mother's spirit admitted from the other side that she was terrified of her husband when they were here on earth and did nothing about the abuse, even though she knew full well what was going on. Out of guilt, anger, and fear she too turned on the daughter, physically and emotionally abusing her, always beating her, dominating her, putting her down.

"On the other side, the parents are now punishing themselves. When they first came through in that reading, they seemed very sheepish. Something was obviously on the father's mind. I could feel it. I could sense it. He kept apologizing to his daughter for not being closer and for abusing her. At first I thought he was admitting to physical abuse. But then he went on further and admitted, 'I took advantage of my daughter.' When he said that, I started getting the feeling that he meant he'd molested her. Then he came right out and said to me, 'I sexually abused her.'

"I was hesitant about repeating to the young woman what her father's spirit was telling me. At first I held back. But finally I told her what her father said. She became hysterical. She was with a girlfriend at the reading, and she put her head on her friend's shoulder and cried and cried. I could sense for her it was a relief to finally hear them admit what they had done to her and to confront them, so to speak. Now they had both apologized. It was important for her to hear this so she could realize that she did not do anything to deserve that type of mistreatment.

"When the parents came through," George continues, "they had a 'sponsor' with them, a higher entity to help them to face their responsibility and their grievous wrongdoing. That's what made me feel they were on a dark level. Basically, the daughter forgave them, but she had to hear from *them* that they were wrong. They had to admit that *they* were the ones who had the problems and were sick.

"In yet another reading, a father came through and claimed he, too, was sexually abused as a child by his father. In turn, *his* father confessed to sexually abusing his son. Now the father and son have reunited on the other side. The father projected a low light. He has got a lot to work out on the other side, something like being in a psychiatric hospital here. The father's sins can be overcome, but it has to be done at his own pace. It could take a long period of time: eons, even, by our standards."

What happens on the other side to a person who is not the abuser but stands by and does nothing to help a victim?

George answers, "Hindus believe if someone is drowning, that's their karma. You shouldn't interfere. But the other side has told me, No, that is not correct. You *should* try to help.

"In the case of children abused by parents who grow up to be abusers, they are just as much to blame even though they are acting out what happened to them. The other side says to me that two wrongs don't make a right. There are plenty of people who suffered abuse but didn't repeat the pattern with their own children.

"The mother who is apathetic, who did nothing, was at fault because she knew the abuse was going on and did not make any effort to stop it. We not only have free will, but religion and society have also set up rules and regulations that prohibit certain kinds of behavior. Spirituality tells us we have the choice to take our own direction, and if we take the wrong path we can only blame ourselves."

8

Direct Communications

John Elliot, an engineer with a physics background, was intrigued but skeptical as he read *We Don't Die*. He'd never been interested in the paranormal. In fact, were it not for the sudden accidental death of his son David, he'd never have even picked up the book. As far as he was concerned, there was no way that this George Anderson fellow could receive messages from the dead. His scientific training taught him that in order to accept such an incredible claim, he would have to see what he terms "measurable phenomena going on." And the only way that could happen is if he had a reading. Again, this was something he'd never considered doing before. But like so many people, his attitudes were changed by death.

It was February 1988 and winter recess at the high school seventeen-year-old David Elliot attended in Penfield, New York. David was one of John and Nancy Elliot's six children. For years David, a strong and athletic six-footer, had begged his parents to let him go skiing with friends, but his parents always said no, feeling the sport was too dangerous. When they finally relented, he was thrilled.

He traveled with several friends to a mountain ski area about thirty miles from home. Ski conditions were fair at best, for it had rained the day before, leaving the trails slick with ice. Many other skiers, discouraged by the slippery surfaces, headed back home. But not David, who couldn't wait to hit the slopes. In his excitement, the teenager ignored conditions and warnings. Skiing slowly down a narrow trail, he lost his balance and slammed into a tree with such force that his aorta, the main artery to the heart, snapped, causing one lung to fill with blood. A short time later he was pronounced dead at the scene.

Reading the book, John was struck by the many similarities between his son and David Licata, the teenager whose story opens *We Don't Die:* Besides sharing the same first name, both boys were high-school soccer stars, tall and good-looking, and died in tragic accidents (Licata the victim of a hit-and-run driver) that occurred during February school recess. Finally, each boy had a parent with the same first name. A man of logic, Mr. Elliot believed these similarities were nothing more than coincidence.

One afternoon he awoke from a nap, disturbed by the details of a vivid dream in which he saw his son's and David Licata's images merging in George Anderson's mind. Both boys were wearing their soccer uniforms and carrying soccer balls. *Your son's name is David; he liked to play soccer,* George told him, adding that David Licata was relaying this information.

John told his wife and a friend about his dream. When the friend asked, "What would make you believe this is for real?" John replied, "I'm a tough cookie. George Anderson would have to give me the name *David.* If they're really over there, they can hear this conversation. So I want them to give me the name David, but through a vision of the David [Licata] in the book."

"That would be incredible, John," his friend answered. And indeed it would be.

Over the next few months the dream remained ingrained in John's mind. Yet if you had asked him, "Do you believe in a hereafter?" he'd have insisted no. And if you had asked him about the stories in *We Don't Die,* he'd have told you that's precisely what they were: stories. Inexplicably, one day he felt compelled to call the Licatas, getting their number from information. He spoke to Mr. Licata, and the next day Nancy talked to his wife, who told her how to contact George. In neither conversation did they mention John's unusual dream.

Mr. Elliot, identifying himself to George's assistant only as John, received an appointment for a group discernment. The day of his reading, he drove seven hours from upstate New York to Long Island, accompanied by his teenage sons Mark and Jack. Nancy had decided not to come, so John brought along a portable video camera. While the boys took seats across the room, he sat down near a wall outlet and set up his camera.

George introduced himself, then began that evening's discernment. After about forty-five minutes of conveying messages to various subjects, the psychic medium glanced in John's direction.

"The man in the back of the room: You've lost a child."

John, still skeptical, deliberately did not answer.

It had been raining and thundering all evening; suddenly a bolt of lightning illuminated the sky. George had to stop, calmly explaining to the startled group, "When there's a lightning storm, I lose the signal from the other side. The communications have stopped, but they should come back in a few minutes."

The unexpected interruption set John to hypothesizing that if George's psychic messages could be temporarily "disconnected" by lightning—a brilliant flash of light caused by the discharge of atmospheric electricity—his ability conceivably might work off *something* electrical or electromagnetic. *Interesting*, he thought.

Moments later, George resumed, his ability restored. He turned again to John.

"You lost a son, correct?"

"Yes," John answered.

George then discerned that the spirit was attempting to explain that he was killed in some type of accident.

"Was your son away from you at the time?" he asked.

John misinterpreted the question, thinking George meant that David had not been living at home at the time of the fatal accident.

"No," he answered.

After laboring several more minutes with John's reading, George moved on to other people in the room. One of those he soon went to was fifteen-year-old Jack Elliot.

"Your grandparents on your father's side have passed; they're around you," George said.

Jack nodded.

"Do you take the name Madeline?"

"Yes, that's her! My grandmother; my father's mother," Jack answered excitedly.

"Donald. Do you take the name Donald?"

"Yes, that's my grandfather, on my father's side."

John observed, incredulous. George continued with other details, accurate messages, all of which Jack acknowledged. Then he correctly discerned that Jack had lost a brother.

Several minutes later, George completed Jack's reading and directed his attention to other subjects. A short while later he came to thirteen-year-old Mark Elliot.

"You're an athlete. There's a lot of running in your sport," George said.

"Yes," replied Mark, an avid soccer, lacrosse, and basketball player.

"Wait a minute." George paused. "The same grandparents are going to you as went to the boy next to you. You guys are brothers."

"Yes," said Mark.

"Now the young man I saw before is coming back, so I assume you lost a brother, too. He's there with your grandparents."

"Yes," Mark answered.

"Watch your back during athletic activity," George said the spirit cautioned.

"Okay," the boy replied.

"Does anyone take the name Maureen?" George asked.

"Oh God, yes!" Mark answered. "That's unbelievable!"

"It's your brother, and he wants you to know that he's aware of the relationship with *Maur-een,*" George said in a singsong voice.

George's accuracy was uncanny. Shortly before David was killed, Mark had been dating a girl named Maureen. Whenever she phoned Mark, and John answered, he teasingly called "Hey Mark, it's *Maur-een!*" in precisely the same singsong intonation David's spirit had instructed George to use.

"Does the name David mean anything at all?" George asked.

"Yes," all three Elliots answered simultaneously.

"Who said yes?" George queried, turning around.

"All three of us," John replied.

"Is that your son?" George asked.

"Yes," John answered.

"Because the message is coming from David." *David*

Licata. "It's so incredible, it really scares me. I just realized it. This is really wild! What sports do you play?"

"Soccer and lacrosse," Jack answered.

"Lacrosse," George repeated.

"Soccer and lacrosse," Jack corrected.

"You do play soccer."

"Yes," Jack acknowledged.

"This is really freaky," George remarked.

From the startled look on George's face, John Elliot sensed what was about to happen. Looking into the lens of his video camera, John said softly, "I think I know why."

"Now, for anybody who has read the book *We Don't Die,*" George went on, "David Licata appears next to you! He's holding a *soccer ball* and is wearing a soccer uniform. That's what makes me give the name David and bring up the sport soccer. After I said, 'Do you play a running sport?' and you answered 'Yes,' I asked, 'Do you play soccer?' I looked again, and I saw David Licata's spirit appear. I said to him, 'What are *you* doing here?' He answered, 'To give you the clue for the game soccer.' Then he asked me, 'What's my first name?' 'David.' That's when he said to me, 'That's their brother you're trying to get a hold of: David.' "

Turning to Jack and Mark, George said, "I've got a message from your brother David. It's about time he came through with his name. Maybe he had a little help on the other side from David Licata, who helped me to get the message across. Yes, definitely, your brother David is coming through."

John Elliot was speechless. George had related the entire contents of his dream as well as the sign he'd "requested."

Later on, George asked John, "Do you take the name Robert?"

"Yes!" It was his older brother, an Air Force pilot, killed in Vietnam in 1968. Now he and David, born two years later, were together on the other side. Likewise, David's grandparents Donald and Madeline, who'd also died before he was born, had met him on the other side when he came over.

As John and his sons drove home in silence, John mulled over what he'd just experienced. *Incredible! Unbelievable.* He repeatedly told himself that "seeing is believing." The thought comforted him.

The encounter was less shocking to Jack, who'd attended the reading already believing in an afterlife and in George's ability to discern spirits. His younger brother, Mark, on the other hand, neither believed nor doubted. Of the three, their father was the most excited by the evening's events. He still hadn't told either of his sons about his dream.

Unlike his wife, a devout Roman Catholic, John had drifted away from God. "I can't believe," Nancy often said to him, "that you, the grandson of a Baptist minister, don't believe in God." He did now.

A month after her husband's and sons' reading, Nancy Elliot went to George, having never revealed her last name. Accompanying her were her eleven-year-old daughter, Karen, and David's best friend, Jerry, also a soccer player. When the two arrived at George's house, they entered separately and took seats apart from one another so that George would not know they had come together. They were careful to avoid eye contact.

"There's a young male spirit walking up and down this row," George said, pointing to Jerry. "Now the spirit is going from you to that woman."

George turned to Nancy. "The spirit is going back and forth between the two of you. Are the two of you related?" George asked them.

"No," they answered.

"What's going on?" George asked, confused. "It's the same spirit going between the two of you. You two do know each other."

"Yes," each admitted.

"Do you know a young male that's passed on?"

"Yes."

"He gives me the name David. He keeps showing me my cousin's face, and he tells me to take both his names, Mark and David." George explained this cryptic clue. "My cousin in Virginia is named Mark David. I'm seeing his face in front of me, psychically, and he's telling me to take his first and middle names."

George was correct, of course, for the names Mark and David were two of Nancy Elliot's sons. This degree of corroboration is all too rare, but there have been hundreds of cases like it, where family members are read independently, sometimes years apart, and yet receive the same information.

George moved on to Jerry, delivering a message from his deceased grandmother Mary: Be wary about receiving a future traffic ticket. She also predicted that Jerry would be getting a new car. He had no such plans, he claimed. She then cautioned him about his driving. She also said that she saw him signing a contract at some time in the near future and reminded him she was his guardian angel.

The latter comment was a comfort, Jerry thought, but the predictions made no sense to him. Two weeks later, however, the teenager received not one but two summonses for speeding, the first he'd ever gotten. Then shortly thereafter he lost control of his car and veered off the road, totaling his car. Miraculously, he was not injured.

Of course, kids have accidents, and it could be argued that Jerry's grandmother's warnings may have turned into a self-fulfilling prophecy for him. How, then, do you explain the enigmatic prediction about a contract? That proved accurate on February 16, 1989—exactly one year to the day that David Elliot was killed—when Jerry signed a contract to play soccer as part of an athletic scholarship from Marquette University.

Today John Elliot accepts that there is another level or dimension, and that his son David is watching over the family from there, acting, in George's words, as a guardian angel to his brothers and sisters. At first John told himself that his dream was nothing more than a series of random images. Now he can't help but wonder, Was it *his* dream, or was his son using the dream to communicate thoughts to him?

There is no question that David somehow knew of not only his father's desire to hear of the dream, but also the dream's actual content. Had it really been "just" a dream, or was it, as John believed, a message from his son: a direct communication.

Since the Elliots' readings, George had another in which the spirit gave information contained in a previous dream. He accurately discerned that a young woman's five-year-old son, Robert, had been killed when a car jumped the curb and hit him and a friend as they played on a neighbor's front lawn. "Your son appears to you in dreams," George said to the distraught mother. "You've been dreaming about him, he says."

"Yes," she replied. "I have been dreaming about him."

"Because he says he comes to you in dreams. He says Leonard is with him on the other side. Leonard or Lenny."

"Yes, Lenny was a friend of my son's, a playmate. He passed on also, from illness."

"Your son says that he and Lenny are playing together on the other side. They're together."

The woman simply nodded. After the reading, she told us that one of Robert's aunts had recounted to her a dream in which he said, "I met a little boy named Lenny on the other side. He's my friend. We play together." Not knowing her nephew truly had a close friend named Lenny, the aunt thought little of the dream except to note its vividness. Robert's mother was amazed that her son came through in the discernment to deliver the same message he'd given to his aunt in her dream.

At another point in the reading, George said, "The little boy—your son—said he knew he was going to pass on."

"He told me the day before [he was killed], 'Mommy, I'm going to die,'" she said. "I told him, 'Don't talk that way! Mommy doesn't want you to die!'"

George, who along with everyone in the room was stunned, answered, "He knew he would die in the sense of this world. But remember: he's still alive in the next stage."

Parapsychology literature is filled with cases of direct communication. Often these are "crisis apparitions," or spirits that appear to the subject at or around the time of the spirit's death, or at a time when we may need to feel their presence, such as a holiday or anniversary. A bereavement counselor says that many of his clients remark, "I felt her presence," "I saw him in the bedroom," "I smelled his favorite cigar tobacco," "I smelled her favorite perfume," "I saw him appear." Then they ask him, "Am I losing my mind?"

Therese A. Rando, a clinical psychologist widely respected for her bereavement studies, is the author of *Grieving: How to Go On Living When Someone You Love Dies*. She writes, "Studies find that over half of all bereaved people report some paranormal experience. If it happens to so many, it cannot be considered abnormal." That surprisingly high percentage is cited in several surveys on the subject, and is even greater among widows and widowers.

The very nature of the paranormal, of course, puts it outside the parameters of science's ability to explain such experiences. But the fact that so many bereaved report that they see, hear, or in some manner sense the presence of their departed loved ones suggests it is an important component of our experiences here with our loved ones in the hereafter.

After a young woman was killed in a plane crash, her mother reported to George this paranormal experience:

"Since my daughter died," she said, "I have seen around me at night when I go to sleep a lot of swirling lights. Consistently there's something going on around the room; something peculiar is definitely going on right around me.

"A friend of mine and I were away together several months ago," she continued. "We spent two nights sharing a room. It was about two o'clock in the morning, and next to my bed was a flash of light that lasted about twenty minutes. The next night it happened again. We both saw a shadow outside the window, then flashing lights started again. Something was going on in our room that was not . . . *normal*. If I didn't experience it, I would have thought it was my imagination. After the lights stopped, we thought it must be my friend's mother, who had also passed on, and my daughter. We thought they must be together. It was a most peculiar experience."

A young man who lost his father in an accident shared this experience with George:

"I took my father's death very badly. There was this one song that I always associated with him. He would sing it; it was his favorite. Several times after he was killed I heard that song on the radio, at times when I least expected it, including the night of his wake. It made me cry, but I felt like maybe he was still around, so it made me feel better. On the other hand, I always thought things like that were coincidences.

"Then about a year after his death I was going through a very emotional personal crisis that involved my career and my health. It could even have affected my relationships, it was so serious. One evening I was totally drained by everything going on, I felt totally overwhelmed and started to cry. *If my father were still alive*, I thought, *he'd be able to help me.* Then, I don't know why, I looked up and said, 'Dad, please help me. Can you hear me? Please, Dad!' Then I calmed down and a few minutes later turned on the radio. Yes, there was that special song, and I knew it meant my father had heard me. I cried with relief as I listened to it. I swear to God, it felt like my father was in the room with me at that moment."

Are these experiences merely coincidental, or are they communications from loved ones who've passed on?

George frequently tells subjects in readings that those on the other side are trying to communicate with them directly. Of one subject, a woman, he asked, "Have you been dreaming about your father recently?"

"Yes, I have."

"Because your father says that he's been coming to you in your dreams," George explained, "to let you know he's okay in the next stage and that he's closer to you than you think."

In 1980, my coauthor, Patricia, and her boyfriend (now husband) were vacationing in a secluded cabin in upstate New York. They had no telephone and hadn't spoken to anyone from home in five days. Early one morning Patricia awoke from a disturbing dream in which her father, John, came to her and said, "This is it: I'm checking out. I love you. Good-bye." Then he turned and walked away.

At breakfast, as she was telling Philip about her dream, a knock came at the cabin door. It was the property owner, saying she'd received an urgent call asking her to phone her family immediately. When she reached her sister Mary, she was told that her fifty-nine-year-old father had died of a heart attack earlier that morning.

The ways that spirits sometimes communicate their presence to George can be, to say the least, unusual. During a reading for a family whose son had passed on, George psychically detected the scent of a cologne. He also claimed to psychically see a bottle of cologne sitting on a dresser in his upstairs bedroom, which is directly above the room in which he conducts readings.

"It's the cologne I use," he said. "That's what I'm psychically seeing and smelling. It's Polo."

Polo, both parents quickly confirmed, was their son's favorite cologne.

Through the years, George has heard thousands of direct-communication accounts. His advice to those who have had such experiences is, "Don't expect anything concrete to fall on your head. It might be a very simple experience. Sometimes somebody could be trying so hard to feel the person who's passed over, they miss the forest for the trees."

People who see George can't help but wonder, *If George can discern my loved ones so clearly, why can't I?* It's a valid question, and the answer is that spirits are probably around us more than we know. During one reading George told a young woman her deceased father spiritually walked her down the aisle the day of her wedding. After the reading, she told George how badly she'd wanted her father to be there with her and how sad she was that cancer had taken his life just months before her special day. "I did feel him there that day," she admitted, "but I couldn't be sure it was he." Once George relayed her father's message, the young bride knew that what she'd felt was real, not just a figment of her imagination.

Of these experiences, George says, "That's what God is all about. That's the true experience of God, letting someone come across from the other side for a loved one left behind."

The prevalence of contacts through dreams suggests that spirits choose to come through when our intellectual defenses are lowest. Also, as you'll see in appendix one: The Electroencephalogram Test, during a contact with the other side George's brain-wave patterns simulate those of someone who is dreaming. Yet George is wide awake and alert. Could this be a key to the riddle? Are our dreams more than dreams? Are we actually in touch with the other side more than we realize? The answer to all three questions may very well be yes.

People often ask, "What is it like to be George?" Many think that if they could tap into the psychic abilities he has, death would somehow be easier for them. As the following story shows, loss is the same painful experience for all of us.

"George, I'd like you to meet Father John. Father John, this is George Anderson." With that introduction by a mutual acquaintance began a warm friendship between George and Father John Papallo that was to endure even into the afterlife.

Father John was a Franciscan Capuchin priest whose wide boyish face and warm smile gave him the appearance of a man at least ten years younger than his forty-four years. Like all Capuchins, he dressed simply in the traditional brown floor-length robe and sandals. Rosary beads hung from a waist cord.

Father John was the Catholic chaplain at the Kings Park Psychiatric Center on Long Island. In addition, he worked tirelessly on behalf of homeless teenagers and other troubled youths. As anyone who met him could attest, he was a beloved man.

The priest first heard about George through our cable-TV program *Psychic Channels*. So many people had told him of George's wonderful spiritual work with the bereaved. Father John reasoned that either George was engaged in some miraculous work of God or he was perpetrating a cruel hoax. Perhaps it was all an act contrived for television. If so, those who had gone to George were being conned, something he would not tolerate.

Father John confided in a friend and parishioner, John Smith, that he wanted to learn more about George's psychic gift, though he admitted to worrying about how his superiors would react if they discovered his interest in the psychic medium.

"Father John was terrified that the Church would come after him, but he was also a man of conviction," Smith recalls. "I think Father John was fascinated by the afterlife. I remember that in his homilies, he spoke about his dad's preparation for death. His father was ill with cancer at that time."

Each month when George devoted a ninety-minute live TV program to psychic readings for studio audience members and viewers phoning in, Father John observed from the audience. As he watched reading after reading, he came to realize that George was sincere and his ability genuine. "It's like watching mini-miracles occur every time George comforts someone with his ability," he told a friend. Frequently, after George's TV programs, Father John could be found comforting and counseling that evening's subjects. No one who asked him for counsel and guidance was turned away. It seemed to help the priest as well. "The day after his father's death," John Smith recalls, "Father John seemed at peace."

Father John had little difficulty in reconciling George's psychic ability with his religious training and personal beliefs. After all, he reasoned, the gifted Padre Pio was also a Franciscan Capuchin, and Pio's long history of psychic and mystical feats—discerning spirits, bilocation, healings, stigmata—had been widely witnessed and documented over many years. Father John confided to friends that he believed in miracles and had long felt there was much beyond what the human eye could see and what religion and science could understand.

"God knows our needs," he said, "and He is always there for us when we are most in need. George offers the gift of comfort. In some cases, the souls on the other side have a greater spiritual need to talk to us than we do here, because God wants them to work things out that they did not work out here on the earth. So it is also a gift to the souls who are passed on that brings peace to them and to us on earth, so that all of us can go on in peace and hope. George gives the hopeless hope, the godless God, the disturbed, peace. In this day and age we need to know that there is a God and a heaven."

For George, Father John's recognition of his ability and good work provided a needed boost to his confidence and helped him spiritually. Over the next two years George and Father John became good friends.

"When he saw what the ability was doing to help people," George says, "his attitude was, as the Bible says, 'By their fruits ye shall know them.' When things come out well, when people are comforted, that's when you know it's of God."

Their conversations eventually led Father John himself to ask for a reading. "We talked about his relationship with his late father," George remembers. "During the reading, his father came through from the other side. I could see him psychically kneeling next to Father John, as if he were in confession.

"I recall seeing Saint Francis and Saint Clare, the founders of the Franciscan order, around him, telling me he was going into a new line of work that would be very spiritual. But the fact that he was a priest made me kind of cynical about the message. Of course he was doing spiritual work and could always be reassigned elsewhere; that's a priest's life. *What else is new?* I thought to myself."

Following the reading, Father John called George several times with questions about life after death. Once George joked, "Father, if you pass before me, make sure you give me a concrete sign that there is a hereafter. Make it something special." Both men laughed.

"In a later conversation," says George, "he told me he had a dream in which his father came to him. There was a lot of the color silver in the dream. I told him silver is a very spiritual color. In the dream, his dad kept telling him that he was going to go through 'a radical change of work,' though it would continue to be spiritual. I recall saying to him, 'Well, Father, it could coincide with the message I got for you when Saint Clare and Saint Francis appeared. They also said there would be a change with or in your work.' Again, I thought nothing of it.

"Father John was so devoted to his work. He was creating a rehabilitation center for young people with substance-abuse problems. His heart and soul were into helping those people and the patients in the psychiatric hospital. He was worried that maybe the messages in the reading and his dream meant that the Franciscan order would send him somewhere else. He was concerned about his vow of obedience if that happened.

"When Father John was having many trials with someone he was working with, I received the impression, spiritually, for him to pray to Saint Philomena. It seems that when he started praying with her, asking for her prayers to guide him, that things started working out very well. Everything suddenly started falling into place. I remember him saying, 'Oh, that's Saint Philomena. She always comes through one way or another.' In fact, the last thing I gave him was a biography of Saint Philomena."

One April evening during the live television program, George saw the Angel of Death appear over that part of the audience where Father John sat. Thinking that symbol could go to any of a number of people there, George let it go.

"On Monday, May 1, 1989, I was doing readings for a group of bereaved people," George recalls. "There was a terrible storm outside, and it was raining heavily. I glanced at my watch. It was about 10:20 in the evening, and Father John came into my mind. It was as if he walked through the room and said something to the effect of 'George, I'm here.' I thought I was daydreaming. I took it to mean that I was just thinking about him."

At about 4:00 the next morning George was startled awake by the sound of pounding on his front door. When he opened it, a friend of his blurted out, "Father John was killed last night in a car accident!"

"I realized," says George, "that the time I had seen him appear earlier in the evening was about an hour after his passing."

The priest was riding in a car when it skidded out of control on a winding, rain-swept road and collided with an oncoming vehicle. Father John was killed instantly, as was the driver of the other car, a young, pregnant mother of two.

George and I, as well as my wife Chris and our friend Elise, were all devastated by Father John's death. George was especially shaken. He admits that despite his work with the bereaved and virtually lifelong communications from spirits, funerals and wakes unnerve him. "It took me two hours to go into the room at the funeral parlor where Father John's body was laid out and to walk up to the coffin," George says, the memory still fresh in his mind.

"When I went home that night, I said to myself, 'Here's an opportunity.' I prayed to Saint Philomena on Father John's behalf. And I also asked him, 'Father, give me a sign that what I'm doing is of God. That it is God's work and that I'm doing the right thing and that there is another side. And that you're okay. But you must give me the sign through Saint Philomena. I don't care what, just something to do with her.'

"The next morning I attended the funeral mass for Father John. The first reading was taken from the Book of Wisdom in the Bible, and I wasn't really paying attention until the priest started reciting it:

The souls of the just are in the hand of God, and the torment of death shall not touch them. In the sight of the unwise, they seemed to die; and their departure was taken for misery; and their going away from us for utter destruction. But they are in peace. And though in the sight of men they suffered torments, their hope is full of immortality. Afflicted in few things, in many they shall be well rewarded, because God hath tried them and found them worthy of Himself. As gold in the furnace He hath proved them, and as a victim of a holocaust He hath received them, and in time there shall be respect had to them. The just shall shine and shall run to and fro like sparks among the reeds. They shall judge nations and rule over people, and their Lord shall reign forever.

"As the priest delivered that first reading, it dawned on me where I heard it before," George says. "It really was the sign, because the last thing I gave Father John was that biography of Saint Philomena, the very first page of which opens with that exact quote.

"I sat in church, stunned. I knew it was Father John, and I immediately felt tranquil and comforted. He was okay. This was his sign to me. He brought it through exactly as I had asked, through Saint Philomena. After all those years and so much experience with the other side, I never would have suspected it would be something so concrete.

"Two weeks after the funeral, I received a package in the mail containing a statuette of Saint Philomena. Somebody who'd come to me for a reading went out of his way to find it and send it to me. The man who sent it said he found it through Saint Philomena's Church in Pittsburgh. I felt that was the tail end of the sign."

Only after Father John's death did George put together the pieces of his psychic clues. As we have discussed earlier, psychic symbols can sometimes have three or four different meanings. They are much like the symbols we frequently dream in. It becomes George's task to interpret the psychic symbols. There were so many questions.

Why did George see the Angel of Death the night Father John was at the TV studio, only days prior to his death? Did George mistake a vision for a daydream when he thought about Father John less than an hour after he was killed?

In his reading for Father John, George relayed the priest's

father's claim that he saw his son making "a radical change of work." Later the priest told George about a dream in which his father conveyed the same message. George now comprehended the meaning of both the dream and the psychic reading. "Obviously Father John was being prepared to pass over."

All of these signs raise the question, Could Father John's death have been prevented?

"I have to say no," George says. "Because it was probably his time to pass on. It doesn't have to do with the circumstances; he could have passed on from a heart attack. The irony is that when I spoke to him a short time before he passed, he told me he had gone to the doctor because he hadn't felt well. He had high blood pressure and some digestive problems. I told him to stop smoking. Well, that's not what killed him."

So many people have experienced premonitions of a loved one's death. Among the readings in this book, several subjects told of theirs. The young mother whose five-year-old seems to have predicted his own death no doubt wonders how he knew, and why. Was there anything she could have done for him? Or anything George might have done had he correctly interpreted the clues he was given? Can death ever be predicted or prevented?

George answers, "Usually, no. You can only hint at it if it's rather obvious. Generally, we're not meant to know when it's our time." Apparently, this is another aspect of death we must simply accept.

Some months after Father John's death, a friend and parishioner of his went to George for a reading. Father John came through from the other side. His experiences with George, he said, "prepared me for the transition to the next stage." There Father John is as busy as he was here, tirelessly continuing the work he had begun on earth.

A Question of Faith

When Police Officer Scott Adam Gadell was murdered on June 28, 1986, he had the tragic distinction of being the first New York City cop shot and killed in the line of duty by a crack dealer. Sitting in his patrol car on a dark, crime-scarred ghetto street, he was approached from behind and gunned down at point-blank range. He was only twenty-two years old.

His mother, Carol Gadell, recalls the moment she learned that her son had been killed by a bullet to the head. "I became numb. My whole body seemed to have died. I couldn't move. My brain was not able to function. I couldn't see or hear. There were people around me. Their mouths were moving, but I heard nothing.

"I went for counseling. I'm thankful my family and children and my friends were there for me. Among families of slain police officers, there's a great deal of support, and that's helped me. I also belong to Parents of Murdered Children. They've listened to me talk, and I've repeated the same thing over and over a hundred times, but I love them and they love me, so they were able to deal with my loss."

But as is so often the case, Mrs. Gadell and her husband needed something more. Sensing this, a clergyman suggested that they see George. After their reading, Carol Gadell explained what it had meant to her. "George told me that Scott has greeted many other people on the other side since he got there. His grandparents were there to greet him. Then, in turn, he greeted a lot of other police officers who were subsequently killed and came over. They're all with him now.

"George told me that Scott is with us at all times. We can't see him, but we do feel his presence. Scott told him also that he felt his family has suffered a great deal of pain and that he was sorry for us and for the suffering we've gone through. Scott never said he wanted revenge in any way. He did feel that justice would prevail, if not here, then in the hereafter. It's a comfort to me knowing that Scott is all right and that he's there with other people and that he's taking care of them and they're taking care of him.

"[In the reading] George knew who Scott was named after, his grandfather. Then he psychically saw a blue suit and other uniforms in my house, including a military uniform. My husband wears a uniform, too. He's a bus driver. George said, 'I see so many different kinds of uniforms.' Then George brought out that Scott was a police officer.

"I've come to terms with what's happened to this extent: I feel Scott's at peace, so I have to be at peace," the slain officer's mother says. "I feel that this is hell we're living in here on earth. Scott's in a better place, and someday I will be there, and he will be there to greet me."

In another reading for a slain policeman's parents who've requested anonymity, George told the father, an ex-cop, and his wife, "There's a loss of a son."

"Yes," the man acknowledged.

"Your son or someone is in uniform."

"Yes."

Later, after discerning that their son was a police officer, George said, "There's injury to his head."

"Yes."

"He says he's sorry he couldn't—that he didn't—go down fighting."

"Yes, I understand," the man answered.

"He was killed in the line of duty, he tells me."

"Yes."

"It was more like he was killed in cold blood."

"Yes."

"I hear shots. Gunshots."

"Yes."

"He was shot in the head? Because there's pain or pressure to my head."

"Yes."

"Is there a Bobby or Bob? Robert?"

"Yes."

"Is he another cop? Your son calls to him. They must have

been friends. He also calls to his grandparents. They're living."

"Yes. They were close."

"And he calls to a girl. He was seeing her, dating her. I'm seeing the symbol of hearts and roses," George explained.

"Yes," the woman answered.

"You were in uniform, too?" George asked the father.

"Yes," he acknowledged. "I was a police officer also."

"Your son thanks you for your constant prayers. You've been praying for him."

"Yes."

"He asks you to tell his friend Bobby's wife that you've heard from him, if she's open to this."

"Okay."

"Your son calls to both of you. He says he's over the anxiety of passing. He says, 'I do love Dad best of all. I hope I don't hurt anyone's feelings.' "

"Okay. We understand."

"He calls out to Shirley."

"Yes, that's my name," the mother said.

"Do you take the name Craig?"

"Yes, that's our son!" she exclaimed.

"Your son says he followed in your footsteps," George said to the man.

"Yes, that's right," he acknowledged.

"He says he became a policeman like you. He's the only one of your children who did."

"Right."

"He calls to William."

"Yes. That's my dad; my son's grandfather."

"Who's Frances? He says, 'Frances.' "

"That's his grandmother," he replied.

"There are a number of other slain policemen with Craig. They're all around him on the other side. They were all given Saint Michael awards there. That's like a spiritual Purple Heart for the sacrifice they made, giving their lives in the line of duty. Saint Michael the Archangel is the patron of police officers," George explained. "He's with a grandfather on the other side; he's calling him Poppa."

"Yes, that's what he always called him," the woman said.

"Your son thanks you for all you've done for him since his

passing. He says he's okay, and he's settled with himself. He asks you to pray for him, of course. He sends his love."

This hero cop's parents found their reading extremely comforting. Yet like so many others who've come to George, they wondered initially if consulting a psychic medium was "right." The number of subjects who agreed to participate in this book only under the guarantee of anonymity attests to the lingering social stigma attached to those who in any way venture into the psychic unknown.

People seem especially concerned about where and how George's ability fits in with traditional religious beliefs. One afternoon not long ago, a pastor of a local Catholic church invited George to lunch with him and several other priests in the church's rectory. It was an occasion that earlier would have been unthinkable. Although local clergymen often refer parishioners to George, most organized religions are officially opposed to what he does.

This group of priests had recently visited George's home to observe several psychic readings. They had heard from others in the community about his gift. They watched quietly, offering neither endorsement nor opinion. But the very fact that they came and were open to his work meant a great deal to George, who'd been raised in the Catholic Church.

George eagerly accepted their invitation. Much to his surprise, he did most of the talking during the meal. He described the afternoon as a "spiritual exchange" among him, the five priests, and two seminarians. His hosts appeared more interested in listening and questioning George about his psychic ability than offering their personal views. Their conversations reflect much about organized religion's sometimes contradictory views of psychic phenomena, even within one specific order.

When the youngest of the group, a seminarian, remarked that psychic ability was a relatively newly discovered phenomenon, the oldest priest gently but firmly reminded him that psychic gifts, specifically discerning spirits, have been known and recorded for centuries.

The pastor, having recently observed George, commented that he'd noticed how comforted subjects appeared after their readings. "You're giving them something that's touching them, something beyond what we the clergy can do, I admit. They're comforted. Their faces show it," the pastor said.

Next, the group of clerics eagerly asked questions of George. "What's the difference between your ability and what's called 'spiritism'? " one asked.

"I don't conjure or consult with spirits," George replied. "There are no Ouija boards or séances. I strictly discern or distinguish spirits. I don't summon them."

"What's your opinion of hell?" another inquired.

"I do feel it exists. It's a very low level of existence. You have to want to put yourself there by severely breaking God's law. Murder is an example of that kind of transgression. You condemn yourself to hell by hating God and what He represents, which is all that's good and positive."

"How has this made you closer to God?"

"Because I get to 'see' God in action through the experience of psychic readings. I get to see and feel what God is all about, firsthand, through the exchange between me and the spirits, and then in the comfort a bereaved parent receives, or a lonely elderly person who's lost a loved one."

"Do you literally see the saints?"

"At times, yes, I see the saints. Other times they appear as saints or visionary pictures to provide me with a clue to some aspect of the psychic reading. When a saint actually appears, it's projected in front of me as a being of overwhelmingly celestial light."

"What about the other side? Are there different levels?"

"There seems to be seven spiritual levels, apart from two darker levels many call hell. There's an introductory level where souls arrive to begin their move up to the higher level. There are normal, or average, levels where most souls go next. Following that are levels of higher light. The highest planes are the celestial levels. People like Mother Teresa would move immediately to the highest, celestial levels. However, most of us can work our way up because, as Christ promises, we can become one with God."

"Have people converted to religion because of their experiences with your ability?"

"Several people have written to tell me they have. A man in upstate New York [John Elliot, father of David] converted to Catholicism after he heard from his son who'd passed on. The man had been an agnostic. A young woman wrote to say that she, too, converted after hearing from her sister who passed tragically. But I tell people that the decision to convert must be their own, not mine. A young Jewish woman asked me if I thought she should convert to Catholicism. I told her to first look more deeply at her own religion before changing. If anyone wants to convert, I advise him or her to see qualified clergy. Religious faith is a personal experience between you and God. You have to do what's best for yourself. I prefer to keep my religious beliefs to myself."

"Have you ever seen heaven or Jesus?"

"I've sensed Jesus Christ by feeling His presence during readings. I've both seen and sensed heaven, as you call it. My glimpses of heaven, or the other side, are that it is very beautiful and serene. It seems to be a perfect place. It's not unlike the way many people have described near-death experiences in which they report rising out of their body, going through a tunnel, and being met by a deceased loved one, surrounded by bright lights and colors."

The priests and George also discussed the history and tradition of apparitions in the Church, such as the visions seen at Lourdes and Fatima. "Saint Paul saw Christ in a vision," one of the priests reminded the group.

The men spoke about biblical prophecies and saints who could discern spirits. "Therefore," said one priest, "there should be no conflict between George's gift and what the Church teaches."

George thought the older priests seemed more accepting of his ability and his answers to their questions than the young men. They appeared to have a better comprehension of mysticism and seemed to need less complicated explanations than their younger brethren. George felt the more experienced clerics understood and accepted that "this is how God works."

Not surprisingly, not all religious leaders agree—in large part, we believe, because aspects of psychic phenomena place the spiritual experience within the sole control of the individual. Following a psychic reading, many people do reexamine their religious beliefs. For those who came believing in life after death, there is confirmation. For former skeptics, atheists, agnostics, and those dissatisfied with organized religion, a reading can throw long-held assumptions into chaos. Some come away feeling slightly different about life after death; others are shaken to the core. In either event, each subject decides for himself what the reading meant.

Despite all the seeming overlaps between the content of George's readings and long-held beliefs, he endorses no particular faith. People from such diverse religious backgrounds as Buddhism, Shintoism, Islam, and Judaism have had readings with no less emotional impact because George "spoke the language" of Christianity. He relayed meaningful messages from loved ones to people of all faiths and opinions.

Much of what George has learned from the other side reinforces traditional Christian beliefs: the continued existence of a soul after physical death, for example. At the same time, the absence of God as a judge of souls or a fiery, torturous hell of punishment directly contradicts the tenets of some sects. The very idea that homosexuals or drug abusers will not be made to suffer after death is in itself repugnant to the more judgmental. In the past year several of George's friends in the priesthood have been told unofficially to be more discreet in their dealings with him. This concern on the part of a local bishop ostensibly came after a single complaint from a Fundamentalist minister. The old adage about avoiding discussions of religion is sound advice, yet we find it impossible not to address some key questions George is often asked.

Since *We Don't Die,* George has undergone a change in attitude toward organized religion, though he remains a steadfast spiritual Christian. As a result of seeing and knowing so many bereaved people, he feels an acute need to address what he views as the harmful, crippling attitude toward death many people have learned through organized religion.

Many people will say that you cannot have a belief in an afterlife and the other side, without a belief in religion and/or God.

"You can have a belief in the afterlife on the other side if you want to believe and know God and believe in Him spiritually. When it comes to organized religion, I don't belong to any tribe. I consider myself a person who is trying to be spiritual the best way I can. I'm no better than anybody else, and I don't know it all. However, I don't feel that you need to be of a certain religion to have a certain belief.

"I had a woman come to me from Japan for a reading. She asked if she could bring me something from her country. I said, 'Can you bring me something on the beliefs and teachings of the Shinto faith?' I don't want to become a Shintoist, but I want to learn about their spiritual beliefs. She also wrote to me, 'Would you be interested in Buddhism, too?' I said, 'Most definitely. I would like to learn.' Just as if somebody came up to me and said, 'I'd like to learn about Jesus Christ. Can you give me some information or books to read?,' I'd say, 'Of course.' I wouldn't try converting that person to Christianity. But he or she can learn *spiritually* from what Jesus Christ had to say."

What about the atheists and agnostics who say there is no God and no afterlife?

"See you on the other side someday!

"One of my most interesting readings concerning atheists was one I did for a visiting Russian government official years ago. In it, the spirit of a man named Josef came through and explained that he had been a close friend of the subject's family when the official was a young boy. It seemed he had cared for and helped raise the child while his parents worked.

"What I found interesting was that Josef had been a staunch communist and atheist while on earth. His spirit admitted that, like millions of Soviet citizens, he had believed that death was final and that there was no God. In other words, Josef had no doubt that there was nothing beyond the communist state.

"But now, from the other side, Josef acknowledged that there is, indeed, life after death and that God does exist. Josef explained that when he died, at first he thought he was dreaming or hallucinating, but he eventually realized he was alive in the next stage. He was initially confused, because he'd been conditioned all his life to believe otherwise. More relatives and friends of the Soviet official also came through from the other side with similar messages. The experience heartened me. For a Russian citizen raised in an officially atheistic state, details of an afterlife—and messages from there—are not everyday occurrences!

"Nearly two years after that reading, I received a letter from a Soviet institute in Leningrad, inviting me there so that their scientists could test my psychic abilities. Of course, the Soviets have studied the paranormal for decades. I was greatly looking forward to going, but things didn't work out, because I would have had to spend at least a month there. Perhaps in the future.

"The point is, I almost imagine the millions upon millions of souls crossed over who were convinced there was no afterlife. Think of their surprise! I always tell people, 'We're all going to croak sooner or later, so one of these days someone's going to be proven wrong. And I can guarantee you it won't be me.'

"There *is* life after death. These people *do* live on, and you *will* be with them again someday. Have your grief, accept the fact that you're going to miss them, but don't feel that just because the coffin is sealed and buried that you have to forget about them. Certainly still bring them up in family conversation and talk about them as if they're still here, because in a sense they still are.

"I think so many times we feel that death is such a termination, such an ending, that we have to end it, we have to die with them and forget about it. I don't think we have to. Live on with them, as the person is living on in the next stage of life. As I explain to people, it's as if your son went away and joined the Peace Corps: you know he's in Africa someplace, but you're just not going to hear from him as often as you did in the past. Accept the fact that your loved one is living in another stage of life, that she is there, and that one of these days you're going to join her, when your time comes."

What do you say to those people who have a religious persuasion—Fundamentalists, especially—who would suggest that what you're doing is the work of the devil? Do you see yourself opposed to what religion says, or do you see more similarities than differences?

"The only thing I would say to people like that is: Organized religion has never had any use for me; I don't have any use for organized religion. No one has the right to make me justify my spiritual beliefs. They're protected under the First Amendment of the U.S. Constitution: a point too many Americans seem to be losing sight of. As far as I'm concerned, what's between me and the Lord is my business and His, and I don't discuss it. Religion is a private thing, and I want to keep it that way. We have something in common: We disagree, so we'll just have to agree to disagree.

"The fact is that when grief overwhelms, rigid religious dogma is quickly laid aside. For example, a Fundamentalist Christian minister in a small southern community lost his young wife to cancer. He contacted me, which is clearly in defiance of his denomination's prohibitions against mediumship. But he needed to hear from her once again, to know she was safe and at peace.

"From the other side, his wife said to me that she was in Christ's light. I told her husband that she kept reading a psalm back to him. She kept telling me that she was reading him the twenty-third psalm, 'The Lord is my shepherd . . .'

"He told me that no one could possibly know that. What ultimately convinced him beyond a question of a doubt that it was his wife present from the other side was her mentioning that psalm. He explained that as she lay dying, in a coma, he sat at her bedside reading to her from the Bible. He selected Psalm 23. They were alone in the room at the time.

"She told me that she felt that this [psychic reading] was an experience she would never have had on earth. She admitted that as a religious Fundamentalist she would have questioned someone like me and would have asked, 'Is this the work of the devil?'

"One evening I accepted an invitation to observe a widows and widowers bereavement support group at a local church. There were about twenty-five people present, all of them seeking answers to their respective losses within their faith by sharing their experiences.

"During a question-and-answer period, a middle-aged woman said, 'Father, tell me: I just have to know that my husband is alive and that I'll be with him again someday.' The priest did not reply. I sat quietly for a few moments, then I just started seeing red. It seemed so insensitive. *How, I wondered, is there not a simple explanation offered her*

*within Catholic teaching that her husband's soul is safe and at
peace, and that they will eventually be reunited?*

"When I couldn't contain my frustration, I really surprised myself! I rose to my feet and declared, '*I* can guarantee it. Your husband *is* still with you, and you *will* be
together again. He will meet you when you pass on. Lady,
I'll prove it right here and now. Don't just believe in God;
know there is a God!'

"All eyes in the room were on me. Suddenly I realized
what I'd done and sat down, a little embarrassed but wanting to see if she or anyone would accept my challenge to
demonstrate a reading. Unfortunately, no one did. Looking
back, I realize that they and the priest probably thought I
was nuts.

"I hadn't meant what I said as a boast. I just wanted to
reassure her that her husband was still very much alive on
the other side and waiting for her. Later, people did make
appointments to see me privately, but I still want that one
widow to know in her heart that her husband truly did not
die."

*A woman who was devastated by the loss of her son asked me,
"Why does God take our children?" A lot of people would
disagree with you, but I know you would say, "God doesn't do
that."*

"No, God does not. I'm sorry to have to say this, but I'm
not really surprised that people feel that way. Most people
come to me because they have experienced tremendous loss.
Parents who have lost children especially say that the first
thing that fails them is organized religion. It doesn't matter
whether you're Baptist, Catholic, Presbyterian, Jewish,
whatever. For one thing, I feel, and a lot of bereavement
support groups agree, that the clergy are not really well
trained to handle bereavement. I'm sure there are clergy out
there who will disagree with me, because there are surely
some exceptional clergy who do a marvelous job. But I'm
talking about overall, and that's my observation.

"A woman I met went to a Christian church-oriented
bereavement weekend after losing her husband. All she got
out of it were Bible quotes—which she could have read

herself at home—and an envelope in her room for donations. Since these people are supposed to represent God, she couldn't understand what their hang-up with death was. 'Why are they afraid of it?' she asked me. 'Why are they unsure of it?'

"She was brought up very, very strictly within her faith and was very secure in her faith. But when her husband died, she felt she had to sit back and say to herself, 'Wait a minute, I have to question things now, because these people aren't sure that there is a God. They don't know how to answer you.'

"As I tell bereaved parents when they come to me, 'Don't think that God has consciously, deliberately singled out your family. Why would God do that?' If that's His way of proving love, as many organized religions would have you believe, that's hardly the work of an enlightened, all-positive being.

"To the parents who ask, 'Why did God do this to me?' I say, 'God did not do that *to you*.' I know what I'm about to say may sound flippant, but I want people to think hard about this. I ask them, 'Do you really think God has nothing better to do than to sit around and say, "Ah, I think I'll kill Mrs. Jones's son; she needs a good lesson. Let's have him get killed in a car accident. We'll bring him over to the other side. Maybe she'll learn how to be a better Christian." ' I simply can't believe that.

"I had a woman come up from Texas, and I was appalled—but not surprised—when she told me this: She had been a very devout Baptist. After her son died in a car accident, one of her congregation's deacons told her he'd been killed because 'obviously' Jesus called him home as a way to bring to her attention that perhaps she wasn't a good enough Christian!

"Now, if that's how Christ works, I'm an atheist. If that's how God works, I'm an atheist. Usually I try so very hard to keep my emotions and personal feelings out of it, but I couldn't help saying to her, 'Do you believe that? That's not what Jesus Christ is all about; that's not what He represented. If you read your Bible carefully, or any of the teachings of Christ, the complete essence of God is the sense of compassion, love, and mercy.' "

•   •   •

What about guilt? For example, there was a young couple whose infant had passed before he was baptized, and they were torn up about that, terribly.

"The parents were afraid that the baby was in limbo, because he had not been baptized. I just looked at the parents and said, 'Do you really believe that? Do you really believe that God is so unloving and unmerciful that He would confine an innocent child "in limbo," because he didn't have water sprinkled on his head?' Again, attitudes like that only add to people's pain, as if it weren't enough that their loved one had died.

"Society and organized religion supposedly teach us how we should live, how we should organize our lives, what we should do. Yet institutions cannot prepare us for these tragedies. Nothing can.

"You should recognize and accept that to a certain degree, you're never going to completely 'get over it.' Some people believe, definitely, in a life hereafter, and they come to me to be reassured of what they already believe. I can't tell you how many parents have come to me and said they were considering killing themselves because they just had to know that the loved one was okay over there."

You spoke to a man from California whose fiancée was murdered. All he wanted to know was, Did she still love him?

"People need reassurance. It's human. They need that comfort. And if using me as the instrument—as I always say, through Saint Philomena's prayers and God's grace—can achieve that, that's fine."

There was a very dramatic reading you did for a young woman who was sexually abused for many years at the hands of her father. And now he comes through from the other side and says, "I'm sorry." All of a sudden he has this wisdom on the other side that he didn't possess here.

"He probably had the wisdom here, but he didn't want to apply it. Anybody with half a brain knows that you don't sexually abuse your children. But if he chooses to take the negative path, that's his choice."

•   •   •

And should she forgive him? He did apologize.

"Yes, she should, for her sake more so, but for his also. This relieves her of a tremendous amount of guilt and negativity that's been haunting her since childhood, and it clears the slate on both ends. But more importantly, it can put the individual at peace. As always, though, it's her decision."

Why is the other side so forgiving? Why don't souls come through angry or bitter at those who hurt or wronged them here on earth?

"Certainly there are such spirits out there, and I've heard from a few. But because I always pray for only the highest and best to come through, I hear from such spirits rarely. Before every private reading or group discernment I quietly say a prayer to the Holy Spirit as well as requesting Saint Philomena's prayers and intercession.

"This is the prayer: 'Breathe in me, O Holy Spirit, that my thoughts may all be holy. Act in me, O Holy Spirit, that my work, too, may be holy. Draw my heart, O Holy Spirit, that I love but what is holy. Strengthen me, O Holy Spirit, to defend all that is holy. Guard me then, O Holy Spirit, that I always may be holy.'

"By saying this prayer I hope to attract only the highest and best from the other side, those that are with God or making a sincere attempt to find God through recognition of their faults."

How does the other side advise us to handle the grief, the anger, the guilt, that whole range of emotions the bereaved experience?

"It's very hard to answer that, because, again, they seem to frown on telling anybody what to do. They always leave it up to the individual to make his or her own choice. The other side is very 'pro-choice,' in the sense of people making their own decisions. They encourage acceptance. They suggest to subjects that they are certainly still 'alive' and at peace, that they will be with them. They do give them hope, but they don't tell them how they should handle it."

•   •   •

Yet sometimes they do advise us. Look at these examples, in some recent readings: The parents from the other side said, "Drive carefully." A child said to the parent here, "Daddy, give up the anger." And I recall a son who'd passed on saying to his mother, "Let up on my brothers and sisters, let them live their lives, stop being so domineering." They do give advice.

"Yes, they do, but it's not in the form of an order. It's advice or a suggestion. It's ultimately up to the receiver to take it or leave it."

And other times they don't tell us what to do; they let us have our own experience.

"Definitely. They never formally tell us what to do. They basically drop an idea into our heads, and if it is meant to blossom, it will. The point is, it has to become our idea to follow it up."

Sometimes they go into the future; other times not. I know of one case where a grandparent warned a teenager, "Drive carefully; you're going to lose that car." And he was later involved in a terrible accident.

"I'll always temper such a message with my cynicism, saying, 'Well, all of us should drive defensively, but this is what they're stating.' Other times, they do foresee the future, but it doesn't happen that often, and I try to dissuade people from relying on something a loved one says from the other side any more than they would if that person were still alive in this dimension. From what the other side has told me, we probably have more free will than we realize. Of course, there's not much you can do about an earthquake, another crazy driver on the road, or those flukes of physics we call accidents. But a lot of what the other side is trying to teach us is to think for ourselves."

Does the other side ever say what purpose there is for being here on earth? A lot of people even question what this is all about here.

"I've asked that several times, and they have said to me that this is school, this is the proving ground, this is where we, of our own free will, have chosen to come to try earning spiritual 'points,' or progress. You can stay on the other side and earn those spiritual points, but, believe it or not, life on earth is the short cut. This life is an excellent proving ground. There are so many good things here, but as we all know, also much that is difficult, heartbreaking, and painful."

What you're saying is, when we are on the other side, we are making the choice to come back. Is that what I am to understand? It's our decision to be born?

"It seems we make that choice through God's grace and help. You throw yourself into a situation here on the earth where you're affected by everything: different peoples, different persuasions, different life-styles. You cannot be a perfect soul until you've experienced and harmonized yourself with everything that life here has to offer, and I mean *everything*, good and bad. Remember, as I've told many people, the greatest lesson to learn here is acceptance, of others and of ourselves, of the good things that happen to us and the bad. But remember that through it all, our loved ones are always here for us, even on the other side."

The next logical question would be, Is there such a thing as reincarnation?

"I am basically open-minded to the belief in reincarnation. However, the reason I would not encourage people to be overly enthusiastic about reincarnation is because I feel we should concentrate on doing our best in *this* life. Don't worry about who you were or might have been in a past life or who you could or might be in a future life. As the Chinese proverb states, 'It is already later than you think.'

"There is plenty of evidence that reincarnation exists, or at least that millions of people throughout history have believed so. The New Testament's books of Matthew and John contain passages suggesting a belief in reincarnation. Further, there is good reason to believe that the early Christian Church removed many references to reincarnation from the Scriptures for purposes of theological control.

"Many great figures in world history were believers in reincarnation, including Saint Francis of Assisi, Voltaire,

Benjamin Franklin, Thomas Edison, Henry Ford, and General George Patton, who was, he felt, a Roman warrior in a past life.

"One problem I find with reincarnation as it is discussed today is the popular emphasis on who or what we were in previous lives. It seems that everyone was a king or queen or someone famous in a past life. No one seems to have been the individual who shoveled out the king's barn. But that doesn't diminish reincarnation as a valuable concept."

If you are reincarnated, can you still come through from the other side?

"I have to say I don't know. However, souls on the other side have told me that families or people you know and love always stay together. Love is more powerful, so the soul who passes before other loved ones will wait for them. Remember, there is no conception of time on the other side, as we know it. As to whether or not they all reincarnate to live together again, I can't really say, but it would seem consistent.

"All I know is that I've never gotten a message from the other side in which I've been told 'Jack's not here. He's reincarnated.' However, souls have said from the other side that they've heard rumors about the doctrine of reincarnation. It depends on their soul growth, because a higher entity who is very enlightened may totally understand the doctrine of reincarnation.

Do the evil ever come back? Are the evil ever reincarnated?

"Yes, but when? A Hitler will be in hell at the darker levels on the other side for eons of time. As the Buddha taught, one cannot escape the results of one's actions. Again, what that means for us living on earth is not entirely clear."

Do we choose whom we will be reincarnated as?

"From what I understand, yes we do. But it's not been made clear to me yet what our choices are, or how or why we arrive at them. I certainly do not believe, as some New Age gurus do, that a person who suffers from a dreadful disease, such as AIDS, or has abusive parents 'chose' those circumstances. It's a very complex subject, one experts have debated for thousands of years. I wish the other side would tell me more about it. Maybe someday."

What would be your complaints, if any, about a belief in life after death?

"It really troubles me when people 'dwell on the grave' or put all their energies into what they'll be doing in the next life. I believe that it's our responsibility to do our best— whatever plane we're on—to make that world a better place for everyone. Unfortunately, I've seen too many people who simply dismiss what's going on in this world, who say 'it doesn't matter,' because the 'real' or 'better' world awaits them after death. Well, maybe yes and maybe no. One thing I've learned from the other side is that what we do here really does count toward our soul's progression over there, and I don't mean just going to church regularly. While here on this earth we should work to make it as productive and pleasant as possible, not only for ourselves, but for the generations that follow. I don't believe, as many organized religions preach, that these two 'worlds' are unconnected. We should be using our individual intelligence and our energies to protect the environment, for example, to learn to get along much better than we do. It seems only logical that our opportunities for spiritual development here would be greatly enhanced if we could ensure the Earth would support our descendants and all God's creatures for centuries to come. Or if we could banish prejudice and war forever. Even though we know there is life after death, we should live as if this is the only life, and work for harmony in everything we do."

Appendix One

THE ELECTROENCEPHALOGRAM TEST

George continues to be studied by experts in various medical and scientific disciplines interested in demonstrating evidence of psychic-mediumistic ability. Over the years, the tests and experiments have included thermography, computer tests to determine the statistical probabilities of George's accuracy, sympathetic pain, experiments dealing with electromagnetic energies, and psychological studies.

The main drawback to testing George's ability is that no one knows why or how it works. In order to devise a test of any type—be it a brain-wave test or a blood test—you must know what you're testing *for,* what results can emerge, and what information those results convey. Because we know and understand the hormonal changes of pregnancy, the specific appearance of microbes and viruses, and the characteristics of nerve damage, scientists have devised tests for them. In contrast, psychic phenomena are so little understood, no test for them exists. There *are* experiments, like J. B. Rhine's famous Zener cards used to measure ESP (extrasensory perception). But these provide only a means of comparing one person's performance at identifying the unseen card against other people's and a statistical mean. The tests in and of themselves cannot "prove" that someone has psychic ability, where it comes from, or how it works. All they can show is that psychic ability exists and the degree to which one person or another might have it.

In countless instances, the bridge to knowledge was a piece of equipment or a new technique. After all, stars existed "unseen" long before the advent of the telescope, and "invisible" microbes long before the microscope. Perhaps one day there will be a test for what George does. Until then we can use tests and experiments to show what he is *not* doing (as we've noted, George scores miserably low on ESP and telepathy tests) and to give us some idea of what happens to George when he uses his ability.

In 1984 George underwent a series of tests using a heat-sensitive diagnostic imaging device, to measure differences in body temperature. Reading after reading, the thermography test showed George's body "heating up" in those areas where and at exactly the instant he claimed to be experiencing sympathetic pain or sensation. There is no way George could have created these "hot spots" voluntarily. Clearly, something was happening, but what? For now, we (and George) are at least partially satisfied knowing that something is happening and science is gradually making strides to understand it.

From the very beginning, George and I have believed that whatever the key to his ability, it lies somewhere in his brain. The amount of new information about the brain seems to grow daily, thanks in part to advanced imaging methods.

Several months after *We Don't Die* was published, George met Dr. Joseph Casarona, a neurologist and then acting chief of a New York City hospital's neurology department. After witnessing George's readings, Dr. Casarona invited him to be tested in an attempt to see if any evidence of his psychic-mediumistic ability would manifest on an electroencephalogram, or EEG. An electroencephalogram charts brain-wave activity by measuring the electrical activity produced from the top layer, the gray matter, which comprises the outer cerebral cortex. During the course of a day, our brain waves change many times, depending on what we're doing, even what we're thinking about. Presumably, any unusual brain-wave activity in George during readings would show itself on the EEG.

There are four brain-wave states: beta, alpha, theta, and delta. Beta is the "awake state," indicated on the EEG as between 14 and 30 cycles per second, or cps. Deep relaxation of mind and body produces alpha waves at 8 to 13 cps. Theta waves indicate drowsiness or very deep relaxation, often unconsciousness (between 4 and 7 cps). Delta, the deep-sleep state, or unconsciousness, shows as .05 to 3.5 cps. Simply put, the more active and alert your brain is, the greater number of cycles per second show up on the EEG. Each night as you drift from alertness to light sleep to deeper sleep, your brain waves gradually slow down.

The EEG is also used to detect and diagnose problems in the brain. Certain types of brain disease and damage can cause atypical brain-wave patterns. In addition to watching the EEG for brain-wave variations during readings, Dr. Casarona would be looking for any signs of brain abnormality or damage.

"Regardless of whether the manifestation is psychiatric or psychic," explained Dr. Casarona, "my overall interest in this is observing the electrical activity in the brain and localizing it to a specific area within the brain. By doing this, we can interpret how and where these particular energies are affected by George's psychic abilities. I had absolutely no expectations at all of what we might find."

During the three-hour session, which was videotaped, the doctor was assisted by an experienced EEG technician. Once in the hospital room containing the EEG equipment, George was instructed to lie on his back on an examining table. He was told to make himself comfortable but to remain as motionless as possible so as not to cause any interference with his EEG recording.

While electrodes were being attached to George's head, he quipped, "I look like Frankenstein's monster!" And he did. Before George did any readings, the doctor took a sample EEG to establish a baseline, or a record of George's normal brain-wave patterns. This "normalized EEG" showed George's brain-wave activity to be in the alpha, or deep relaxation, state. There was nothing unusual about that. As the technician observed the EEG's printed graph, an anonymous subject selected by Dr. Casarona was brought in for George to read. George had never met the young man before.

George correctly discerned that a close male friend of the subject had passed on from cancer. The subject's father too came through, apologizing to his son for not being closer to him and admitting that he should have been more understanding. He also said he realized after his death that he had been "insensitive." George gave the young man's father's name, Joseph, and a message from him: "You should be wearing glasses, but you're not." The subject acknowledged that all the information was correct. He was clearly moved by the experience, responding emotionally to each of George's statements.

The EEG technician remarked that she was very surprised to see George's brain-wave activity slow down during the reading, although he remained fully alert. Once the reading ended, George's brain-wave activity returned to normal.

Next Dr. Casarona brought in a second anonymous subject: a youthful-looking man with dark, curly hair and dark eyes. He was dressed very casually in jeans and a white T-shirt bearing the Italian flag.

George correctly discerned that despite his youthful appearance and casual dress, the subject was a medical doctor, an internist, who worked at the hospital. And despite his wearing the colors of the Italian flag, George psychically heard the man's deceased relatives speaking Yiddish. The subject admitted he was Jewish. George also correctly discerned that the doctor—who wore no wedding band or other jewelry—was married, with a child.

Again the EEG graphing showed that even though George remained fully awake and alert during the reading, his brain-wave activity slowed down. And, again, as soon as his communication with the spirit world ended, his normal brain-wave activity resumed.

The brain-wave abnormalities were shown to come from two different parts of George's brain. "With each subject, there was a different EEG response during the readings, both of them abnormal," Dr. Casarona explained. "George's EEGs showed that the temporal and parietal lobes in the right side of his brain went into a very slow brain-wave activity—the theta [or drowsiness] state. In each reading the changes initiated in the right side of the brain. In the first reading it was localized to the right parietal lobe, the upper-back area of the brain, which is often called the sensory or passive part, because the body's sensory receptors originate there. In the second reading, this activity was seen in the right temporal lobe, an area approximately parallel to the temples. Hearing, memory, emotions, sense of self and time, even déjà-vu experiences, originate there.

"Such slow activity as we saw in George during the readings is not always abnormal in an EEG. However, it usually appears symmetrically, in both the left and right hemispheres. In George's case, the slow-wave activity was consistently on the right side of his brain. Therefore, I would consider this activity an abnormal finding."

As most people know, the right side of the brain is more intuitive, more emotional, if you will, than the left.

"In the second reading, slow-wave activity was followed by a sharp spikelike activity, which is often seen in those patients with seizure disorders, such as epilepsy. That too was found on the right side of the brain, asymmetrically, which is not generally a normal finding. Once again it ceased at the end of the reading.

"It was strange, because looking at the record of the second reading, I would have thought that it represented a more emotionally intense reading. In fact, in terms of content, the first reading was much more emotional. But it should be noted that both readings were very accurate. I would have expected the intensity of the slow-wave activity to increase with the intensity of the reading."

I asked Dr. Casarona if he expected to see these discrepancies from one subject to another.

"I was taken back," he admitted. "I didn't expect changes this blatant. And I didn't expect two very distinctive changes with the different subjects."

Could George have consciously induced these brain-wave changes through meditation or some other deliberate means?

"No, not in a unilateral sense on one side of the brain," said Dr. Casarona. "And the patient should not be wide awake and talking during these EEG changes." The reason for this is that the brain's two hemispheres work independently and then communicate with each other. "The right side of the brain is the passive side; it is involved with thinking, feelings, and organization. The left side is the active side, responsible for motor activity, talking, and personality," the doctor explained. "So it doesn't shock me that the slow-wave activity we saw began in the right side of the brain and was then communicated to the left side, where it was manifested verbally. That makes sense to me. What we saw in George's case was that even though he was alert, talking, and responsive with his subjects, the EEG records themselves were of someone who was going into a drowsy, dream-like state."

So why doesn't George become sleepy when his brain waves show he is in a sleeplike state? As a matter of fact, George says that during readings he feels wide awake, or, as he puts it, "charged up."

"It can't be explained at this time," said Dr. Casarona. "There *is* an absolute discrepancy between the EEG record and George's clinical state. To interpret that at this particular point would be a little precocious. But we do have it documented with these readings and videotapes.

"You cannot fool an EEG," he asserted. "Even if you induced George's brain-wave changes with psychoactive drugs, the findings would show symmetrical changes [in both brain hemispheres] and a clinical subject would be in a drowsy state. He would not show George's unilateral, asymmetrical changes. His is a grossly abnormal finding. Looking at this particular record, if I knew nothing about the subject, I would have said this patient has a right-cerebral dysfunctional abnormality, perhaps an underlying tumor, a blood clot, or a subdural hematoma . . . in other words, significant brain trauma from a past injury. We see the slow-wave activity in those cases because the brain cells are fewer and they conduct at a slower pace. Therefore, these abnormal EEG results would imply a structural lesion. But in George's case, the abnormality normalizes at the end of the reading, thus negating the possibility of a pathological structural abnormality."

George and I told Dr. Casarona about his childhood case of chicken pox, the resultant high fever and temporary paralysis, which were followed by George's first psychic experience. "That could imply the possibility of some brain damage, after which George's brain would have begun to heal itself," the doctor observed. "This healing results in connective tissue that forms a scar in the brain. The nervous tissue tries to replicate itself to replace the tissue that is damaged. Of course, it's never in the original structural state that it was prior to the [damage]. This sometimes results in a 'rewiring' or 'restructuring' of the brain tissue and its neuro-anatomical connections."

Scientists tell us there is a large portion of the human

brain that we do not yet understand, and that theoretically we have abilities not yet comprehended. For example, we do not fully understand memory, instincts, or dreaming. We asked the doctor if perhaps the key to George's ability lies somewhere in that as-yet unmapped terrain.

"The brain has capacities that we don't yet understand," Casarona concurred. "The brain basically works on a wiring system. There are billions and billions of circuits. If the circuits are not working properly or if there is damage to some of them, this results in 'misfiring.' There's a possibility that the damage from the chicken pox could have left George with some kind of brain damage, which led to a rewiring of the cortical circuitry. Of course, we don't know if George had that psychic ability prior to the insult when he was a child.

"We need to open up our horizons further," the doctor continued. "Things can happen that we don't necessarily understand. But we must allow ourselves to be open to the possibility that they might exist even though we can't explain them. In other words, if it is raining out, it is my decision to choose whether or not I accept to believe it. Something really is going on, and we now have some of the scientific basis for it. George's EEG records indeed showed that despite his being alert, active, and awake, his record was that of a sleeping person. That's not what we are taught one is supposed to see."

Appendix Two

SAINT PHILOMENA

Many people who have been to George for psychic readings have taken note of his interest in and devotion to Saint Philomena. In one corner of the room where he conducts readings, George has a small shrine to and statue of her.

George has long had an interest in the saints of the Catholic Church. Many of those declared saints by the Church over the centuries are documented to have had psychic gifts and experiences including astral travel, the abilities to discern spirits, heal, levitate, bilocate (appear in two places at once), prophesize, and experience clairaudience and clairvoyance.

"Shortly after *We Don't Die* was published in 1988, I was praying one night," George recalled. "I heard a female voice say that because she was martyred at age thirteen, she knows in her Christ-like compassion how it feels to die tragically and leave grieving loved ones. I was impressed that the voice I heard was that of Saint Philomena."

Briefly, this is Saint Philomena's story:

In 1802 excavators digging in an ancient Roman catacomb unearthed a tomb on which were written the words LUMENA/PAXTE/CUMI. When the tiles were rearranged in their proper order the Latin read, PAX TECUM, FILUMENA, or, translated, "Peace Be with You, Philomena." Also inscribed on the tiles were a lily, arrows, an anchor, and a lance, all traditional symbols of virginity and martyrdom. Inside the coffin lay the remains of a young girl, perhaps twelve or thirteen years old, and a vial of her dried blood. These were removed and sent to the Vatican.

In 1805 a priest from Naples, Italy, requested and received the relics of Philomena. He enshrined them in his church in

Mugnano, near Naples. No sooner were Philomena's remains placed there than unusual, even miraculous, events began to occur. Favors were granted to those who had prayed for her intercession. These increased so greatly in number that in 1837, only thirty-five years after she had been exhumed, Philomena was elevated to sainthood by Pope Gregory XVI, who called her the "wonder worker of the nineteenth century." What made Saint Philomena especially remarkable was that except for her name and her martyrdom, nothing was known of her life. She became the only person in Catholic Church history to become a saint solely on the basis of her heavenly intercession rather than anything else she had done during her mortal lifetime besides martyring herself for Christ.

Philomena's name and popularity soon spread worldwide. At one time there were well-known shrines to Saint Philomena in Pennsylvania, Wisconsin, France, and England. A recent shrine to her was begun in 1987 at the Queen of the Angels Church in Dickinson, Texas.

Some of the most profound reports of visions of Saint Philomena and her heavenly interventions come from the French priest John Vianney, himself later sainted and known universally as the Curé of Ars, the patron saint of priests. His gifts as a confessor and director of souls made him world renowned. He demonstrated an uncanny knowledge of the afterlife and could discern the souls of those who had passed on. Saint Vianney is credited with being largely responsible for encouraging devotion to Saint Philomena, and she appeared to him from heaven on several occasions. He described her as appearing out of a cloud "surrounded by glorious heavenly light" so bright that it made her look almost transparent.

The story of Saint Philomena is not without controversy, however. In 1961 the Catholic Church removed her feast day from its calendar, supposedly for a lack of historical evidence about her. Also removed were the feast days for Saint Christopher and Saint Catherine of Alexandria. However, contrary to popular misconception, removal of their feast days does not mean these saints were "desainted" or otherwise demoted. It was simply a liturgical directive to make room for modern saints, not a denial of sainthood. Saint Philomena *is* a saint. Prayers to her have never been and are not today discouraged by the Church.

George said, "I found out that Padre Pio, the modern-day mystic and healer, was very devout with Saint Philomena. I think the reason I'm also attracted to her is because her story is like one big psychic experience."

On two separate occasions, visions of Saint Philomena were seen in George's home. One day shortly after he had completed psychic readings, George saw the spirit of a teen-age girl wearing a white tuniclike gown with olive-green trim. Her shoulder-length reddish-brown hair was parted in the middle. She radiated white light and appeared to George to be "suspended" off the floor. But no sooner had George made eye contact with her than the vision disappeared. It had lasted mere seconds.

On another occasion a friend visiting George's house had virtually the identical experience. She, too, witnessed a fleeting vision of a young girl dressed in a long, white gown, and emanating from her was a comforting illumination. Startled by the vision, she told George about it, not knowing that he had observed the same vision a few months earlier. Her description matched George's exactly.

George has no doubt that both times the visions were of Saint Philomena, which he often sees or senses during psychic readings. She appears as a sign for a distressed girl or woman, a troubled marriage, unhappiness in the home, or problems with children. She can also be the symbol for someone with the name Philomena or its variations, such as Phyllis, Fannie, or Faye. Her appearance may also indicate that a subject has great devotion to her. If she appears over someone's head and then seems to move away, it is likely a sign that the individual is emerging from a despairing situation. Saint Philomena can also be the sign of a happy birth or that a couple wishes to have children.

While George endorses no specific religion, he still remains devoted to Saint Philomena and encourages others to pray to her. "Usually the recommendation I give," he said, "is to pray to her for thirteen consecutive days. Many people have told me their prayers have been answered. If Saint Philomena wants to let you know that she is going to answer your prayers, or that she is near, many people report hearing a knocking sound. It has come to be known as 'Saint Philomena's knock of assurance.'

"Let me just emphasize, it doesn't matter what religious faith you are. God is universal, God is one, and Saint Philomena is praying to God on your behalf. I look upon her as a comforter of the bereaved. As Saint John Vianney said of her, she brings joy to the sorrowful.

"I think for me, personally, Saint Philomena is a tremendous inspiration for my faith. I basically consider her my heavenly advocate. She's the patroness of my work, especially with the bereaved. I feel she does indeed bring joy to those who are grieving."

For more information about Saint Philomena, please write: National Confraternity of Saint Philomena, P.O. Box 1303, Dickinson, Texas 77539. The confraternity, however, does not endorse or support George's work or beliefs in any way. Nor does the confraternity have any relationship, personal or business, with him.

Appendix Three

GLOSSARY OF PSYCHIC SYMBOLS

AIDS—the word appearing over a subject's head indicates either that the spirit passed from the disease or that the subject suffers from it.

an airplane—work-related (the subject or spirit works with airlines or travel) or future travel.

Angel of Death—a passing is imminent.

apples—ripe apples mean the subject is "ripe for a job change." When George sees an apple core, it signifies the core, or the heart, of a matter.

artist's easel—work or study of art.

automobile accident—can mean an automobile accident, any accidental passing, or a passing that was swift and unexpected, like an accident.

bells, ringing—someone on this side or the next is on the alert, usually waiting for someone to pass over.

birth of a baby—the subject is about to embark on a new beginning.

black—when the subject appears to George to be surrounded by black, it means that someone close to him or her will pass on in the near future.

black spots—around an individual or around a particular area of the body usually indicate cancer, either in the past, present, or future.

blood—violence, a violent incident, or death.

blood, seen bursting—a stroke or other vascular problem, such as an aneurysm.

blood cells—a disease related to the blood cells, such as leukemia or AIDS.

books, a hand writing—work, study, or strong interest related to writing; work around books, as in a library.

bread—abundance.

314

broken heart—romance gone bad, a broken love affair.

car wheel—auto accident or car trouble, either in the recent past or the foreseeable future.

cards—a large deck of playing cards indicates that the spirit of the reading had or the subject will be making a big deal in business.

classroom or school—the subject may be a student or is or will be learning something that will enhance his or her career.

clear water—usually in a glass or in a stream, a symbol of "clear going" in the future. A positive sign.

computers, electrical wiring, machinery—references to the careers of the subject or the spirit.

contracts—legal papers are being signed, either in the present or the future.

currency, piles of money—money coming to someone through an inheritance, job, or gift. May also mean that the subject or spirit works with or around money, as in a bank.

dawn—a new start is foreseen for the subject.

dog, or dog barking—indicates that the spirit was met and greeted on the other side by a deceased pet dog.

drink, on the rocks—indicates that the subject should exert caution in a relationship ahead.

eight ball—someone is being overshadowed by a problem or caught up in a difficult situation.

Empire State Building—New York City.

Felix the Cat—this cartoon character's appearance indicates that the subject will be hearing good news ahead.

a finger placed to closed lips—advises a subject to keep quiet about a situation.

French Revolution—radical changes are foreseen.

glass of milk—relaxation is needed.

green fields—money or abundance.

gun—psychically seen weapons almost always indicate the means by which the communicating spirit was killed. Sometimes George will see a double-barreled gun, indicating that the person in question has been hit twice by tragedy.

hands tied—a spirit's way of communicating, "There's nothing you can do about it."

hearts and roses—a love affair.

Sherlock Holmes—the subject or the spirit was involved

with some kind of police or detective work, either in uniform or undercover. Also may mean one is searching for an answer or solving a mystery.

horn of plenty—abundance ahead.

ice cubes—advises subject to "keep cool."

knife—see *gun*, above.

lemon—a large lemon on wheels suggests car trouble for the subject.

letters of the alphabet—a specific letter appearing psychically over the subject's head is a clue to a key word, such as the first letter of the spirit's name.

lightning bolt—something shocking and unexpected.

Lourdes water—sign of healing, related to the health condition of subject.

medals—symbolize "awards" or progress on the other side.

mercy killing—indicates the subject or spirit was involved in a mercy killing, often spelled out.

musical instruments—might indicate that the subject or spirit was a musician, disc jockey, songwriter, music teacher or had a strong interest in music.

musical notes—may indicate someone being "in harmony." See also *musical instruments*.

New York Stock Exchange—someone works at or with the Exchange, or is or will be involved with investments.

nose—a large nose means that someone else is butting into the subject's marriage with future marital upset as the result.

palm trees—travel or a move to a southerly, tropical location.

pentagram—a five-sided star indicates involvement with the satanic.

piano—someone plays either the piano or some other percussion instrument.

priests, nuns, other clergy—indicate that the subject or the spirit was or knew others in religious service.

question mark—indicates some mystery or question about a situation.

rainbow—optimism, a new beginning ahead.

REDRUM—the word *murder* spelled backward indicates that someone has been murdered.

red light—George takes this as a psychic symbol to stop psychic reading, that he is in danger of overexerting himself. This can also have a literal meaning, often indicating that an ignored red light or stop sign played a role in an auto accident.

rosary beads—generally mean that the spirit, regardless of religion, is asking for prayers. When the subject or spirit is Catholic, they usually refer to the rosary of someone in particular, often identifiable, because George will be shown their color.

roses—white roses are a sign of congratulations or celebration from the other side. The roses may be offered by the spirit around the time of a celebration, anniversary, or birthday. Other times they are just presented as gestures of love or thanks.

Sacred Heart of Jesus—a symbol of Jesus' suffering on the cross, often indicates a spirit died by his own hand.

Saint Anthony—if dressed in black, a symbol of death, loss, or tragedy.

Saint Joseph—the patron saint of fathers, carpenters, and death. His appearance symbolizes a peaceful death, one that occurs during sleep or unconsciousness.

Saint Peregrine Lazosi—patron saint of cancer victims. His appearance indicates that someone has or will die of cancer.

Saint Vincent de Paul—patron saint of charitable societies, his presence indicates that a person was giving while here on earth.

scales of justice—a legal situation in the subject's or the spirit's life.

shamrocks—symbolize that the person in question is of Irish descent.

sinking ship—a situation "rocked your boat."

skull and crossbones—negativity, friction.

Smith Brothers—the famous trademark pair found on boxes of cough drops indicates a subject's or spirit's surname is Smith.

spider's web—being trapped.

spring cleaning—a spirit's way of saying, "Your life needs a complete overhaul."

star—creativity.

Star of David—the spirit or subject was of the Jewish faith.

stripes on shoulder—promotion, as in military service.

suitcases—future travel.

swastika—sometimes seen with the screaming face of Adolf Hitler, coils of barbed wire, concentration camp victims, and the Star of David superimposed over the image. This symbolizes that the spirit or subject were victims of the Nazis.

Switzerland—when George sees a map of this country, it means that the subject is being advised to stay neutral in a conflict.

towels, in knots—a short temper.

triangle—a love triangle, infidelity, adultery.

trumpets sounding—happy news.

turkey—psychic clue that an event occurred around Thanksgiving time.

uniforms—these symbols give clues as to the subject's or the spirit's occupation, and are distinguished by color: white for health and medical workers, blue for police, firemen, military, and so on.

washing machine—health difficulty related to kidney or adrenal malfunction.

wedding ring—a broken wedding ring indicates a marital breakup or discord in a romantic relationship.

windmill—someone has "been through the mill."

wolf—a sign of evil.

X—a large X shown over a scene, symbol, or word that George sees psychically means that it is incorrect, not what it seems to be, or that the subject is being advised not to take some action represented by that symbol. For example, an X over a vision of a wedding might mean that the spirit is suggesting his loved one reconsider an impending marriage.

yellow rings, murky—when these appear around a specific part of the human anatomy, they indicate illness or some malady affecting that area, in the future.

Bibliography

This is actually two bibliographies; one of recommended titles on the paranormal, and another of books about bereavement. We especially thank Elaine and Joe Stillwell for their help with the latter.

The Paranormal

Cayce, Hugh Lynn and Edgar Cayce. *God's Other Door and the Continuity of Life.* Virginia Beach, Virginia: A.R.E. Press, 1958.

Chinmoy, Sri. *Death and Reincarnation.* Jamaica, New York: Agni Press, 1974.

Ebon, Martin, ed. *Communicating with the Dead.* New York: New American Library, 1968.

———. *The Evidence for Life after Death.* New York: Signet/New American Library, 1977.

Ford, Arthur. *Unknown but Known.* New York: Harper & Row, 1968.

Fuller, John G. *The Ghost of 29 Megacycles.* New York: Signet/New American Library, 1981.

Garrett, E. J. *Many Voices.* New York: G. P. Putnam's Sons, 1968.

Jacobson, Nils O., M.D. *Life without Death?* New York: Dell, 1973.

LeShan, Lawrence. *The Medium, the Mystic, and the Physicist.* New York: Viking, 1966.

McCaffery, John. *Tales of Padre Pio.* Garden City, New York: Image Books, 1981.

Martin, Joel, and Patricia Romanowski. *We Don't Die: George Anderson's Conversations with the Other Side.* New York: G. P. Putnam's Sons, 1988; Berkley, 1989.

Meek, George W. *After We Die, What Then?* Franklin,

North Carolina: Metascience Corporation Publications Division, 1980.

Mitchell, Edgar, ed. *Psychic Exploration.* New York: G. P. Putnam's Sons, 1974.

Mohr, Sister Marie Helene. *Saint Philomena: Powerful with God.* Rockford, Illinois: Tan Books and Publishers, 1953.

Montgomery, Ruth. *Here and Hereafter.* New York: Coward-McCann, 1968.

———. *A Search for Truth.* New York: William Morrow, 1966.

———. *The World Before.* New York: Coward, McCann, and Geoghegan, Inc., 1976.

———. *A World Beyond.* New York: Ballantine Books, 1972.

Moody, Raymond A., Jr., M.D. *Life after Life.* Atlanta: Mockingbird Books, 1975.

———. *Light Beyond.* New York: Bantam Books, 1988.

———. *Reflections on Life after Life.* Atlanta: Mockingbird Books, 1977.

Morse, Melvin, M.D. *Closer to the Light.* New York: Villard Books, 1990.

Osis, Karlis, Ph.D., and Erlendur Haraldsson, Ph.D. *At the Hour of Death.* New York: Avon Books, 1977.

Perry, Michael. *Psychic Studies: A Christian's View.* Wellingborough, Great Britain: The Aquarian Press, 1984.

Ring, Kenneth. *Heading Toward Omega: In Search of the Meaning of the Near-Death Experience.* New York: William Morrow & Company, 1984.

———. *Life After Death: A Scientific Investigation of the Near-Death Experience.* New York: Coward, McCann & Geoghegan, 1980.

Sherman, Harold. *The Dead Are Alive.* New York: Ballantine Books, 1981.

———. *You Live after Death.* Greenwich, Connecticut: Fawcett Gold Medal Books, 1972.

Spraggett, Allen. *The Case for Immortality.* New York: New American Library, 1974.

Spraggett, Allen with William Rauscher. *Arthur Ford: The Man Who Talked with the Dead.* New York: New American Library, 1973.

Stearn, Jess. *Edgar Cayce—The Sleeping Prophet.* New York: Doubleday & Co., Inc., 1967.

Sugrue, Thomas. *There Is a River: The Story of Edgar Cayce.* New York: Holt, Rinehart and Winston, 1942.

Taylor, Ruth Mattson. *Witness from Beyond.* New York: Hawthorn, 1975.

White, John. *A Practical Guide to Death and Dying: Conquer Fear and Anxiety through a Program of Personal Action.* Wheaton, Illinois: Quest Books, 1988.

Wilkerson, Ralph. *Beyond and Back: Those Who Died and Lived to Tell It.* Anaheim, California: Melodyland Productions, 1977.

In addition, George Anderson and Joel Martin are the subjects of a chapter in Sharon Jarvis's *True Tales of the Unknown: The Uninvited* (New York: Bantam Books, 1989).

Bereavement

Bolton, Iris, and C. Mitchell. *My Son My Son.* Atlanta, Georgia: Bolton Press, 1983.

Cerza Kolf, June. *When Will I Stop Hurting: Dealing with a Recent Death.* Grand Rapids, Michigan: Baker Book House, 1987.

Gunther, John. *Death Be Not Proud.* New York: Harper & Row, 1949.

Knapp, Ronald J. *Beyond Endurance: When a Child Dies.* New York: Schocken Books, 1986.

Kübler-Ross, Elisabeth. *Living with Death and Dying.* New York: Macmillan, 1982.

———. *On Children and Death.* New York: Macmillan, 1983.

———. *On Death and Dying.* New York: Macmillan, 1970.

———. *Questions and Answers on Death and Dying.* New York: Macmillan, 1974.

———. *Working It Through.* New York: Macmillan, 1987.

———, ed. *Death: The Final Stage of Growth.* New York: Touchstone, 1986.

Kübler-Ross, Elisabeth, and Mal Warshaw. *To Live Until We Say Goodbye.* Englewood Cliffs, New Jersey: Prentice-Hall, 1978.

————. *AIDS: The Ultimate Challenge*. New York: Macmillan, 1987.

LeShan, Eda. *Learning to Say Goodbye (When a Parent Dies)*. New York: Avon Books, 1976.

Lukas, Christopher, and Henry M. Seiden. *Silent Grief: Living in the Wake of Suicide*. New York: Bantam Books, 1987.

Lukeman, Brenda. *Embarkations: A Guide to Dealing with Death and Parting*. Englewood Cliffs, New Jersey: Prentice-Hall, 1982.

Panuthos, Claudia, and Catherine Romero. *Ended Beginnings: Healing Childbearing Losses*. New York: Warner Books, 1984.

Parrish-Harra, Carol. *The New Age Handbook on Death and Dying*. Santa Monica, California: IBS Press, 1989.

Quackenbush, Jamie, and Denise Graveline. *When Your Pet Dies*. New York: Pocket Books, 1988.

Rando, Therese A., Ph.D. *Grieving: How to Go On Living When Someone You Love Dies*. Lexington, Massachusetts: Lexington Books, D. C. Heath & Co., 1988.

Sanford, Doris. *It Must Hurt A Lot: A Child's Book About Death*. Portland, Oregon: Multnomah Press (date unavailable).

Sarnoff Schiff, Harriet. *The Bereaved Parent*. New York: Crown Publishers, 1977.

Schoeneck, Therese S. *Hope for the Bereaved: Understanding, Coping, and Growing through Grief*. Syracuse, New York: Hope for Bereaved (date unavailable).

Scrivani, Mark. *Love Mark*. Syracuse, New York: Hope for Bereaved (date unavailable).

Tatelbaum, Judy. *The Courage to Grieve*. New York: Harper & Row, 1980.